Researching Soci

Researching Social Change
Qualitative Approaches

Julie McLeod and Rachel Thomson

Los Angeles | London | New Delhi
Singapore | Washington DC

First published 2009

SAGE Publications Ltd
1 Oliver's Yard
55 City Road
London EC1Y 1SP

SAGE Publications Inc.
2455 Teller Road
Thousand Oaks, California 91320

SAGE Publications India Pvt Ltd
B 1/I 1 Mohan Cooperative Industrial Area
Mathura Road, Post Bag 7
New Delhi 110 044

SAGE Publications Asia-Pacific Pte Ltd
33 Pekin Street #02-01
Far East Square
Singapore 048763

Library of Congress Control Number 2008932496

British Library Cataloguing in Publication data

A catalogue record for this book is available from the British Library

ISBN 978-1-4129-2886-1
ISBN 978-1-4129-2887-8 (pbk)

Typeset by C&M Digitals (P) Ltd, Chennai, India
Printed and bound in Great Britain by TJ International, Padstow, Cornwall
Printed on paper from sustainable resources

Contents

Researching Social Change

Questions about change in social and personal life are a feature of many accounts of the contemporary world. While theories of social change abound, discussions about how to research it are much less common. This book provides a timely guide to qualitative methodologies that investigate processes of personal, generational and historical change. It showcases methods that explore temporality and the dynamic relations between past, present and future. Through case studies, it reviews six methodological traditions: memory-work, oral/life history, qualitative longitudinal research, ethnography, intergenerational and follow-up studies. It illustrates how these research approaches are translated into research projects and considers the practical as well as the theoretical and ethical challenges they pose. Research methods are also the product of times and places, and this book keeps to the fore the cultural and historical context in which these methods developed, the theoretical traditions on which they draw and the empirical questions they address.

This book is an invaluable resource for researchers and graduate students across the social sciences – especially in the fields of gender, youth, family and community studies, education, health, and qualitative methods – who are interested in understanding *and* researching social change.

Acknowledgements

There are many people who have helped us in the development of this book. The project began in 2004 with a seminar at London South Bank University on 'Researching Continuity/Change: Qualitative Perspectives', at which we mapped out the basic structure and themes of the endeavour. We would like to thank those who contributed to the day, and Patrick Brindle, our editor at Sage, who was there from the start and has guided the project along the way. During the writing process we have appreciated conversations with many of those whose work we have described, including: Julia Brannen, Janet Holland, Sheila Henderson, Lyn Yates, Harriet Bjerrum Nielsen and Diana Leonard. We have also benefited from the constructive comments of an anonymous reviewer and our own readers, who in addition to those already mentioned include Sean Arnold, David Goodman, Mary Jane Kehily, Naomi Rudoe and Katie Wright, with valuable research assistance from Claire Charles and Glenn Savage. We would like to acknowledge the enabling role of the Faculties of Health and Social Care at the Open University and Education at Deakin University, as well as the University of Melbourne Graduate School of Education. We appreciate the support of the editorial and production staff at Sage. Last, but not least, we thank our families for helping us find, make and steal the time needed for the travelling, talking, reading, writing and editing that is this book.

1

Introduction:
Researching Change
and Continuity

This is a book about researching change in personal and social life. It showcases methods that privilege the temporal. We hope that you will be able to use it in a range of ways. Through case studies you will see how different methods work in practice, as well as understanding these as located in particular times and places. In combination, the chapters will give you an understanding of the epistemological and ethical dimensions of research that seeks to capture dynamic processes. This is not a book about using research to make change (Greenwood and Levin, 2006), or even researching people who are changing the world (see Andrews, 2007). Rather it is a book about the kind of research that we do and we admire, qualitative research that takes temporality seriously.

The genesis of this book is shaped by some of the temporal motifs that we explore within it – coincidence and remembering. Coincidence in that we met in 2000, finding that we had both designed studies that sought to explore common processes of personal and social change, that we shared methodological and theoretical interests in temporality, discovering the same conceptual tools to help us in this work. We soon became aware of others thinking along similar lines and converging trajectories of academic and popular thought, seeking to forge a dynamic understanding of social processes. It was at this point that we decided that we would like to write a book about the challenges of researching social change, drawing on the qualitative research traditions that had shaped us and that we employed in our own practice. This undertaking was an expression of friendship, a desire to collaborate and to make concrete our meeting and our affinities.

The project also demanded that we locate this endeavour in time and place, leading us to trace different research traditions and to re-engage in literatures and to remember what had come before and how we had arrived at this point. This remembering was both personal and academic, and we have enjoyed the opportunity to map the literatures that surround our chosen methodologies, to discover and rediscover classics and to bring these to a contemporary audience. In this introductory chapter we outline some of the theoretical and methodological motifs that run through the book. We then outline the structure of the book and the rationale for its organization.

Telling stories about social change

In 1965 the British historian Peter Laslett published a book called *The World We Have Lost* in which he critiqued the tendency of Marxist accounts to read the past through theory. He criticized the way this work employed linear histories in order to focus on the assumed rupture of industrialization and the creation of a mass society from one based on the family as the unit of life and the home as the site of industry. Laslett's solution was to replace the narrative approach of 'recounting history' with a comparative approach in which pre-industrial and contemporary society are counterposed, enabling the analyst to see more of what is the same then and now, as well as what is different. He recognizes that such an approach may 'seem unhistorical in the final sense, since it abandons the method of explanation by telling a story' (1965: 232), yet warns against the seductions of nostalgic narratives. In his words:

> there is more to it than a wrong account of how things have changed. Our whole view of ourselves is altered if we cease to believe that we have lost some more humane, much more natural pattern of relationship than industrial society can offer. [...] In tending to look backwards in this way, in diagnosing the difficulties as an outcome of something which has indeed been lost to our society, those concerned with social welfare are suffering from a false understanding of ourselves in time [...] historical knowledge is knowledge to do with ourselves, now. (1965: 236–7)

In 2007, the British historian and sociologist Jeffrey Weeks played on Laslett's title in a book called *The World We Have Won* in which he seeks to challenge what he sees as a widespread popular and academic 'nostalgia for a more settled and ordered moral culture than we apparently have today' (2007: ix). The target of Weeks' polemic is not the historical materialism of Marxist sociologists, but a body of cultural pessimists (in which he includes moral conservatives, communitarians and radical scholars) who fail, in his view, to recognize and celebrate 'changes in sexual and intimate life that are transforming everyday life and the rapidly globalizing world we inhabit' (p. ix). For Weeks, we are living 'in a world of transition, in the midst of a long, convoluted, messy, unfinished but profound revolution that has transformed the possibilities of living our sexual diversity and creating intimate lives' (p. 3). His book provides a balance sheet of the gains and losses that contribute to the character of these changes over a 30-year period. His project is not simply to show that things have changed, but also to argue that they have changed for the better. In constructing his case he warns against a series of myths: the *progressive* myth which 'all too readily forgets the contingencies of history, the tangled roads that have brought us to the present'; the *declinist* myth associated with moral conservatives which 'celebrates a history that never was, a world that was not so much lost as nostalgically reimagined to act as a counterpoint to the present'; and a *'continuist* myth' associated with feminist and queer scholars who 'stress the recalcitrance of hidden structures, but in doing so forget the power of agency and of the macroscopic impact of subtle changes in individual lives that makes up the unfinished revolution of our time' (2007: 7).

Weeks argues that each of these positions 'occlude what seems to me to be the inevitable reality: that the world we have won has made possible ways of life that represent an advance not a decline in human relationships, and that have broken through the coils of power to enhance individual autonomy, freedom of choice and more egalitarian patterns of relationships' (2007: 7). Echoing the sentiments of Peter Laslett, he cautions against theoretically-laden accounts of social change, instead arguing that it is only by gaining 'a handle on the links, the tendencies, the interconnections of past and present in our present history and our historic present that we can measure our gains and losses, the successes and failures, the possibilities and intransigencies, the pleasures and dangers' (p. 3). For Weeks, having a sense of the past enables us to hold 'the present to account, denaturalizing and relativizing it, demonstrating that it is a historical creation, suggesting its contingency' (p. 3).

In counterposing these two examples we can see how enduring are questions about the status of claims regarding social change and continuity, involving debate over political positions, theoretical frameworks and empirical methods. While the targets of the two polemics are different, both share a scepticism towards the theoretical and sentimental narratives that shape the way in which temporal processes are conceptualized, as well as sharing an interest in the ways in which empirical practices can contribute towards and disrupt our understandings of the interplay of past, present and future. These are sentiments that we share, although we are less motivated by a desire to demonstrate or celebrate/mourn change than by exploring practical strategies that may enable us to document, imagine and represent temporal processes and to explore the relationship between personal and social dynamics.

Methods and moments

We write this book in an interesting cultural moment, characterized by a proliferation of increasingly anxious discussions of social change and the future. Theories of postmodernity, late modernity, high modernity and reflexive modernity all point to an epochal shift equivalent to the industrial revolution that is in the process of transforming economic, material, social and personal relations. Whether such accounts construct this transformation in terms of the 'end' of modernity or the 'beginning' of a new, reinvigorated phase, they nevertheless share an interest in narrating processes of transformation. A vocabulary of detraditionalization, disembedding, reflexivity and individualization constructs an understanding of the individual at the centre of social and historical processes, facing a landscape of increasing uncertainty. In temporal terms, we encounter an 'extended present' (Adam, 2003, 2004) that disrupts modernist temporal orderings (Harootunian, 2007). Brian Heaphy has characterized such theoretical orientations as a 'reconstructive turn' – similar in many ways to 'constructive' founding narratives of modernity (Marx, Durkheim, Freud and Weber) which shared a taste for 'knowing the direction of social change and the part that human agency played with respect to this' (2007: 26). The reconstructive turn is characterized by a shift to a more optimistic tone and to a temporal register that shrugs off the determinations of the past, concerning itself with the ways in which the future is created in the present. Notions such as the choice biography (Beck, 1992) and the reflexive project of self (Giddens, 1991) draw heavily on phenomenological traditions and the notion of the extended present. It is argued that such biographical forms are historically new, existing independently of the past, without memory, roots or traditions.

Our contemporary moment is also characterized by the recognition of our implication in discourses of change and self-consiousness as to the contingency of our knowledge claims. Heaphy suggests that this ambivalence arises from a 'deconstructive turn' – the coincidence of poststructuralist 'incredulity' towards grand narratives (which turn upon the notion of modernity as movement with a direction; Heaphy, 2007: 65) and other deconstructive impulses (initially simple and increasingly radical) emerging from feminism, queer and postcolonial scholarship which problematized the claims of social science to neutral, objective and legitimate knowledge. Central to both intellectual trends has been Foucault's proposal for genealogies that make the present strange by identifying discontinuities and contingencies that give rise to particular power/knowledge relations that in turn produce regimes of truth and subjects. The deconstructive turn leads to a reflexive and ambivalent position from which 'sociology must acknowledge that it is involved in narrative production, and that it is in the business of producing contingent knowledge that is open to contestation and, at best, can provide the basis for diverse interpretations of the social world' (Heaphy, 2007: 43).

The work of US political theorist and feminist Wendy Brown (1995) captures the ambivalence of this position perfectly. On one hand, she warns feminism of the dangers of its own narratives, in which injuries of the past are perversely defended in that they provide the basis for identities in the present. Yet she also calls on feminism 'not to reproach the history on which it is born' (1995: 51), suggesting that it is possible to maintain an attachment to subjectivity, identity and morality without indulging in *ressentiment* (a term derived from the work of Nietzsche to capture the reassignment of the pain that accompanies a sense of one's own inferiority onto an external scapegoat). For Brown, our very ability to create political identities is dependent on our ability to be free from such dependencies in order to imagine a future, which in turn demands a 'sense of historical movement' (2001: 9). Accepting the deconstructive inheritance of poststructuralism and radical difference does not mean abandoning politics, but it does mean relinquishing simplistic historical narratives. Brown argues that 'as the past becomes less easily reduced to a single set of meanings and effects, as the present is forced to orient itself amid *so much* history and *so many* histories, history itself emerges as both weightier and less deterministic than ever before' (2001: 5).

A turn towards time

You will see from our approach in this book that we have been influenced by the reflexive inheritance of the deconstructive turn. We are interested in histor*ies* rather than history, and self-conscious of our own implications in the sociological and empirical narratives that we forge. Yet we do not wish to abandon the project of locating ourselves and others within historical and cultural perspectives, and we seek practical and empirical strategies that capture the interplay of past, present and future while also acknowledging how social, cultural and disciplinary positioning shape the resulting narratives and the questions we ask of methods. In his 2004 book *After Method*, John Law makes an impassioned plea for a new kind of social science methodology that recognizes that methods produce the realities that they understand, and which are able to capture 'the ephemeral, the indefinite and the irregular' (p. 4). In Law's words, 'we need to find ways of elaborating quiet methods, slow methods, or modest methods. In particular, we need to discover ways of making methods without accompanying imperialisms' (p. 15). In this book we have not sought to invent new methods, but instead have looked at what we already have, but which we believe have some of the qualities outlined by Law. These are all methods that capture something of the fleeting character of the ephemeral and the interplay of the subjective and objective dimensions of time. They are methods that through different forms of 'duration' – in fieldwork and/or analysis – recognize movement, exchange and dynamic process.

Twenty years before Law, in an introduction to a collection of papers on historical psychology, Kenneth Gergen (1984) identifies three 'romances' or underlying myths about time that circumscribe the discipline. The first of these is the privileging of synchronic over diachronic analysis – a focus on static entities (such as social class) rather than states across a temporal period (such as social mobility). The second is an adherence to research methods which truncate temporal patterns rather than allowing for periods/flows of time. Here Gergen points to how familiar features of everyday life all require extended time horizons: whether this be phenomena at the micro-level ('holding a conversation, playing games, teaching a lesson, having a fight, making love' (p. 8), or phenomena that take place against a wider time horizon ('getting an education, developing friendships, carrying out a romance, raising a child, getting ahead occupationally'), or even those macro-phenomena that qualify as historical and social changes. The third romance about time is what he terms 'the privileging of phenomenological immutability over temporal contingency' (p. 8) – the search for laws rather than situated meanings and the attempt to exempt the research process from a contingent location alongside the data. More than 20 years later, we feel that the turn towards time in social research, of which this book is a part, goes some way towards overturning these romances. This is an interdisciplinary impulse, and in privileging sequential patterns one is better able to articulate the temporal and the spatial. It is a methodological project that needs to be historically aware, drawing on insights and traditions from across the social sciences and the arts, requiring recognition of its place at the intersection of a number of methodological and disciplinary histories. For historians, this may appear naïve, but a generous reading of the field can recognize its necessity.

Methodological motifs

The book reviews six methodological traditions: memory–work, oral/life history, qualitative longitudinal research, ethnography, intergenerational and follow–up studies. These are overlapping approaches; some of our case studies could have appeared in more than one chapter and the same 'methods' are employed within the different traditions. In reviewing these approaches we have become aware of a number of recurrent themes, which are, in turn, implicated in our theoretical orientation. Before outlining the structure of the book we discuss each briefly.

Historicizing of method

Research methods are the products of times and places. They have histories and the forms of knowledge that they produce are in turn productive of power–knowledge relations (Alastalo, 2008). The 'invention' of questionnaire-based survey methods and ethnographic fieldwork at the end of the 19th century enabled representations of the present, replacing a reliance on narrative and library-based approaches, which Peter Burke (1992) describes as an expression of a new moment in modernity and a shift in influence from the old Europe to the new world. The rise of biographical and narrative methods in the 1980s and 1990s spoke to the rise in influence of new social movements and a turn to subjectivity within western cultures and across academic disciplines. More recent talk of the 'crisis in empirical sociology', including anxieties about the lack of purchase of survey and interview methods in the face of commercial information technologies or real-life documentary genres, can be seen as yet another moment in this history of social research methods (Savage and Burrows, 2007). Talk of a 'descriptive turn' in the context of a new empiricism suggests a move away from causality and explanation as an ideal towards more connected, thick and theorized accounts (Latour, 2005; Savage and Burrows, 2007).

Each of the methods we feature in this book have had their moments in the sun, when they produced enthusiasm with researchers giving rise to new forms of representation and understanding which in turn forged a new sense of possibility. Memory-work thrived in the 1980s yet is rediscovered regularly in different places. The heyday of oral history coincided with the heyday of feminist and socialist reclaiming of their pasts. Qualitative longitudinal methods are popular as we write, and ethnography has a complex history spanning the last century, both reviled and reclaimed in different times, places and disciplines. Intergenerational approaches which emphasize psychic and material transaction become salient in moments of crisis and rapid change. With the rise of digital technologies the potential of data archiving and data sharing becomes more compelling, and as the Baby Boomers mature they become increasingly interested in revisiting their earlier studies. By attempting to tell the story of a range of different research approaches, each of which has some purchase in capturing processes of continuity and change, we hope to show the ways in which research methods are themselves historically situated techniques producing situated forms of knowledge.

Historicizing the subject, including the researcher

Much has been written about the role of the researcher in producing knowledge in research encounters and their role in producing reflexivity (Denzin and Lincoln, 2005). Our explorations have helped us understand why the researcher can never be outside the process of knowledge production and data generation. By thinking in temporal and historical terms, both the researcher and the researched are located together within a hermeneutic circle. The extent to which we actually *notice* the presence of researchers in research accounts or data depends in part on the methods employed and the genre of reporting. For example, a deliberate commitment to reflexivity and accounting for oneself in the data produces an autobiographical representation of the researcher. The production of field notes as part of data generation forges a voice that can be represented directly or indirectly in research accounts. Revisiting data (whether in follow-up or secondary analysis studies) or revisiting oneself, as in returning to one's earlier work, in qualitative longitudinal research or memory-work, also provides a way of producing the persona of the researcher as part of the data record. If we take the perspective of the intellectual biographer (of self or others) we could see the researcher in their choice of subject matter, or theory, and more subtly in what is and what is not seen in the data and the kinds of recognitions and omissions that characterize the stories they tell (Coslett et al., 2000; Stanley, 1992). Recent moves within psychosocial approaches to research that construct the research subject as defended also alert us to the reciprocal dynamics of transference and projection within the research encounter, as well as the implication of the defended researcher in the production and analysis of material (Frosh et al., 2002; Hollway and Jefferson, 2000; Lucey et al., 2003; Walkerdine et al., 2001).

Dynamic temporal relations

Research methods, the data they generate and the interpretations that we make from them are characterized by a dynamic relationship between temporal registers. While it can be necessary for analytic and everyday purposes to distinguish the past, present and future, they are inseparable, constitutive of the temporal flow (Elias, 1992). Philosophers of time have conceptualized this in different ways. The key point that we take from this work is the distinction between an objective measurable 'clock time' and an understanding of time as experienced subjectively. Bergson, for example, distinguishes between *temps* (a spatialized orientation to time characterized by extensity) and *duree* (a temporalized orientation characterized by intensity) (Ansell Pearson and Mullarkey, 2002). Heidegger provides an ontological concept of existence, '*Dasein*', which is constituted by an orientation to the future (existentiality), an orientation to the past (facticity) and an orientation to the present (ensnarement) – corresponding respectively to the experiential modes of pursuit of the future, bearing the past and acting/drifting within the present (Farrell Krell, 1993). These concepts were influential in the formation of phenomenology and the psychologies of G.H. Mead and William James, and more recent theoretical engagements with temporality acknowledge their continuing legacy (Grosz, 2004, 2005).

The notion that the past and the future are always apprehended in the present has not always found its ways into empirical paradigms. Although different methodological strategies may emphasize different temporal registers (for example, oral history may appear to be about the past), the interrelating dimensions of past–present–future are always in operation. So accounts of the past are created in relation to the demands of the present and in their telling evoke a possible future. Despite our recognition of the indivisibility of past–present–future, the book is organized to show how different approaches privilege particular temporal perspectives: Part 1, *Remembering* (methods that seek the past through memory and narration), Part 2, *Being With* (methods that seek to capture the present and the unfolding of events and lives), and Part 3, *Inheriting* (methods that are oriented to the future, yet which approach it by exploring the passage of time and relationships between generations).

Another element of this dynamism concerns the dual aspect of continuity and change. Traditionally social theory has been schematized as either explaining continuity or explaining change (for example, via distinctions drawn between conflict and consensus theories). Yet empirical research regularly confronts us with the paradoxical nature of phenomena which express aspects of both (Crow, 2008). So, for example, the idea of the 'invented tradition', a term coined by historians Hobsbawm and Ranger, helps us see how the creation of national celebrations which appear to establish continuity with the past are in fact highly modern phenomena speaking to the future. As Paul Connerton observes, beginnings demand recollection, and we tend to hear the 'echo of tradition at the moment of its de-authorisation' (1989: 9). Fred Davis characterizes this paradox in terms of nostalgia, suggesting that in times of rapid change we tend to assuage 'apprehension of the future by retrieving the worth of the past' (1979: 71), and that this 'allows time for needed change to be assimilated while giving the appearance … of meaningful links to the past' (p. 110). Conversely, phenomena that appear to be entirely 'new' also speak to the past. So, for example, the formulation of the 'magical solution' generated by cultural studies accounts of youth culture in the 1970s showed how teenage skinhead culture could be understood as existing in conversation with the culture of the parents and the loss of traditional working–class communities (Hall and Jefferson, 1976). These kinds of understandings of the interdependent dynamic between continuity and change, which are rooted in empirical awareness of how lives are lived and cultures work, offer a way of thinking about change where the past and present coexist and where social reproduction is a situated and emergent accomplishment.

An articulation of contingency and relatedness

Abstraction is a tool for social research, and tends to work by taking the individual out of the social, or evacuating the social from subjectivity. Both, in turn, produce and sustain the theoretical problem of the relationship between structure and agency. These kinds of abstractions are useful, pragmatic and misleading. Doreen Massey (1993, 1994) has written about this in terms of tendencies, on the one hand, towards privileging the spatial (i.e. relationships of structure, social location, coexistence) and, on the other, of privileging the temporal, generally expressed through an emphasis on the individual, process, contingency and how things pan out over time. Certain methods are good at the former (such as cross-sectional methods), and certain methods are good at the latter (such as longitudinal and narrative approaches). Combined, they enable a three-dimensional perspective, yet this is static. Massey argues that movement needs to be introduced, to achieve a four-dimensional sociology that articulates the two and keeps them in motion. In our view, this is an inviting and ambitious approach, one which opens up possibilities to show the coalescence of place, time, subjectivity and the social: explaining why certain stories can be told and heard at certain moments, and the consequence of this. Each of the methods we consider in this book sheds some light on aspects of Massey's four-dimensional sociology and suggests both the promise and value of this approach, but also the difficulty in achieving the required level of analytical and methodological complexity across different types of research projects.

Various attempts have been made to capture this articulation of contingency and relatedness. For example, in earlier work Julie explored the value of Bourdieu's concept of habitus, which can be understood as 'socialized subjectivity', the dispositions and embodied 'ways of being', including values and ways of comporting oneself, which are formed in interaction with 'social fields' – how individuals 'become themselves'. She experimented with a temporalizing of the 'formation of habitus over time' within which individuals may 'improvise' (McLeod, 2000). To do this, she drew on Harriet Bjerrum Nielsen's appropriation of Freud's metaphor of the 'magic writing pad' through which resources are gleaned from experience and cultural forms to elaborate the kind of woman that one wants to be. These inscriptions are made metaphorically onto a page, to be overlaid with others, as they become available. Yet each inscription leaves a mark, or indentation, on a soft wax block behind the sheet of paper. While the page is wiped and overlaid with new inscriptions, all are accumulated into a less conscious yet more enduring record. The two dimensions of gender identity and gender subjectivity exist in a dynamic and dialectic relationship over time, giving rise to gender as a process. It is a 'dialectic which results in the "magic" situation that change does not exclude permanence, and permanence does not exclude change. Without inscription there is no change in subjectivity, without the wax block there is no subject for the identity work' (Bjerrum Nielsen, 1996: 10).

We do not propose a single theoretical framework or resolution in this book. Concepts and theories arise within chapters, led by the kinds of research questions posed and the methodological solutions pursued. Any number of theoretical frameworks could be relevant to the endeavour of this book, and our choices are a deliberate reflection of our wish to embed theory within the purposes of particular projects.

Organization of the book

We have approached this book as a joint endeavour involving a division of labour. We have taken a lead on different chapters, each addressing one methodological approach within a section. Julie has taken responsibility for chapters on oral history, ethnography and follow-up studies and Rachel for memory-work, qualitative longitudinal research and intergenerational studies. We have shared the task of editing as well as the job of creating an introduction and conclusion for the book and writing Chapter 8 on 'Time, Emotions and Research Practice'. The book is organized into three parts, representing different temporal registers. In the first part, 'Remembering', we explore methods that focus on the past, memory-work and oral history. Chapter 2 tells the story of memory-work through three examples: the original experiments of German feminist Frigga Haug and colleagues in the 1980s, the adaptation of this method by a group of Australian feminist psychologists in the 1990s, and finally a cultural studies approach represented by the work of Annette Kuhn. The chapter provides a guide to the method as well as exploring differences and commonalities in its use. Chapter 3 takes as its focus oral and life history approaches which employ interviews in order to capture biographies and testimonies that offer a window on the past. It creates a case study clustered around the *Bringing Them Home* report (1997), which gave voice to Indigenous Australians forcibly removed from their families (the Stolen Generations). We explore the complex relationship between experience and narrative, the impact of narrative accrual, and life stories as testimony and a form of inheritance. The second case study examines a life history study of New Zealand women teachers informed by Foucauldian genealogy and feminist theory, and considers how these approaches de-familiarize the present and interrupt linear accounts of history, progression and change.

The second section of the book, 'Being With', showcases two qualitative research strategies which privilege the present. Chapter 4 explores qualitative research that is longitudinal, and which seeks to walk alongside research participants over a determined period of time. Again we seek to place the method into historical and cultural context, asking why and how such approaches are gaining in popularity. We illustrate the potential of the method through examples taken from our own work into young people's lives, showing the way in which personal change can be connected to broader institutional and social processes as well as reflecting on the challenge of analysing, storing and sharing such data sets. Chapter 5 on ethnography explores the way in which a frozen 'ethnographic present' has become the focus of contemporary critique and how this is being extended in order to engage with questions of change as well as continuity. Through two exemplars of ethnographic studies, both informed by feminism and representing different moments in feminist theory and social research, the chapter illustrates how the method can be used to privilege a focus on action, performance and the passage of time, and in doing so reveal the contingency and construction of that which may be taken for granted or assumed as natural.

The third section of the book, 'Inheriting', engages with two research strategies that speak to the future, capturing the passage of meaning and experience between generations. The first of these, Chapter 6, explores cross-generational research and qualitative studies of intergenerational chains. The chapter begins with an exploration of sociological approaches to generation, before considering two examples of intergenerational research in depth: a Norwegian study of three-generation chains of women and a four-generation study of English families. The chapter provides insights into the methodological challenges of such studies as well as outlining how data generated from such studies can enrich and complicate understandings of personal and social change. Chapter 7, 'Revisiting', looks at the shifts between generations of researchers. Here we consider the growing interest in returning to social science studies of the past. This may involve a new set of researchers or the original researcher(s) at a different stage in their life course. Such studies raise a range of compelling practical and epistemological questions about the possibility of recreating the original research context as well as the promise of new or re-contextualized data as a means of documenting social change.

The penultimate chapter in the book – 'Time, Emotions and Research Practice' – provides a case study of research analysis in practice, mobilizing some of the techniques and orientations described throughout the book. By returning to two troubling and related research incidents after a period of several years, we explore the ways in which research encounters can be interrogated retrospectively in order to better understand the 'present' that 'was'. Through critical examination of a performance of racism in a focus group we explore some of the ethical dimensions involved in conducting and writing about research, showing the recursive and iterative character of analysis and how the subjectivity of the researcher can be a resource for this work. The book ends with a conclusion in which we review the themes of temporality, change and continuity and the characteristics of the research traditions we have explored in this book.

By placing our chosen methods within a wider context of their intellectual histories we hope to have gone some way towards holding the dynamic between determination and hermeneutics – showing how the past influences the present and how the present shapes what we see as the past (Connerton, 1989). Methods may simultaneously help us think about processes of continuity and change while also being recognized as claims to knowledge. In our view these are tensions to be recognized rather than resolved, and they can be productive of rich accounts, not simply of relativist dead ends. What we offer in this book is a practical guide to a range of methods that have enormous potential if used thoughtfully and reflectively. We also offer a series of essays on the way in which different methods have arisen and the kind of insights that they may offer, including the theoretical palettes that they may inspire. We hope that the book encourages people to do research that not only privileges temporality, but which goes some way towards the kind of four-dimensional sociology envisaged by Massey: 'the point is to try to think in terms of space–time. It is a lot more difficult than at first sight it might seem' (Massey, 1994: 264).

PART 1
Remembering

2
Memory-Work

[O]ld-fashioned-looking men wearing black suits and hats as if they had to keep their past with them at all times so as not to lose it. (Kiran Desai, 2006: 81)

The paradox of memory is the same as that referred to by the 'hermeneutic circle': the past structures the present through its legacy, but it is the present that selects this legacy, preserving some aspects and forgetting others, and which constantly reformulates our image of this past by repeatedly recounting the story. (Paolo Jedlowski, 2001: 41)

These two quotes point to the complexity of temporal relations, as well as the facility of literary modes of expression to capture such coexistences. Our aim in this book is to map a range of academic approaches that can capture the dynamic relationship between the past and present, characterized both by determination (the past shaping the present) and hermeneutics (the present constructing the past) (Connerton, 1989). Yet we recognize that the language of social science is not always best suited to express the subtleties of temporal processes, and for this reason we employ literary examples along the way. In this first section of the book we explore two research methods which take memories as a raw material for the project of researching social change: memory-work[1] and oral/life histories. Our approach locates these methods in times and places, showing how the generation of knowledge about personal and social change forms part of wider cultural and political agendas. Through examples, we tease out some of the practical and epistemological challenges of working with memory. Memories are indirect and unreliable evidence – in Freudian terms, they combine manifest and latent meaning, and the capacity to remember is posed as an alternative to a compulsion to repeat. Yet it is the very complex and subjective character of memory that makes it such a rich source for exploring temporal processes.

In this chapter we consider memory-work, a technique for the exploration of relationships between pasts, presents and futures that is closely tied up with the development of the women's movement. Memory-work has had many moments of popularity in different academic communities. Here we provide an overview of the very different ways in which memory-work has been exercised and adapted, explicated through three examples: the work of Frigga Haug and colleagues (*Female Sexualization*), the work of June Crawford and colleagues (*Emotion and Gender*), and the work of Annette Kuhn (*Family Secrets*). In telling a story of memory-work, we seek to demonstrate how methods and ideas emerge in concrete situations, yet are creatively appropriated and transposed into new contexts, giving rise to situated knowledge claims.

These examples all share a relationship with emancipatory politics, and fall within two disciplinary traditions: social science and cultural studies. The methods themselves are fluid and adaptable. Although the work sometimes gives rise to remarkable products, the most important outcome may in fact be the process – the making of collective intellectual endeavours. While the various memory-work projects within this overall history have concerned themselves with the relationship between popular culture and personal memory, the group itself becomes the vehicle for other, hidden histories of the changing relationship between radical movements and academic cultures. It is possible to see parallels with the project of oral history described in Chapter 3, where a methodology was looked to for the promise of political transformation, yet in this case the methodology of memory-work was also understood to have the potential to transform subjectivity and consciousness.

We have engaged in memory-work as a complementary research practice for 10 years, with regular memory-work becoming a vital part of communication within research collectives, feeding into the accumulation of a reflexive understanding of our investments in our topics of research, or connections with and differences from each other as well as directly into methodological and theoretical development. In writing this chapter we have become aware that we are arguing *for* the method, and through describing and comparing the projects, detailing their methods and recognizing their limitation, we hope to show the potential of memory-work as a method for exploring the intersections of social and personal change.

A Collective Work of Memory

As far as we are aware, the term 'memory-work' was coined by Frigga Haug and colleagues in a book published first in German as *Frauenformen* 1 and 2 in 1983, then in English translation (by Erica Carter) as *Female Sexualization* (1987). It was reprinted in 1992 and then republished as a Verso Classic in 1999. Haug and colleagues were a group of West German feminist socialists – some were also academics – who worked together on the autonomous women's editorial board of the Marxist journal-cum-publishing house-cum-intellectual forum *Das Argument*. *Female Sexualization* was the result of a two-year project, and the preface to the English edition provides a retrospective account of how the group came together and how they worked in what were heady political times. The overall ambition of the women's editorial group was 'reconstructing scientific Marxism along feminist lines' (1999: 23), and a series of 'projects' were established on a range of themes to this end. What is reported in the book is the result of the project that explored how 'sexuality is constituted as a separate sphere of existence' (p. 34).

Attempts to 'locate' the memory-work of Haug and colleagues for English readers is assisted by an extensive foreword written by Erica Carter for the 1992 English edition. In presenting memory-work to a British audience in the 1990s, Carter seeks to translate three main elements. First, we are introduced to the 'Germanness' of the project, and Carter reflects on the difficulty of translating some of the key theoretical terms, and of smoothing the translation between a language of scientific Marxism and an increasingly post-Marxist consciousness. Second, Carter repositions Haug and colleagues theoretically, in line with academic frameworks salient to this new audience. So, for example, our attention is drawn to the impact on the group of the work of the Birmingham Centre for Contemporary Cultural Studies (BCCCS) (for example, McRobbie and McCabe, 1981; Willis, 1981) and their appropriation of Althusserian perspectives on how we come to desire or own oppression and in doing so remake inequality. This dynamic and psychoanalytically-influenced approach to understanding the way in which agency is active yet constrained is linked by Carter to a second influence on the group – their reading of Foucault and the notion that power is fluid and circulating. She suggests that the authors draw productively on these ideas for their exploration of the body as a site of discourse, facilitating an understanding of ideology as mediated in and through the material. Third, Carter positions the reader's orientation to the practice of memory-work as a resource in feminist engagements with postmodernism and in particular providing feminism with a means to understand how memory is 'mobilized collectively' while avoiding the construction of the kind of 'linear historical development towards liberation' (1992: 14) which had been the focus of so much political and intellectual critique.

The English translation is divided into three parts, opening with an account of the memory-work employed by the collective. The introduction explains that the decision to privilege the methodology of the project was made late in the day on the advice of the typesetters, who suggested that the intended opening chapter (an engagement with Foucault) was perhaps too dense and uninviting. It is thus that the book opens with an extensive discussion of method (Chapter 1), in which the problem of the book is posed as 'the way in which human beings construct themselves into the world … the threads of that development and the points of their interconnections in our memories' (p. 52). This is followed in Chapter 2 ('Displacements of the Problem') by sections representing a series of projects undertaken by the collective into aspects of female embodiment and their relationship to feminine socialization: the hair projects; the body projects; the slave girl projects; legs projects; and notes on women's gymnastics. The main resource in these projects is written memories and analysis of those memories, although photographs are also drawn on.

The group describe their work as being based on two premises:

1. *The subject and object of the research are one.* Rejecting the criticism that memories are too subjective a resource for social science, they treat them as evidence of identity formation – the focus of their investigation. But this does not mean simply treating 'experience' or narratives of the self as unproblematic; rather they recognize that such narratives will gloss the kinds of contradictions, silences and ruptures that are of interest to the analyst. The generation and analysis of memories of embodiment is offered as a way of disrupting and getting into these places.

2. *The research should be a collective process.* The authors argue that group analysis enables the boundaries of forgetting to be made visible. It also enables the construction of the collective subject – 'historical contemporaries engaged in reconstructing the mosaic of experiences by which we were trained to enter society' (p. 58). The more diverse the group, the richer the insights.

The authors clearly state that there is 'no single true method' (p. 70). 'In our experience new modes of analysis express themselves continuously' (p. 70), and 'what we need is imagination' (p. 71). They do, nevertheless, reflect on their method and share the lessons that they learned. These are not laid out as a recipe but have to be gleaned from the text, which we summarize as follows:

The principles of memory-work

• *The importance of good research questions* is central to their approach. Questions should not simply reproduce normative notions. So, for example, in their sexuality project they began by questioning 'how is sexuality constituted as a separate sphere of existence?' (p. 34) which, in turn, helped them construct the projects. They contrast this with an approach that takes sexuality at face value and enquires simply into topic areas such as 'loss of virginity' or 'sex education', questioning whether such an approach could produce anything useful beyond stories of painful recognition and disappointment.

• Another focus is on the development of *techniques for reducing prejudice.* Despite their view that memory-work is predicated on there being no subject/object split, they also seek a systematic approach and practices to ensure that the subject is not 'prejudiced'. Their approach here is shaped by psychoanalytic insight that treats self narratives as based on 'continuities that are manufactured retrospectively in the mind' (p. 48). These techniques for reducing prejudice in the creation of memory texts include focusing on a specific situation (rather than life in its entirety), using the third person (thus approaching past selves as a stranger) and attempting to escape the constraints of relevance by describing everything and anything. They also suggest juxtaposing past and present rather than seeking to forge self narratives, thereby avoiding value judgements and deliberately attempting to imagine the motives and position of all involved.

• Their methodological approach is also distinguished by a *focus on form.* Their discussion of the methods pays a great deal of attention to language and writing. This includes noticing the genres employed, the use of cliché, metaphor and popular sayings, and treating these as evidence of the imbrication of the social within the personal. In seeking to get past these popular discourses, their work is also characterized by a search for an authentic voice, based on the view that women's voices and the voices of the everyday have been silenced in literature. The writing of memories and rewriting of memories represents an attempt to forge the missing voice.

We have found it interesting to revisit this text, 23 years after it was written and possibly 10 years since we looked at it properly. In the light of subsequent appropriations of memory-work we are struck by how open and unprescriptive the method was, involving a range of practices from critical group reading through to writing exercises. We are also struck by the extent to which the book is a product of its own time and place, reflecting a coming together of consciousness-raising practices and the generation of theoretical insight. Some of the language is dated, and the political optimism jars, exposing its absence in contemporary climates. Yet it is not as theoretically naïve as one might have feared, with the exception, perhaps, of the search for an authentic female voice through writing.

In recent years an increasingly critical perspective has developed within feminist theory regarding the use of experience and 'consciousness-raising as a mode of discerning and delivering the "truth" about women' (Brown, 1995: 41). Wendy Brown describes consciousness-raising as operating as 'feminism's epistemologically positivist moment. The material excavated there, like the material uncovered in psychoanalysis or delivered in confession, is valued as the hidden truth of women's existence – true because it is hidden, and hidden because women's subordination functions in part though silencing, marginalization, and privatization' (1995: 41). Brown's position poses a challenge to methods such as memory-work which 'demand the right to use experience as the basis of knowledge' (Haug et al., 1999: 34). Brown points to the 'sharp but frequently elided tensions between adhering to social construction theory on one hand, and epistemologically privileging women's accounts of social life on the other' (Brown, 1995: 41). For Brown, the danger of consciousness-raising (and standpoint perspectives) is that the knowledge gained from such approaches 'while admitting to being "situated", cannot be subjected to hermeneutics without giving up its truth value' (pp. 42–3).

To what extent does the approach of Haug and colleagues fall into this trap? Certainly, the practice of collective memory-work originates in the kinds of consciousness-raising practices that were a familiar part of the women's movement of the time. Haug distinguishes their 'memory-work' from less sophisticated group endeavours and conscious-raising groups that failed to take a critical approach to the object of their enquiry (in this case sexuality) or to theorize insights made available by the practices of retrieval and collective analysis. The methodological and political agendas in relation to which *Female Sexualization* was written differed from those of today. Their arguments were with positivism rather than post-structuralism. They had to demonstrate that the use of their own subjectivities as a raw material for the production of knowledge was valid, that it was not – in their words – 'prejudiced', which may go some way toward explaining their investment in distancing techniques. Theoretically, they were very much concerned with hermeneutics, the indivisibility of subjects and structures and the impossibility of standing outside of these processes. Yet, politically, they expressed an investment in a relatively unproblematized feminist project, including ideas of forging an authentic female voice in their writing.

Haug and colleagues walk a fine line in relation to Brown's charges of feminist positivism, which itself is the culmination of a long series of intense debates with feminism regarding the status of experience, 'voice' and their relationship to politics and agency (Ramazanoglu and Holland, 1999; Scott, 1992). Certainly their approach is based on a critique of female experience as absent from existing knowledge, and memory-work is offered as a way of generating knowledge from female experience, for the direct purpose of changing women's lives. Memory-work in this sense is understood as an intervention in the world, an emancipatory practice, and not simply as a tool for the collection or creation of data. The categories 'women' and 'feminism' are treated in an unproblematic way. Yet, in their defence, they do not understand the memory stories produced in the work as transparent or 'true' in any way. In particular they are critical of the part played by narratives of the self in 'making sense' of contradictions, pointing to the collective interrogation of memories as central to destabilizing these narratives: 'we set out to investigate the process through which we have formed ourselves as personalities, rather than the way that things "really" – objectively – were' (p. 40). Undoubtedly their approach is inspired by their attachment to notions of false consciousness and the operations of the unconscious rather than by a critique of the fiction of the unitary subject. It is a position that is resonant of the theoretical and political climate of western Europe during the 1980s.

To what extent can we understand their project of memory-work as an investigation of social change? As we will explore in the following chapter, historical discourse has played a vital part in the formation of feminism as an intellectual and political project. Central to this has been the use of both historical and anthropological methods to demonstrate *specificity in formations of femininity* (De Beauvoir, 1949/1997; Rubin, 1975). It was perhaps the primary achievement of second-wave feminism to demonstrate the non-universal, socially-constructed character of gender, and the way in which such formations were and are articulated through other historically and culturally defined formations of social class, ethnicity, sexuality and place, and so forth. The project of revealing social construction was so successful within feminism that it undercut feminist claims as to a common subject: be that 'woman' or 'feminism'.

The work of Haug and colleagues emerges at exactly this turning point in the history of western second-wave feminism. Their project is engaged with questions of social change in complex ways. The group take as their focal point the process of 'socialization', the passage from childhood to adult femininity. They do not treat this as a natural or universal developmental process, but rather one in which they are active agents operating within historically-defined parameters. Working as a collective and a generational cohort enables them to identify those historically-defined parameters. The fact that they have come together to review this process through memory-work also locates them within a project of change for the future. They act on the idea, indebted to psychoanalysis, that in understanding how they came to be as they are today, they are also intervening in their own futures. These women are both studying and inciting themselves as a generation that is self-consciously engaged in progressive transformation. The 'we' that their investigations represent is both the specific 'we' of the group and, through theorization, an abstract 'we' encompassing 'women', 'sexualization' and 'socialization' in the collective.

An Australian appropriation of memory-work

In 1985/6 Frigga Haug visited Macquarie University in Australia as a visiting scholar and gave a series of seminars. In attendance were feminist psychologists June Crawford, Una Gault and Sue Kippax. They had been working together (with

Jenny Onyx and Pam Benton) in a reading group exploring critical ideas in social psychology. Inspired and challenged by the ideas and practices presented by Haug, the women began working as a memory-work group, exploring the theme of 'emotion', the outcome of which was published as *Emotion and Gender: Constructing Meaning from Memory* (Crawford et al., 1992). This book, in turn, played a critical role in disseminating and popularizing a particular approach to memory-work to an international audience.

In their introduction to this volume the group provide an explanation of how their project developed. The origins are quite distinct from the culture of Marxist–feminist activism of Berlin in the early 1980s. Here the account is of a group of feminist academic friends, all of whom experienced marginalization within their mainstream psychology departments, and who wanted to explore new ideas beginning to stir within critical social psychology. They described themselves as 'academics, and psychologists, and women' (p. 1) who have managed to sustain a regular commitment to collective work in the 'interstices of full time paid work and the endless work of young and older children and sick or ageing relatives, of overseas study and travel, of political commitments' (p. 1). Explaining their debt to Haug, they credit her with developing a method that is 'empirical but not empiri-cist' (p. 4), 'a feminist theory that was more than a critical analysis of existing society, one that incorporates its own method for empirical research' (p. 4). Discussing their enthusiasm for working with written memories, the group explain that 'We liked the feminist political orientation. We liked the collective way of working. We were intrigued by the collapse of the subject and object, by theory and method, by the idea of becoming our own subjects' (p. 4).

In a different time and place, Crawford and colleagues inevitably put memory-work to different use. The book, written collectively at the end of four years of group work, represents their creative appropriation of the methodology. It is a version that is more circumscribed than the range of practices described by Haug et al. (1999), focusing specifically on the collective analysis of written memories. The method is also presented in a much clearer and more schematic way, as a set of 'rules'.

Memory-work rules

They divide memory-work into three phases:
Phase 1:
Write a memory[2]

1. of a particular episode, action or event
2. in the third person
3. in as much detail as is possible, including even 'inconsequential' or trivial detail (it may help to think of a key image, sound, taste, smell, touch)
4. but without importing interpretation, explanation or biography.
5. Write one of your earliest memories. (p. 45)

All but the last of these injunctions are derived directly from Haug (although in the original they are much more extensive and discursively presented). The last injunction was added by Crawford and colleagues, who in exploring emotion from a psychological perspective considered themselves to be looking at a developmental process that is most active in childhood. As such, they wanted to excavate memories from this period.

It is also interesting that while the group let go of much of the flavour of Haug's original methodology, they retained and amplified the concern with avoiding 'prejudice'. In their introduction they acknowledge that in using an approach such as memory-work they were 'denying the imperatives of our training', asking whether they could also 'remain rigorous' (p. 4). They emphasize Haug and colleagues' warning against the beguiling coherence which biography brings. 'Coherence hides resistance and in this way works against the method' (Haug et al., 1987: 41); a method in which the analysis 'has to be seen as a field of conflict between dominant cultural values and oppositional attempts to wrest cultural meaning and pleasure from life' (Crawford et al., 1992: 47). Thus memories are to be written in the third person and interpretation avoided in the initial stages. The choice of the authors to employ pseudonyms in the book is explained as both an attempt to maintain anonymity but 'more importantly, it helps resist the temptation to write biography' (p. 6).

The gestation of a written memory could take up to a week. Once memories were written, the group would convene for *Phase 2*. Crawford and colleagues offer a set of rules for this stage of the memory-work, yet note that 'we did not adhere to all of them strictly' (p. 48).

1. Each memory-work group member expresses opinions and ideas about each memory in turn, and
2. looks for similarities and differences between the memories and looks for continuous elements among the memories whose relation to each other is not immediately apparent. Each member should question particularly those aspects of the events which do not appear amenable to comparison. She or he should not, however, resort to auto-biography or biography.
3. Each memory-work member identifies cliches, generalizations, contradictions, cultural imperatives, metaphor … and
4. discusses theories, popular conceptions, sayings and images about the topic.
5. Finally, each member examines what is not written in the memories (but what might be expected to be), and
6. rewrites the memories. (p. 49)

Again they clarify that 'it is important that autobiography and biography which emphasize individual aspects of experience be avoided. What is of interest is not why person X's father did such and such but why fathers do such things' (p. 49).

Phase 3 of the process is that 'in which we evaluate our attempts at theorizing' (p. 51), and for Crawford and colleagues this involves a comparative consideration of accounts generated by different episodes of memory-work and a recursive conversation between their memory-work and the psychological literature on emotions. Writing the book was one of the outcomes of this final phase. They observe that in an ongoing memory-work group these phases would run concurrently.

Reflecting on the particular character of this group's appropriation of memory-work is revealing of the ways in which research methodologies evolve as they move across times and places. Most striking is the way that they take what is a messy, unboundaried and highly politicized practice and make it into a 'technique' that can be used by others. Undoubtedly this will have been the result of attempting to extract, share and justify a method within their particular disciplinary framework – psychology. Crawford et al. report that they not only had their own memory-work group but also set up others to work in parallel, where they might act as facilitators and/or researcher/members. They were successful in securing competitive research grants to undertake empirical research using memory-work methods. Crawford and colleagues effectively 'transcribe' memory-work from its original genre of Marxist feminist activism to institutionalized academic feminism within which they are able to maintain the hermeneutic character of the methodology.

Although their version of memory-work was very schematic, the team saw these methods as contributing to the wider methodological project of promoting social constructionism within a psychological framework. Where Haug et al. employ the language of the sociologist in their concern with agency, structure, reproduction and change, Crawford and colleagues considered the method in the light of social psychological concerns with intersubjectivity that were current in the early 1990s (referring to the classic work of Mead and Vygotsky revisited in the then contemporary work of Shotter). They express excitement with the potential of the method to capture both the 'I' and 'Me' dimensions of the self, suggesting that in Phase 1 of the process the self talks with itself, and in Phase 2 the self responds to itself as others respond to it. The collective mode of analysis is seen to be critical in mirroring and confirming the collective condition of the self that is captured in memories, with analogous processes observed in 'the commonness of the episodes and the common sense reached' (p. 52). Both the 'I' of the written memories and the 'Me' of the group discussion are constituted socially, confirming for the group the 'intersubjectivity that proceeds subjectivity' (p. 52).

Why we remember

Crawford and colleagues are particularly interested in the collapse of the distinction between the subject and the object, which they identify as the hallmark of memory-work. It is this that locates memory-work for them within a hermeneutic epistemology and in opposition to an atheoretical empiricism. They are cautious in making claims for the generalizability of insights generated through memory-work, arguing that 'plausibility', 'credibility', 'recognition' and theoretical generativeness may be more appropriate claims for the method. In a chapter called 'Remembering and Forgetting', the group engage in an extended discussion regarding the veracity of memories, and how they mediate the relationship between the present and the past. On the question of veracity they are clear that there is a distinction between real memories and real events and that the focus of memory-work is 'the process of construction … the search for intelligibility, not the actual event' (p. 151). They are also clear on the question of reality vs construction. Memories are reconstructions of past events, and in memory-work 'we are not seeking to uncover the nature of

the event itself but rather the meaning that the event had for us then and now'
(p. 152). They endorse an approach that understands the self as constructed out of
memories. We do not remember everything, and what we remember is highly selective. Drawing on a wide body of psychological literature, including the writings of
Freud on repression, Crawford and colleagues argue that we tend to 'remember
episodes of unfinished business' (p. 154). The mundane is generally not remembered,
nor is the resolved. Such memories can be retrieved, but may only be accessible
indirectly. Following Freud they also observe that repressed material, or more consciously suppressed material, may be forgotten and/or unavailable. They summarize
their view as follows:

> The ways in which the memories we produce in our memory-work, the building
> blocks for our theory of self, represent a biased selection of all the experiences
> that ever happened to us. The bias is a meaningful one. … Nevertheless in
> theorizing our memories, we are concerned at the possibility that there were
> experiences which we do not remember and therefore do not produce in
> memory-work which were important in our construction but were not reflected
> upon, as were those which we produced. (p. 159)

In discussion of an example of a repressed memory they suggest that one of the
reasons that a memory may not be available to a particular trigger may be that this
cultural framework, within which to make the experience intelligible, was not
available to the individual at the time.

The work of Crawford and colleagues is part of an ongoing tradition within
social psychology in which experience and subjectivity are interrogated within
changing theoretical landscapes (Gillies et al., 2004, 2005; Stephenson and
Papadopoulos, 2006; Stephenson et al., 1996). This discussion has shown how
Crawford et al.'s project differed from that of Haug and colleagues (being less
Marxist/sociological; more boundaried; more focused on technique; more engaged
in questions of subjectivity and psychology), but also some of the ways it was
similar (shared focus on socialization; structure/agency; theoretical generation; a partial constructionism/partial hermeneutics; concern with distancing techniques;
avoidance of auto/biography). Although Crawford and colleagues were using their
childhoods to explore meaning, the outcome of their project does not bear much
light on questions of social change, other than in contributing further towards an
understanding of emotion as 'constructed' and thus neither universally produced nor
determined. These themes are brought into relief when we compare this Australian
appropriation of memory-work to a UK cultural studies tradition, influenced by
Haug and colleagues as well as by others.

Family Secrets

The original English translation of *Female Sexualization* (1987) was published by
Verso in the series 'Questions for Feminism', edited by a group that included

Annette Kuhn. Kuhn went on to publish another landmark example of memory-work in 1995, *Family Secrets: Acts of Memory and Imagination*. There are clear connections between Kuhn's approach and that employed by Haug and colleagues, although Kuhn herself does no more than cite *Female Sexualization* as an example of further reading. Kuhn takes the method in a very different direction from that taken by Crawford and colleagues, into a tradition shaped more by the arts than the social sciences and connecting to oral history, cultural studies and psychoanalysis. This section begins with a description of the main components of Kuhn's approach before considering its antecedents and some of the developments that came in its wake.

Acts of memory and imagination

Memory provides material for interpretation, to be interrogated, mined for meaning and possibilities. It involves active staging of memory; it takes an enquiring attitude towards the past and its (re)construction through memory. (Kuhn, 1995: 157)

In stark contrast to the approaches of Frigga Haug, June Crawford and colleagues, Annette Kuhn's memory-work project embraces auto/biography, understood as a tool through which it is possible to detect the traces of the collective and the historical and not an obstacle to such understanding. Kuhn's own project draws on a range of primarily visual raw materials, including her family photograph albums and the traces of their use over the years, including inscriptions on the backs of pictures, and the cutting down and reordering of photographs. She also draws on films, music and paintings, as well as a range of sensory triggers and media through which versions of the past are represented and consumed. She describes her approach as treading 'a line between cultural criticism and cultural production' (p. 4), driven by a concern for the way in which memory shapes the stories we tell, and what it is that makes us remember.

For Kuhn, memory-work can be an individual activity. In fact, she luxuriates in the accessibility of the method, describing memory-work as requiring 'the most minimal resources and the very simplest procedures. Making do with what is to hand – its raw materials are almost universally available – is the hallmark of memory-work's pragmatism and democracy' (p. 7). Moreover, memory-work is 'easy to do, offers methodological rigour, and is fruitful in countless, often unexpected, ways' (p. 6).

A recipe for memory-work

Kuhn provides her own 'recipe' for memory-work, which can be usefully compared to others. Her assumption is that the project will begin with a photograph:

1. Consider the human subjects of the photograph. Start with a simple description, and then move into an account in which you take up the position of the subject. In this part of the exercise, it is helpful to use the third person ('she', rather than 'I', for instance). To bring out the feelings associated with the

photograph, you must visualize yourself as the subject as she was at that moment, in the picture: this can be done in turn with all of the photograph's human subjects, and even with animals and inanimate objects in the picture.

2. Consider the picture's context of production. Where, when, how, by whom and why was the photograph taken?

3. Consider the context in which an image of this sort would have been made. What photographic technologies were used? What are the aesthetics of the image? Does it conform with certain photographic conventions?

4. Consider the photograph's currency in its context or contexts of reception. Who or what was the photograph made for? Who has it now and where is it kept? Who saw it then, and who sees it now? (p. 8)

Although Kuhn suggests the use of the third person in the exploration of the image, she does not do so as a 'distancing technique'. Rather she encourages the memory-worker to identify promiscuously with everyone and everything in the image, as an exercise in imagination. Perhaps this is because her way into the social and collective is not through the process of socialization or development (as with Haug et al. and Crawford et al., respectively) but through an examination of the form of cultural production. Thus we are encouraged to see evidence contained within the form of the photograph, its genre and technologies of production. We are then invited to stay with this photograph through the passage of time and to investigate the part that it plays in the construction of contemporary memory and identity. Rather than seeking to escape the 'coherence' of the biographical, Kuhn seeks to explore the situated practices through which these stories are constructed.

In the course of the book Kuhn adopts a number of different approaches, which accumulate to provide a layered memoir in which memories are traced from origins to application. Examples include her reflections on an image of herself from childhood. The photograph was taken originally by her father, a semi-professional photographer, and for Kuhn it is a record of their adoring and exclusive relationship. This image is traced through its place in a family photograph album created by her eight-year-old self, in which all images of her mother were eradicated. Subsequently the album and the image are revised by her mother who, through rearranging, cutting and inscribing, imposes her own account of the family story. Photographs continued to play a part in her communications with her estranged mother, and are used by Kuhn as ways of attempting to understand her mother's investments in a particular version of her daughter – as well-dressed, neat and slim. The simple image of her childhood self, holding a bird in her hand, with crossed-out notes on the back of the photo, is the site of conflict over memory, about which there is no last word. For Kuhn 'in the process of using – producing, selecting, ordering, displaying – photographs, the family is actually in the process of making itself' (p. 19).

An auto/biographical approach

Kuhn's approach is indebted to the ideas and the practices of psychoanalysis, and she takes from this field a rich vocabulary for considering the operations of memory: accretion (how memories accumulate meaning over time), condensation (how meanings intensify and become 'simpler' over time), secondary revision (the way in which we create retrospective narratives to fit with present needs), repression (material that is 'forgotten' or pushed into the unconscious), and melancholia (an inability to let go of what is lost – a form of hyper-remembering). Her investigation of her family photograph albums is inevitably also an investigation of the unique psychic constellation that is her own family. Yet in accepting the autobiographical she also enables us to gain access to specific details of the past and to the ways in which biographies are enmeshed in history. Hers is a biography firmly located in time and place – postwar London – and shaped by a painful process of social mobility. It is an account that captures the interplay of personal and social change. Kuhn's interest in the representation and evocation of memory extends beyond her own biography, yet it always starts with her experience. Beginning with herself enables Kuhn to see beyond herself, whether that be to read from the image of herself in her special 'coronation dress' through to the creation of popular nationalism, or the familiarity of a world before her birth evoked through the trigger of the image of a burning St Paul's Cathedral. Kuhn employs memory and the connections that are evoked through it (including what Barthes describes as 'piercings' that appear to transcend historical or biographical time) as a way to navigate through the incessant and iterative flow that is popular culture. Paradoxically, although she is much more autobiographical than either Haug et al. or Crawford et al., her approach also speaks more directly to an interest in social and historical processes such as social class, educational mobility, nationalism and the operations of nostalgia.

In the opening pages of the book Kuhn explains to the reader:

> The family secrets are indeed mine – in a manner of speaking; and like all such things, they have roots in the past and reverberations in the present. None of which can be understood until the memories behind the secrets are brought to life and looked at closely. This calls for a certain amount of delving into the past, and for preparedness to meet the unexpected. What is required is an active and directed work of memory. (p. 3)

In beginning with 'secrets' rather than simply with memories, Kuhn's approach demands that the autobiographical is the route taken into memory-work. It is an approach that prioritizes the present, and the idea of 'unfinished business'. Kuhn speaks of memory as 'a position or point of view in the current moment' (p. 128) and memory-work as 'working backwards – searching for clues, deciphering signs and traces, making deductions, patching together reconstructions from fragments of evidence' (p. 4). The autobiographical is also the medium through which to apprehend others, to imagine their motives and perspectives and to unleash this material into our inner world.

Kuhn ends *Family Secrets* with six theses about memory, insights that she has gained through her involvement in memory-work, summarized as follows:

1. *Memory shapes our inner world* (there is a relationship between memory, the psyche and the unconscious).
2. *Memory is an active production of meanings* (the past is not simply there to be retrieved. Memory is always staged, shaped by 'secondary revision', an account that is always discursive).

3. *Memory texts have their own formal conventions* (non-linear/sequential/synchronous, counterposing/contrast).
4. *Memory texts voice a collective imagination* (although our route to the memory may be individual, the memory itself is, as argued also by Haug et al. and Crawford et al., imbricated with the social/ collective).
5. *Memory embodies both union and fragmentation* (here Kuhn points both to the way in which memories provide a sense of coherence, but also how the proliferation of memory texts facilitated by media technologies undermine this promise of coherence as it becomes increasingly hard to forge narratives of self).
6. *Memory is formative of communities of nationhood* (it is difficult to know whether Kuhn wants to suggest that there is a privileged relationship between memory and nationality or whether she was able to use memory-work to explore nationality, in the same way that Haug et al. used it to explore sexualization and Crawford et al. to explore emotion).

Kuhn locates her exercise in memory-work within a tradition of 'revisionist biography', in which she includes key texts such as *Truth, Dare or Promise* (1993), Liz Heron's collection of feminist stories of childhood, the oral historian Ronald Fraser's *In Search of a Past* (1984), feminist historian Carolyn Steedman's *Landscape for a Good Woman* (1986) and photographer Jo Spence's *Putting Myself in the Picture* (1986). These are all examples of the use of memory as a resource for accessing the historical and cultural, but also use the personal as an interruption of more traditional academic discourse. Kuhn talks about feminist and socialist 'outsider biographers' engaging in critical deconstruction of the autobiographical self, for whom there is a gap between the 'I' that writes and the 'Me' that is written about of this generation. Memory-work is presented as an 'instrument of conscientisation: the awakening of critical consciousness through their own activities of reflection and learning, among those who lack power' (p. 9).

Memory-work: family characteristics

Looking across these examples of 'memory-work', it is clear that although they are recognizably within a 'family' they differ considerably and on most counts. These differences are shaped in part by the time, place and disciplinary context in which the exercises in memory-work take place. From this perspective it is difficult to see memory-work as a single method – as Haug and colleagues observe, there is no 'true method'. Yet in creating and refining guidelines, different researchers have productively drawn attention to different potentialities within an overall methodology. In juxtaposing these approaches we seek to further enrich an understanding of what could be done with and through memory-work.

What all the approaches have in common is an embracing of a hermeneutic epistemology which recognizes that, when dealing with memory, the past is apprehended through the subject. Inherent to this hermeneutic position (in which subject and object are one) is an understanding of time as subjectively experienced. This refers to the temporality described by Bergson as *durée*, in which the past is not simply 'out there' to be retrieved but which must always be evoked subjectively and through the present. In each example of memory-work discussed in this chapter it is recognized that the selection of memory (acts of remembering/forgetting) and representation of memories (in albums, as narratives, genres, mediated by popular nostalgia/moral panic) are practices of *a* present. As such, both are shaped by the context and communities within which and for whom the remembering takes place (Halbwachs, 1950/1992). One criticism of the consciousness-raising roots of memory-work is that such approaches to excavating 'experience' privilege it over other kinds of knowledge: 'admitting to being "situated" … without giving up its truth value' (Brown, 2001: 42–3). As we raised early in this chapter, this is a serious challenge to memory-work, but one to which it can respond confidently if not conclusively. Certainly, all the approaches to memory-work described here go a long way in 'situating' the material generated. The different memory-workers tend to do this through problematizing the relationship between the memory text and associated narratives, yet in different ways. In the social science tradition, both Haug and colleagues and Crawford and colleagues employ distancing techniques to disrupt the formation of autobiographical narratives. Within the cultural studies tradition, Kuhn embraces the autobiographical in order then to treat is as a cultural product, historicized in time and located within space. Whether the memory-workers 'give up the truth value' of the memories they are working with is another matter. All respond to the question of veracity within the terms of their discipline, understanding memories as constructions and as 'raw material' for the work of social, psychological and cultural analysis.

Yet the question of the veracity of memories or what Hacking (1995) calls 'memoropolitics' has become a volatile and politicized subject, with a history of its own. Memory-work as a method for the generation of memories has to be understood as coexisting with a wider culture of remembrance and testimony within which it has become possible, for example, to 'excavate' and tell stories of sexual abuse and survival (Plummer, 1995; Reavey and Warner, 2003). In 2001 Frigga Haug reflected on her dismay during a visit to Canada in the early 1990s as to the inability of her students to distinguish between an invitation to participate in memory-work and an invitation to reveal experiences of child sexual abuse. Haug understands this as a symptom of the growing individualism of the feminist movement which focuses on personal confession and the crimes of individuals rather than on global economic processes. In a subsequent response to her article, Jane Kilby interprets Haug's view as attempting 'to re-establish the Marxism underpinning her early and influential writing on memory-work. … For Haug, memory-work is a method that should take us beyond domestic history' (Kilby, 2002: 201). While sympathizing with Haug, Kilby outlines how high the stakes are in debates around memory, and the difficulty of balancing the hermeneutic understanding of the past being shaped by the present (a recognition that our memories are shaped by present-day identities, cultural context and the communities with and for whom we remember) and the determinist position of the present being determined by the past (for example, understanding current identities as the result of events remembered).

Although it may be possible to accept an interplay of hermeneutic and determinist dynamics in social and psychoanalytic theory, such uncertainty and indeterminacy are more challenging within political, legal and evidential terrains. This is a tension that underpins a range of contemporary debates, including the 'history wars', that we will consider in Chapter 3. We can add to this ongoing debate within feminism and other progressive political movements concerning the problems of *ressentiment* – a dependence of feminist/socialist/marginalized identities on the injuries of the past (Brown, 2001) and a desire to be open to imagining alternative futures from the position of an open present, one that is not precluded by particular narratives (Grosz, 2004, 2005).

Conclusion

In this chapter we have traced the development of memory-work as both an empirical practice and a field of theoretical development. The three examples of memory-work discussed are situated within particular times, places and disciplines, and to some extent can be understood as the product of and responses to these circumstances. Together they form a methodological 'family' with a shared hermeneutic approach in which past memories are understood as personal constructions within the present, yet which include traces of the conditions of their production.

Memory-work has its roots in forms of collective consciousness-raising and individual 'conscientization', which both seek to make public previously hidden stories and experiences but which also problematize the self that remembers. All of the approaches are comfortable with the idea of an unconscious, with latent as well as manifest meaning, and recognize a relationship between fragmentary/contradictory memories and narratives that forge coherence. How we orient to our memories is politicized and moralized territory. There is no reason why memory-work should lead inevitably to 'melancholic attachments to the past', but rather it might enable an awareness of the surfacing and diffusing of the past within the present (Brown, 2001). At its best, memory-work insists that we interrogate what and why we remember and forget. And although it invariably begins with the personal, most approaches to memory-work ultimately seek to comment on wider social, cultural and historical processes. It is not only the outcome of memory-work that makes it a popular practice across disciplines and social fields. The process of reading, thinking, remembering, analysing, theorizing and writing alone and together can make memory-work productive as a parallel research practice to other projects, generating ideas tangentially and feeding into the analysis of wider data. As Grosz (2005) points out, perception is enriched by memory, and perhaps it is this generative facility that arises from what Wendy Brown calls 'mindful remembering'. Our own experience supports the comments of Crawford and colleagues who point out: 'what was unexpected, what overwhelmed and excited us, was the strength of memory-work in enabling us to ground emerging theory in our data and their analysis. We found that memory-work worked even better than we anticipated' (1992: 43).

Summary points

- Memories are not simply records of the past, but in their evocation represent the past within the present.

- Memories are *constructions* into which the personal, social and the historical are intertwined.

- Memories are likely to be fragmentary, contradictory and include latent as well as manifest meanings.

- Memories can be distinguished/distanced from the narratives that give memories coherence. It is also possible to explore memories through the narratives that occasion their telling/representation.

- Memory texts can be productively analysed as cultural texts: asking questions about audience, genre, composition, etc.

- The context in and through which memories are produced is always relevant. We remember for and with others, and this will shape what is remembered and how.

- The process of engaging in memory-work can heighten perception and contribute to creativity and theoretical generation.

- The value of memory-work is not simply that it provides access to the personal or the autobiographical, but rather that this is a vehicle for the understanding of social, cultural and historical formations.

Further resources

Fraser, R. (1984) *In Search of a Past: The Manor House, Amnersfield, 1933–1945.* London: Verso.
Fascinating and moving combination of memoir, oral history and self-analysis. Example of how the complexity of memory can be captured through formal writing techniques.

Marker, C. (1998) *Immemory.* Berkeley, CA: Exact Change.
CD ROM created by filmmaker and artist Chris Marker that uses hypermedia techniques to map the kinds of non-linear connections that link memories represented by mementos of a lifetime: childhood books, family photographs, picture postcards.

Radstone, S. (ed.) (2000) *Memory and Methodology.* Oxford: Berg.
Edited collection bringing together leading writers on memory including Annette Kuhn, Frigga Haug and Richard Johnson. Explores the politics of memory, the impact of technologies and the art of memory-work as practised in different disciplines.

Reavey, P. and Brown, S.D. (2006) 'Transforming agency and action in the past, into the present time: adult memories and child sexual abuse', *Theory and Psychology*, 16: 170–202.
Exploration of how theories of remembering can be employed to create new ways of thinking about traumatic childhood memories. Emphasizes the way in which memories are structured spatially.

Smart, C. (2007) *Personal Life: New Directions in Sociological Thinking.* Cambridge: Polity Press. (Chapter 5, 'Secrets and Lies'.)
Exploration of secrets and silences within families, and how new technologies and legal frameworks shape what it is possible to tell and to hide.

Notes

1　This text adopts the compound term 'memory-work' (following the use of Haug et al. and Crawford et al.) rather than the more general 'memory work' adopted by Kuhn, except in direct quotations.

2　Once a general subject matter is chosen, a trigger word is generated. They describe their own process of generating trigger words as an iterative process. Beginning with the trigger 'Sorry', they were surprised not to discover memories marked by guilt and shame. They then tried the trigger 'Transgresstion'. Subsequently they experimented with a directly emotional label, 'Happiness', following this with 'Anger' as a contrast. They used the trigger 'Praise' in juxtaposition with the previous use of 'Transgression' and the situational trigger 'Play' to see if it would produce reports of happiness. Memories of both childhood and adulthood were produced in response to the trigger 'Holidays'. The group advises that around a week is needed to 'gestate' on the trigger and to engage in the first phase.

3

Oral and Life History

'[E]verything starts, not from the archives, but from testimonies', observes Paul Ricoeur (2004: 147): 'we have nothing better than testimony, in the final analysis, to assure ourselves that something did happen in the past' (Ricoeur 2004: x). Whether or not they go as far as Ricoeur, many researchers today work with personal narratives, testimonies and memories. They do so in order to gain access to past experiences that are not documented in other ways, and also because they believe such sources can give them a much richer understanding of the past-present relationship. A focus on individual stories is often accompanied by an interest in how histories are imagined and constructed, and in what this reveals about the time and place in which they are told. This has led, in turn, to questions about why certain things are remembered while others are not, and to sustained reflection on the social and biographical processes of memory and forgetting. 'Memory is historically conditioned, changing colour and shape according to the emergencies of the moment', asserts Raphael Samuel; 'It is progressively altered from generation to generation' (1994: x). In this chapter, we explore oral and life history approaches through these themes of testimony, memory, and the past-present relationship. We begin by charting some of the history of oral and life history approaches from the 1960s and 1970s onwards, and the hopes that animated their development. On the whole, this is a story about trends within the UK and Australia, but there are parallels with developments in Europe and North America, and these, as well as the transnational impact of influential debates about memory, biography and history, are noted. As with the story about memory-work, the chapter offers an account of how social research methods have emerged in a particular time and place, not simply as strategies for documenting change, but also as strategies for effecting and influencing change.

The two case studies discussed in this chapter draw upon different theoretical traditions, yet both engage with life histories to interrogate the politics of the present. The first case study takes as its focus the collection and use of Indigenous oral histories and testimony in Australia, their significance in contemporary race relations, and the socio-political legacy of telling life stories – in the present and for

the future. It offers an example of oral histories that are embedded in wider political struggles and community histories and reviews contrasting methodological and
theoretical approaches to examining these narratives. This first case study is intentionally the longer of the two. This is, in large part, because it demands a greater
level of detail and explication to draw out the complexity of a contemporary and
controversial use of oral histories 'in action'. This provides a unique opportunity to
elaborate central themes discussed in this chapter, such as individual and collective
memory, in reference to a current issue, one that powerfully highlights significant
ethical and epistemological dilemmas in oral history practice and interpretation.
The second case study returns to the genre of an academic research project, and
considers a study that combines Foucauldian genealogy with feminist life history
to examine the experiences of women teachers in New Zealand. In foreground-
ing an orientation to writing a 'history of the present', this case study represents an
approach to historical enquiry that has become increasingly influential and which
brings additional, important dimensions to our discussion of the relationship
between past and present.

We began writing this chapter during a time when issues about the relationship
of history to the present were making headlines in Australia. Intense public debates
about the teaching of Australian history in schools were echoing in the background
as we researched the merits and purposes of oral history and its links to social movements and public histories. A backdrop to these debates about history curriculum
was the 'history wars' (Clendinnen, 2006; Macintyre and Clark, 2003), a series of
heated public disputes among historians and political leaders about how Australia's
history should be written. The former conservative Prime Minister, John Howard,
accused Australian historians of advancing a 'black armband'[1] view of history. This
kind of history, he declared, emphasized negative aspects of Australia's past, particularly regarding the impact of British 'settlement' on and the subsequent treatment of
Indigenous people. A more positive national history was needed, he argued, one that
celebrated Australia's achievements and highlighted commonalities, not differences,
among Australians. These matters were at the base of the controversy about how
Australian history should be taught in schools.[2] The point of contention was not
whether Australian history should be part of the school curriculum (which it
already was), but what kind of history should be taught and whose stories would be
told. These 'history wars' forcibly underlined the political salience of historical
knowledge, showing that historical narratives are about the past *and* the present,
shaped by the time and place in which they are written and circulated. They are also
about the future. The teaching of national histories is linked to citizenship formation and decisions about the knowledge and values deemed appropriate for future
generations. The politics and production of historical knowledge have been central
themes in the development of oral and life history.

Disciplinary contexts and convergences

Both oral and life histories employ interviews to elicit memories, attitudes and
reflections on experiences. Interviews can be collective or individual, in-depth or

unstructured, conversational or relatively structured, depending upon the particular methodological framework and purpose. They can involve a range of prompts – such as photographs or memorabilia – and rationales, and comprise images, sound recordings, written or transcribed text and other artefacts, or what Ken Plummer (2001) evocatively calls 'documents of life'; these can be naturally-occurring documents, such as letters, diaries, blogs, or generated for a specific research project. The conceptual and methodological frameworks for studying this material take many forms, but a common challenge is how to interpret it in ways that illuminate the life of the individual as well as the phenomena or social relations in which they are embedded or which are being explored.

For the French sociologist Daniel Bertaux, the 'object [of study] should never be an individual as such but rather a sociological object; that is a given set of social relations' (1981a: 9). Plummer suggests that 'life story research at its best always brings a focus on historical change, moving between the changing biographical history of the person and the social history of his or her lifespan. … A life history cannot be told without a constant reference to historical change' (Plummer, 2001: 39–40). Consequently, the individual life story is frequently complemented with additional enquiries, such as interviews with others – family, friends, fellow workers – documentary records, photographs and so forth, which in combination with the life story – the story one tells about one's life – comprise the basis for constructing a life history (Bertaux, 1981a; Chamberlayne et al., 2000).

Today oral and life history are part of mainstream research practices, widely studied in universities and taken up in community and social organizations. There are identifiable classic texts, specialized journals and professional associations, as well as histories of phases in the fields' development (Chamberlayne et al., 2000; Perks and Thomson, 2006; Plummer, 2001). This established position contrasts with their more oppositional and outsider beginnings, with proponents challenging methodological orthodoxies and championing the politics of new forms of biographical and historical research.

In these beginnings, as now, oral history and life history shared similar aims and methods, even though they are associated with different disciplinary traditions – the former history, the latter sociology (Thompson, 1981). The two converge on the significance attributed to subjective experience, memories and narratives – life stories – for generating insight into social processes and for bringing the perspective of local and individual experience to macro sociological and historical pictures. 'In giving value to subjective experience, historians and sociologists were discovering common ground' (Chamberlayne et al., 2000: 4). For Bertaux, a key focus of the life history approach was to explore 'the connection between social dynamics and historical change: what is the relationship between individual and collective praxis and sociohistorical change?' (Bertaux, 1981a: 6).

Two further contexts are relevant here. The first is 'recovery' and 'preservationist' oral histories, which include attempts to document folklore or the voices of a generation before they disappear. Indeed, preservationist studies may be more motivated by an interest in protecting and conserving the past than in promoting a transformative political agenda. Other types of 'recovery' projects record a cohort, such as an ageing generation that has lived through momentous or traumatic historical events. For example, the US Federal Writers' Project in the 1930s recorded the memories of former slaves, then quite elderly, and developed an extraordinary archive of slave narratives (Hirsch, 2003; Yetman, n.d.). Another example is the documentation of memories from now ageing Holocaust survivors. In both examples, the knowledge from life histories is also offered in the hope of preventing such events from happening again, to make sure that we do not forget. Thus, a second context is that, although many types of projects share an interest in recovering and recording oral histories for the present, they bring different perspectives to the past–present relationship and the relationship of oral history to social change projects.

Challenging history

As a movement and a method, oral history gained ground during the 1970s amid a flourishing of social, labour and women's history (A. Thomson, 2007). This was a time in many parts of the world when movements for political and social change, such as feminism, permeated universities and challenged traditional forms of knowledge. Concurrently, a radical critique of historical methods from the 1960s onwards (Munslow, 1997) challenged the selection and construction of sources, the role of the archive, the privileging of written documents and the topics deemed worthy of historical investigation: whose past and what kind of experiences and events became recorded as history? New social histories sought to understand the experiences of people whose lives were typically neglected or subordinated in the historical record – women, labourers, the illiterate – and oral and life history methods helped realize these ambitions (Gluck and Patai, 1991; Perks and Thomson, 2006).

In its early days, many historians and sociologists saw life history research as reinvigorating their discipline. Bertaux[3] (1981b) charged sociology with being stuck in a rigid positivism that (unsuccessfully) attempted to replicate the methods of natural science in the study of social dynamics. Others regarded sociology as lost in the abstractions of structuralism, and saw in life history a way to build a more humanist focus on the individual experience within processes of social change (Plummer, 2001). As qualitative researchers now commonly argue, a reliance on survey and quantitative data obscured subjective experiences and offered little insight into how social phenomena were actually encountered and lived (Crotty, 1998; Denzin and Lincoln, 2005). Other kinds of data and methods were needed to understand human experience; quantifying it was insufficient, as was disembodied theorizing.

Similarly, social historians judged conventional historical practice as insufficiently oriented to the experiences of the individual (Samuel, 1994; Thompson, 1978). Paul Thompson argued that social dynamics were typically theorized at the level of structures, not at the level of individual negotiations of them. Our understanding of economic and ideological changes is incomplete without knowledge 'of how such forces interact at an individual level … to form those myriad decisions which cumulatively, not only give shape to each life story, but also constitute the direction and scale of major social change' (Thompson, 1981: 299). Oral and life history were thus interdisciplinary, combining elements of sociological and historical traditions to challenge the conventions of their discipline and to investigate the dynamics of the past/present relationship and socio-historical change via a focus on biographical experience and memory.

Radical traditions

Intellectual excitement and an enthusiastic sense of political purpose animated the renaissance of much oral history writing during the 1960s and 1970s (A. Thomson, 2007). Many practitioners represented their research as offering a kind of emancipatory methodology for eliciting and honouring the voices of the oppressed or silenced, for rescuing history from elites, and ordinary people from oblivion – for telling new stories about the past for the present. Proponents sang the praises of research that enabled the voices of 'ordinary' people to be heard, and for their stories to become part of the larger historical and cultural picture (Hamilton and Shopes, 2008).

Whether motivated by the concerns of socialist or feminist history, many oral historians, coming from diverse backgrounds, shared a desire to create a different kind of history. By excavating stories of oppression and resistance, they sought to transform understandings of the past and to build counter-traditions, which in turn could contribute to reshaping the present, and the future. History 'should provide a challenge, and understanding which help towards change', reflected Paul Thompson (1978: 17).

Further, the growing popularity of oral and life histories challenged the hegemony of academic history. History belonged with the people and in communities, not experts, and in the 1970s and 1980s many public and local history projects flourished, fuelled by oral histories and an associated interest in documenting everyday community life. Joanna Bornat and Hanna Diamond argue that community-based 'extra-mural work has been a defining characteristic of much oral history in the English-speaking world' (Bornat and Diamond, 2007: 22).

Oral history's radical and political ambitions were part of a wider trend in academic and community research. Transformative agendas underpinned many social research approaches that similarly gained in popularity from the 1970s onward and continue to be influential, such as participatory and action research methodologies informed by critical and feminist theories. Oral and life history projects are distinguished, however, by the salience they give to the past in the project of change.

Remembering the past in the present

'Our present *is* history', declared Bertaux (1981b: 35). Oral and life histories represent the past not as a distinct temporal domain, cut off from the present, but as indissolubly connected to the present. What we see in the past – the things we remember or forget – are shaped by what is happening in the present and the

social circumstances in which one is embedded. To an extent, these understandings of the past/present relation were muted, or not typically addressed, in early
oral history projects (Bornat and Diamond, 2007; A. Thomson, 2007). From the
1980s onward, however, these insights began to enter mainstream oral history
research practice.

In our previous chapter on memory-work, we argued that past memories are
always also personal constructions within the present. This argument applies
equally to oral history projects, even when the explicit purpose is not to explore
autobiographical narratives or memories of the self. The recollections of events, or
of working life, community or family relations, emerge in the present, in response
to the concerns and mood of the times, and in the context of the teller's stage of
life and social location. Life history narratives are thus never the simple outpour-
ing of unmediated recollections of the past, but are shaped by multiple factors. In
yet other ways, the present *is* history in how stories that are told or remembered
today become future sources for understanding *this* present – a future past. These
temporal relations have been grappled with extensively in diverse historiographi-
cal traditions (Foucault, 1984; Harootunian, 2007; Koselleck, 1985; Ricoeur,
2004), but our concern here is with the particular perspectives offered by oral and
life history.

The high hopes for oral history were also met by criticisms, from both oppo-
nents and supporters of biographical research approaches. On the one hand, questions about the status of oral and life stories as historical knowledge came from
sceptical empiricists who found fault with the reliance on the inevitably flawed and
partial memories of individual social actors. Are personal stories reliable? Do they
count as research evidence? What about false or distorted memories – is listening
to what people remember and choose to tell us really history? On the other hand,
there were criticisms of what was seen as oral history's own empiricism, evident in
a valorization of oral testimony as the new historical source and window onto the
past, and an attendant neglect of the biographical and cultural dimensions of memory (Popular Memory Group, 1982).

Documenting these debates and limitations is now part of the regular story about
the development of oral history, told as a movement from naïvety to a more sophisticated recognition of research dynamics in the interview and the complex interplay of
memory and forgetting in the construction of collective and biographical histories
(Bornat and Diamond, 2007; Summerfield, 2000; A. Thomson, 2007).

Individual and collective memory

In accounts of the history of oral history, an interest in memory begins to develop
during the late 1970s and early 1980s. Up until that point, debates about oral
history had largely been between preservationists, enthusiasts for its emancipatory
potential, and empiricist sceptics, who questioned the reliability of oral history's
evidence. In many respects, the 'turn to memory' sidesteps these debates by
dwelling on how and why people remember things. The central issue becomes not
whether memories are verifiably true or false, but what memories reveal about

collective and individual contexts and experiences. This led to a focus upon, as US historian Michael Frisch suggested, 'how people make sense of their past, how they connect individual experience and its social context and how the past becomes part of the present' (Frisch, 1990: 188). Most theorists of memory, in one way or another, distinguish individual memory from collective or social memory, and have characteristically expressed more interest in the latter than the former (Hamilton and Shopes, 2008).

Interest in the study of memory also emerged in the context of cross-disciplinary interests in subjectivity and the rising influence of cultural studies, with its focus on the social and discursive construction of meaning. Memory studies now constitute a thriving field of enquiry (Darian-Smith and Hamilton, 1994). Hamilton suggests that there are two broad strands within memory studies: 'The first derives from oral history and the work on group biographies; the second from a concern to document the processes of collective remembering on a national scale' (Hamilton, 1994: 17), and includes studies of material forms such as war monuments or national celebrations. However, the relationship between oral history and memory studies, despite overlapping interests, remains somewhat contested. Hamilton and Shopes observe that, despite significant expansion in both oral history and memory studies, exchanges between the two have been relatively limited, with 'very little published work [that] examines how oral history, as an established form for actively making memories, both reflects and shapes collective or public memory' (Hamilton and Shopes, 2008: vii–viii). One explanation for this, they suggest, is that oral history has been principally concerned with the life story of individuals while 'memory scholarship, unlike oral history, has been largely concerned with memory that is sustained beyond the individual lifespan, most often in memorials, monuments, or rituals [and] is principally concerned with the memory of groups' (Hamilton and Shopes, 2008: x). This understanding of memory scholarship contrasts with the form of individual and group memory-work discussed in Chapter 2, yet both share a focus on memories as not only individual but also as socially-embedded.

One of the most influential interventions into debates in the UK and Australia regarding the relationship between oral history and memory was an essay published in 1982 by members of the Popular Memory Group at the Birmingham Centre for Contemporary Cultural Studies. Entitled 'Popular memory: theory, politics, method' (Popular Memory Group, 1982), it examined the social and subjective dimensions of memory. Its most lasting contributions were an insistence on the cultural and collective nature of memory and an articulation of the relationship between public representations and private memories. Oral history is not about the past, they argued, but the 'past–present relationship' (p. 240), and such histories are 'profoundly influenced by discourses and experiences in the present' (p. 243). While these are now relatively commonplace views, they gained currency in a particular time and place and in response to identified stalemates in researching the interconnections between historical, biographical and social processes.

The social production of memory refers to all the ways in which memories and a 'sense of the past are constructed': academic history is only one element of that production (Popular Memory Group, 1982: 207). 'The social production of memory is a collective production in which everyone participates, though not equally' (p. 207): historical memory is contested and shaped by relations of power and inequality. According to the Popular Memory Group, while distinctions can be drawn between public representations and private memory, there is a symbiotic relationship between the two. Within public representations, dominant memories may be contested but they more or less shape what is remembered individually. This does not constitute a simple opposition between dominant and counter memory, but rather conveys the extent to which popular memories are diffused and infiltrate so-called private or individual memories. In developing these arguments, the essay echoes a longer line of debate about memory, with the concept of 'collective memory', derived from Maurice Halbwach's work (Halbwachs, 1950/1992), in which memory, though experienced personally, is not an individual but a social phenomenon. Building on this insight, Connerton suggests that 'it is through membership of social groups that individuals are able to acquire, localize and recall memories' (1989: 32).

Private memory and cultural myths

The ascendancy of memory studies might suggest, on the one hand, an intensification and proliferation of 'memory'. Yet, on the other, French historian Pierre Nora argues that 'Memory is constantly on our lips because it no longer exists' (1996: 1), having been supplanted by the 'acceleration of history' (p. 2). Nora laments that societies based on memory 'are no more', and that 'the institutions that once transmitted values from generation to generation – churches, schools, families, governments – have ceased to function as they once did'. Similarly, 'ideologies based on memory have ceased to function as well' (p. 2). In contrast to a more dominant view that sees an expansion of memory and its significance in contemporary life, Nora argues that 'our very perception of history has, with much help from the media, expanded enormously, so that memory, once the legacy of what people knew intimately, has been supplanted by the thin film of current events' (p. 2). Memory, Nora declares, 'has become a private affair. As a result of this psychologization, the self now stands in a different relation to memory and the past' (p. 11).

Against Nora's nostalgic sense of loss and decline, others propose a less pessimistic account, noting the continuing vitality and power of social and individual memory. The interplay of collective and individual memory is also part of what gives cultural myths their power, argued Raphael Samuel and Paul Thompson, a decade after the Popular Memory Group (Samuel and Thompson, 1990). Oral historians have particular opportunities, Samuel and Thompson suggest, to 'observe the displacements, omissions and reinterpretations through which myths in personal and cultural memory take shape' (p. 5):

> The individuality of each life story ceases to be an awkward impediment to generalization, and becomes instead a vital document of the construction of consciousness, emphasizing both the variety of experience in any social group, and

also how each individual story draws on a common culture: a defiance of the rigid categorizations of private and public, just as of memory and reality. (Samuel and Thompson, 1990: 2)

What are the implications of these arguments about life story and memory for research practice? First, memories are both individual and social, and manifested, apprehended and sustained in particular life stories. The oral or life history interview therefore can take a dual focus on the collective and the individual, and memories provide a bridge between the two. Second, individual memories, while idiosyncratically interesting, have the potential to illuminate cultural myths, dominant memories and public histories. In telling their story, individuals are involved in a process of making their own history, and speaking back to and co-constructing public or collective histories. The analytic and research focus is thus both on what is remembered – or forgotten – (the content) and on how those memories are told (the form).

Interviews – remembering, forgetting and constructing

A common criticism of early oral and life history interviews was that they overly focused on the content (rather than the form) of what was told in interviews, and on the accumulation of particular details. Looking back, Raphael Samuel and Paul Thompson reflected that such interviews were characterized by a 'naïve realism':

> Inspired by the very abundance of the newly discovered sources in living memory which we had opened up, we made a fetish of everydayness, using 'thick' description, in the manner suggested by anthropologists, to reconstitute the small detail of domestic life: but we had little to say about dream-thoughts and the hidden sexuality of family relationships. (1990: 2)

The aim of such life history interviews was less to reveal the psychological processes of memory and individual emotions than it was to build a sense of the larger social context and structures in which recollected experiences occurred. Further, as the Popular Memory Group observed, oral historians neglected 'the relations of power that enter into the method, unconsciously because not theorized, at every point from the devising of an interview schedule to the presentation of the final explanatory account' (Popular Memory Group, 1982: 223). Yow (1997) observes, however, that since the late 1980s oral historians 'have talked about the interview as a collaborative effort, not between authority and subject, but between two searchers of the past and present' (1997: 69–70).

Most oral historians now, as with others engaged in life story and biographical research (Chamberlayne et al., 2000; Erben, 1998; Hollway and Jefferson, 2000; MacLure, 2003; Plummer, 2001), reject an objectivist view of the interview as a search for facts or uncovering of the true and full story. This is evident in the shift from seeing life history interviews as records of what is remembered, to a greater interest in what is not told, or seemingly forgotten, and the relationship between unconscious and conscious memory (Summerfield, 2000). The work of the Italian oral historian Luisa Passerini has been influential in this regard. Her study of memories of interwar fascism in Italy 'showed how the influences of public culture and ideology upon individual memory might be revealed in the silences, discrepancies and idiosyncracies of personal testimony' (A. Thomson, 2007: 54; see Passerini, 1987, 2002). Passerini attends to the realm of the imaginary, not factual recall, arguing that 'dreams, images, myths, fantasy' shaped and made possible the actual life experiences of her interviewees, and continued to structure and echo across their recollected life stories (Passerini, 1990: 54).

Similarly drawing on the psychology of memory and subjective desires, Alessandro Portelli (1990) described a series of interviews he conducted in which the informants recalled events or told stories about their pivotal role in something that might have happened, but did not, or did not happen in quite the way they remembered. We can fruitfully understand such narratives as 'uchronic stories':

> All these stories are not about how history went, but how it could have gone: their realm is not reality, but possibility. We gain a better understanding of them if we connect them to the great literary form of the refusal of existing history: uchronia. Uchronia is 'that amazing theme in which the author imagines what would have happened if a certain historical event had not taken place'; the representation of 'an alternative present, a sort of parallel universe in which the unfolding of an historical event had not taken place'. (Portelli, 1990: 150)

Such ways of reading narratives emphasize the present time of remembering and its framing of the recalled past experience: we return to this point in Chapter 6 in relation to life histories in intergenerational research.

Intersubjectivity and life story interviews

Such ways of reading life stories shift the weight of attention from a predominantly sociological account of the collective production of memory and public history to one more attuned to the psychodynamic and intersubjective dimensions of memory, desire and history, and to how mythic forms and desires manifest in both the past experience and its recollection. Life history interviews, as with other in-depth interviews, are marked by the desires and reactions of the interviewer as well as of the interviewee (McLeod and Yates, 2003; Schostak, 2006; St Pierre and Pillow, 2000).

The shift from eliciting facts and content to recognition of the productive dynamic of the interview has necessarily contributed to a greater focus on subjectivity – of both the interviewer and interviewee. Passerini, for example, argues that recognition of the process and effects of intersubjectivity is essential:

> inter-subjectivity is at the basis of the interview, which constitutes the oral testimonies, and also at the basis of interpretation. Furthermore, inter-subjectivity is at

the origin of the narrations which we collect, not in the sense that we interviewers generate them … but rather in the sense that the narrations themselves originated in a context of exchange, prior to our intervention. (Passerini, 2002: 4)

As our discussion of memory-work in Chapter 2 suggested, and as we explore in
reference to our own research in Chapter 8, addressing the psychodynamic
dimensions of interviews can provide important clues for developing analyses of
what takes place in the interview itself and what the interview means (Hollway
and Jefferson, 2000; Walkerdine et al., 2001). In terms of researching social change,
links are required between the internal dynamics of the interview and the socio-
cultural setting in which the interview and the narrative arise. One instance of this
in life history research is the Biographic Narrative Interpretive Method (BNIM),
which combines a psychodynamic perspective with an explicitly historical and
sociological frame in order to facilitate understanding of 'both the "inner" and the
"outer" worlds of "historically-evolving-persons in historically-evolving situations", and particularly the *interactivity* of inner and outer world dynamics'
(Wengraf, 2006: 1; see also Chamberlayne et al., 2000). Examining what is or is
not told, remembered or not remembered can illuminate an individual life, but
because memory is both biographical and social, life history narratives have a
wider cultural resonance.

The following case study draws out the some of these themes and the complex
relationship between individual memory, dominant discourses and public history,
showing the cultural power of life stories in contemporary politics. It explores the
impact of oral histories told by Indigenous Australians and reflects on the use of life
stories as forms of testimony and historical record.

The Stolen Generation: Memory and political discourse

'Indigenous narrative memory is held in life stories and life experiences', observed
prominent Aboriginal leader and historian Jackie Huggins (2005). 'The old ones
remember stories, songs, dances and live out their stories to try to live good lives.
Thus Indigenous narrative memory is an organic process, which is a collective
activity, and is essentially a map for possibilities of existence upon which people can
draw to make sense of experience' (p. 3). Telling one's life history has an added
political dimension because of the profound effects of colonization, which simultaneously misrepresented or erased the experiences of Indigenous people by generating
information about 'them', as if Indigenous people had no capacity or authority to
speak or act on their own behalf. Oral history has thus been an important means
by which Indigenous people themselves have told their own histories directly,
rather than have their history told from non-Indigenous or racist perspectives.
Consequently, Huggins argues it is equally important that the gathering and management of these oral histories is organized by Indigenous agencies, as the 'only
way the Indigenous narrative memory can be properly understood is through the

paradigms of Indigenous people' (2005: 3). The challenge is not simply to record the stories, but to know how to interpret them, and to understand the ways in which personal stories are socially embedded. There is not a single 'Aboriginal perspective' that unfolds in the various life stories, and the individual life history is always part of a collective community history (p. 3).

A significant impetus to the collection of Indigenous oral histories came from research for and recommendations arising from the report *Bringing Them Home: Report of the National Inquiry into the Separation of Aboriginal and Torres Strait Islander Children from their Families* (1997). Commissioned by the Commonwealth government, and conducted by the Australian Human Rights and Equal Opportunity Commission, the Report documented the practices and effects of state-sponsored forced removal of Aboriginal and Torres Strait Islander children from their families, and the placing of them with white families or in orphanages and children's homes. Forcibly removed children and their families are known as 'the Stolen Generations'. In some Australian states these practices, described as a form of cultural genocide, continued from 1910 until the 1970s, with devastating effects upon Aboriginal families and communities. Scholars are now turning to studies of trauma and the Holocaust to understand the long-term effects on communities and individuals of the forced break-up of families (Haebich, 2002; Huggins, 2005).

The National Inquiry received submissions from many Aboriginal organizations and over 500 Indigenous people, including those who had been forcibly removed, or had had children taken from them. Many submissions were in the form of life history, offered as testimony to the effects of a policy of child removal.[4] Endorsing the significance of oral histories for present-day communities and future generations, the Inquiry recommended the establishment of appropriate Indigenous agencies to 'record, preserve and administer the testimonies of Indigenous people affected by the forcible removal policies and who wish to provide their histories in audio, audio-visual or written form', (*Bringing Them Home*, 1997: 18).

Within the *Bringing Them Home* Report, testimony and oral histories are drawn upon to convey the impact of child removal on individuals, families and communities. Returning to our framing questions about how oral histories traverse past, present and future, life stories are represented as showing how experiences in the past continue to shape lives in the present, and have ongoing effects on future generations: 'The harm continues in later generations, affecting their children and grandchildren'. Simultaneously, the circumstances of the time shaped how these stories and memories about the past were told and received. These memories were held by families and communities prior to the Inquiry, but its establishment gave formal sanction, albeit long overdue, to these memories, recognizing them as evidence, and saw the telling of – and listening to – them as central to the political process of redressing injustice. The *Report* found that 'The experience of the Shoah Foundation [which houses testimonies of Holocaust survivors] and of this Inquiry is that giving testimony, while extraordinarily painful for most, is often the beginning of the healing process' (p. 18).

The past is very much with us today, in the continuing devastation of the lives of Indigenous Australians. That devastation cannot be addressed unless the whole community listens with an open heart and mind to the stories of what has happened in the past and, having listened and understood, commits itself to reconciliation. (Human Rights and Equal Opportunity Commission, Australia)

Since the publication of the *Report*, the telling of these stories has been instrumental in driving calls for the Australian government to say 'sorry', to formally apologize for past acts of child removal. The former conservative Prime Minister, John Howard, refused to do so, arguing that the current generation could not be responsible for, nor feel guilty about, acts committed in the past – a view consistent with his characterization of the 'black armband' view of history.

As we were writing the final chapters for this book, our reflections on this topic were overtaken by current events. Following the election of a Labor government in Australia at the end of 2007, the new Prime Minister, Kevin Rudd, in the opening of Parliament on 13 February 2008, formally apologized to Indigenous people. This was broadcast nationally – people stopped work, gathered in public places, talked about where they were when they heard it and how it made them feel. In his speech, the Prime Minister retold the story of an Aboriginal woman, Nungala Fejo, who had been taken away as a child. In preparing his speech the Prime Minister met and talked with the Aboriginal woman, and asked her permission to use her story; this represented a symbolically important ethical protocol. These stories from the 'Stolen Generations' contained painful memories; they belonged to people and should be used respectfully, and with their consent. This action – of consulting and seeking consent to use a life story – gained further significance when it was revealed that the Leader of the Opposition, Mr Brendan Nelson, in his speech responding to the Prime Minister's apology, drew selectively upon an oral history from an Aboriginal woman, Faye Lynam, with whom he had not consulted. He used excerpts from her history, and omitted key parts, to lend support to his argument that hearing 'sorry' from white Australians was not what mattered most to Aboriginal people. In the days following, this incident was widely reported in the press, with Lynam objecting to what she saw as Nelson's misrepresentation of her memories. Newspaper reports wrote that Nelson 'stole her dignity when he quoted her without consent'; and Lynam declared, 'How dare he use my words, the bloody bastard. He doesn't realise how much that has hurt, it was a toxic speech' (*The Age*, 16/2/2008: 4).

The use of life histories was thus integral to how the government – and the political party in opposition – framed its apology, and to the public reception of the apology. These stories showed in personal and direct ways how previous policies had affected individual lives, and gave an immediacy to arguments about the need to acknowledge past wrongs in order to look towards a future politics. As the Prime Minister reflected in his speech: 'There is something terribly primal about these first-hand accounts; the pain is searing, it screams from the pages. The hurt, the humiliation, the degradation and the sheer brutality of the act of physically separating a mother from her children is a deep assault on our senses and on our most elemental humanity'.

It is difficult to write about these testimonies in relation to a discussion of research methods, as if methodological lessons can be cleanly abstracted from them. They cannot be, and that is part of the story we are trying to tell about the social location of methods. We are trying to show the political salience of oral histories, and how biographical accounts and memories are caught up in wider socio-historical processes. Methodologies are not decontextualized techniques; they have histories, they develop and become popular in particular times and places, and, as this example suggests, they can be the means to provoke powerful political and emotional responses. Further, the formal apology – which met widespread public support – suggested not only that the politics of the present had changed, but also underlined the power of testimony and life stories to effect that political and cultural change.

Narrative accrual – the circulation and transformation of life stories

We have been considering the impact of individual testimony and life stories, and we now turn to look at accounts about the Stolen Generations from two other perspectives: one informed by an analysis of the social production of memory and the other by psychoanalytic concepts of subjectivity and trauma. This also requires a shift in time, to the period following the publication of the *Bringing Them Home* report in 1997. We begin with an argument from an Australian historian, Bain Attwood, who proposes that in the 1980s and 1990s there was a proliferation of stories about the separation of Aboriginal children from their families, to the extent that this became a major theme in Australian history and had the status of an official, truthful discourse. Rather than seeing this as the uncovering of a submerged history, Attwood examines the social production of what he names the 'stolen generation narrative'. This now powerful narrative emerged and became popular, he argues, in a particular time and as the result of a number of intersecting discourses and events (Attwood, 2001: 183). His stated purpose is not to dispute the existence or effects of forced child removal, but to ask how and why a particular discourse could enter collective memory and become so popular and widespread when it did. There had been earlier stories of child removals, but from the 1970s onward the narrative of 'stolen generations' took hold in an unprecedented way. Accounts of children being removed from families shifted from being local and family stories to becoming national history. By the 1990s, Attwood argues, 'stories of removal were being reproduced again and again, and/or were interpreted in terms of "the stolen generations"' (p. 196).

The historical problem as defined by Attwood is how to explain the conditions that enabled this discourse to be articulated and heard, and to take on cultural and political authority: his task is to understand the 'historicity of the stolen generations narrative' (p. 188). Identified factors include the coining of the phrase 'stolen generation' in an influential essay by the historian Peter Read in the early 1980s

(Read, 1982), the establishment of the organization 'Link-Up' to bring together separated Indigenous family members, growing interest among non-Indigenous Australians in Indigenous art, fiction and autobiography, and the mode of argument and inquiry, including the use of personal testimony, in the *Bringing Them Home* report.

Drawing on theoretical discussions about history and memory, he calls this a process of 'narrative accrual' or 'narrative coalescence', in which a collection of 'minor discourses coalesced into a major, monolithic narrative'. Attwood argues that 'there is always a difference between what happened in the past and what was and is narrated later … history is not the past but always the past represented and re-presented … historical narratives undergo considerable change over time, shifting as the time of their telling changes' (Attwood, 2001: 188). In interpreting memories we need, he argues, a 'methodology that does not naïvely regard texts such as the narratives of the Stolen Generations as simple sources that provide a transparent window onto the past, but which considers them instead as murky texts that require sophisticated readings before they can be said to reveal a past reality or yield insights into it' (p. 211).

Yet Attwood provides few clues as to what such a methodology might be, other than rehearsing arguments about the social production of memory. In doing so, he exposes some of the limitations of this framework when it overly focuses on the sociological dimensions of memory and dispenses with the psychological and biographical effects of particular types of experiences and memories. Further, his account of the social production of a Stolen Generation narrative tends to render family traumas as abstracted historical events that can be examined in a detached way without paying heed to collective and individual emotions. The Stolen Generation narrative may have arisen in a particular cultural climate, but his account fails to make bridges between the generational and the subjective, and the cultural and the emotional.

Life histories, testimony and inheritance

Responding to Attwood's arguments, Rosanne Kennedy (2001) proposes alternative strategies for interpreting oral histories 'not simply as evidence, which places the historian in the role of expert, nor as literature, which makes them marginal for history's purposes of establishing what happened in the past, but as contributions to historiography in their own right' (2001: 117). We briefly consider her adoption of psychoanalytic concepts as employed by the historian Dominick LaCapra to investigate issues of memory, trauma and affect in relation to the Holocaust. LaCapra argues that 'a neo-positivist understanding of history as a dry and sober matter of fact analysis and … a suspicion of memory as inherently uncritical and close to myth … positions history in a purely enlightened realm that may divert attention from the continual need … to examine one's implication in the problems one studies' (cited in Kennedy, 2001: 122).

Kennedy suggests that testimonies, such as those from the Stolen Generations, are not usefully read in a 'forensic' way as a source of historical fact. 'Testimonies should not be evaluated according to the demands of proof or truth', she argues. Rather, she suggests, they 'should be read and analysed for their insights into how people involved in past events interpreted those events and their implications'. Further, the value of testimony for historians is precisely that it is 'situated and embodied'. Dealing with oral testimonies of trauma may generate particular challenges because 'they are laden with pathos' and provoke strong emotional responses (p. 124). Rather than quell such affective responses, LaCapra argues that the historian becomes a kind of 'secondary witness' to a 'past that has not yet passed away' (p. 125). Through a process likened to psychoanalytic transference, the historian tends to 'become emotionally implicated in the witness and his or her testimony with the inclination to act out an affective response to them' (p. 125). Kennedy's discussion suggests that the historian, in working out an affective response to a *history that is still happening*, is contributing to a different kind of knowledge about the past, one that incorporates the subjectivity of the historian as well as the role of the subject in history.

Life histories as stories for the future

We have been discussing two approaches to interpreting 'Stolen Generation' life histories – one emphasizing the social production of memory and narrative accrual, the other the role of life story as testimony and the witnessing role of the researcher. They each illustrate, although differently, some of the ways in which oral histories are about the past and the present, and also invoke the future. Writing about testamentary narratives of traumatic events, Roger Simon argues that:

> as the enactment of historical memory, the movement of testament is always caught up in the obligations expected by the transitive testamentary act – the act of writing, speaking, imaging – so as to bear an educative inheritance to those who 'come after'. It is how one conceives of this inheritance and on what terms one is prepared to engage it that is the critical determinate of the substance of the links between historical memory and civic life. (2005: 5)

Telling and acknowledging testimony represents a form of restitution for the past in the present and a record for the future. Testimony thus cuts across different temporal relations, recording a past which lives on in the present, yet opens up the possibility for a different kind of future in which social relations and civic life could be imagined otherwise. Remembrance does more than invoke the past for the present: it has an inherent futurity:

> At issue … is an anticipation of a future that might become conceivable and concrete yet remains indeterminate, dependent on the substance of time through which testament may be transformed into inheritance. This time of coming-to-inheritance has important implications for the future of sociality. It holds the possibility of a transformative learning that is quite different from the dominant social functions of historical memory, anticipating practices necessary for sustaining

democratic communities. Thus, my concern here is not with memory as a component of the founding ethos of national or communal identity, but rather as a condition for the learning necessary to sustain the prospect of democracy. (Simon, 2005: 5)

We note here two themes that arise from Simon's argument and which we take up in different ways throughout this book. First, testament is understood as a form of inheritance to pass on to future generations. This suggests an inter-generational trajectory implicit in life stories, even in those that are not about the witnessing of traumatic events. Passing on memories is a form of inter-generational inheritance, and the anticipation of their future retelling and remembrance is also likely to frame how the life story is constructed. Second, the idea of memory as connected to a sense of future possibility speaks to our concern with social change, and with methods that both research and effect change. In Chapter 1, we noted Wendy Brown's argument that the ability to create political identities depends on a capacity to imagine a future, which in turn 'demands a sense of historical movement' (Brown, 2001: 9). Life history, viewed in the ways we have been discussing here, enables one to gain a sense of historical movement and of the movement of memories across time.

With our second case study, our focus shifts from memory and biographical processes to consider a genealogical or 'history of the present' framework. First, we explain what distinguishes a 'history of the present' approach; second, we discuss how this approach offers a way of historicizing the phenomenon of life history; and then we briefly consider an example of a feminist life history study that adopts a genealogical approach.

Genealogy and life history

Foucauldian genealogy seeks to problematize the present, examining the diverse contingencies, unpredictable events and conditions of possibility that enable and produce the present. As with reflexive sociology (Bourdieu and Wacquant, 1992; Kenway and McLeod, 2004), the aim is to make the present strange, revealing the '(often quite recent) inventedness of our world' (Burchell, 1993: 279). This involves an historical interrogation of the position from which one speaks and researches, underpinned by the view that 'the best tool to examine and dismantle existing orders is history' (O'Farrell, 2005: 54). A genealogical exposition proceeds according to an analysis of the local and particular, and in Foucault's terms, the method of enquiry is 'gray, meticulous and patiently documentary' (1984: 76–7). Genealogy is distinguished by its opposition to teleological quests for historical origins and grand narratives that produce linear accounts of history as stories of inexorable progress. Instead, genealogy marks out the effects of discontinuities, accidents, reversals in the past and present, and the power/knowledge relations that produce and regulate dominant regimes of truth and 'systems of reason' (Popkewitz, 1998; see also Baker and Heyning, 2004).

Foucault's account of the past–present relation stands in contrast to everyday notions of the past living on in the present. As a method of enquiry, genealogy 'does not pretend to go back in time to restore an unbroken continuity that operates beyond the dispersion of forgotten things … its duty is not to demonstrate that the past actively exists in the present, that it continues secretly to animate the present, having imposed a pre-determined form on all its vicissitudes'. Instead, genealogies should identify 'the accidents, the minute deviations – or conversely, the complete reversals – the errors, the faulty appraisals and faulty calculations that gave birth to those things that continue to exist and have value for us' (Foucault, 1984: 81). In this view, 'history is figured less as a stream linking past and future than as a cluttered and dynamic field of eruptions, forces, emergences, and partial formations' (Brown, 2001: 116). And in pushing discontinuities to the foreground, Brown argues that Foucault's 'history is spatialised – conceptually wrenched from temporal ordering' (2001: 116–17). Consequently, if history does not have an unfolding course then 'it does not prescribe the future' (p. 117).

The project of creating histories of the present is characterized by a profound scepticism about narratives of change – particularly when they are understood as linked to progress – and a desire to reveal discourses as the medium through which claims to truth are made. Histories of the present make no assumptions about who we are and where we have come from; rather they begin by interrogating how subjects are formed in particular times and places, in the intersection of technologies of domination and technologies of the self (Baker and Heyning, 2004; O'Farrell, 2005). So, for example, the modern subject is not seen as the result of an historical process of civilization or emancipation, but as regulated by practices of confession and self-reflection, a self-governing, reflexive individual, who is formed in an era of neo-liberal individualism and the ascendancy of psy-knowledges (Rose, 1999). From this perspective, the life history interview itself is an exemplary technology of the self and manifestation of a culture of the self. Further, Kehily (2002) suggests that 'doing research and being researched provide a … site for the enactment of versions of the self' in which research is a 'modern technology producing subjects who can be "known" through a dynamic where the research encounter provides a performative space for the creation of the self' (Kehily, 2002: 13). Life history research, because of its incitement to tell stories about the self, amplifies the performative dimension of research encounters.

From this theoretical perspective, the current methodological interest in life history can be located as an episode in the history of subjectivity. It represents an intensified focus on individual lives, and provides strategies for examining and constituting the reflexive self. For researchers, the analytic focus may be processes of social, historical and biographical change, but the initial unit of analysis is the individual narrative, and what it condenses or captures or refracts of the wider culture. On the one hand, then, a Foucauldian perspective on the phenomenon of life history emphasizes its form and role as a technology of the self. Yet, on the other, it can be mobilized as a method to frame the analysis of life history narratives as part of a 'history of the present'. In order to explore this paradox, the following case study shows how Sue Middleton adopts a genealogical perspective in a life history study of New Zealand women teachers and the disciplining of bodies and sexuality in 20th-century education.

Teaching biographies: Making the present strange

Middleton's (1998) project was to excavate ideas that informed educational practice in New Zealand in the period from the 1920s to the 1990s. The research encompassed policy and documentary analysis, theoretical review and life history interviews with different generations of teachers reflecting on their experiences as teachers and as school students. Her guiding questions were: 'How are the educational and wider social theories of today's policymakers lived out by teachers and students in schools? Conversely, how do teachers' and students' ideas, resistances, and everyday behaviours shape policy decisions? How is history "written" on the bodies of teachers and students? And how do everyday school disciplinary practices "sexualise" our bodies?' (pp. 3–4). She describes her study as a history of the present, an 'historical investigation of disciplining sexuality in the present' (p. 1). Following Foucault, she argues that 'We have to know the historical conditions which motivate our conceptualisation. We need a historical awareness of our own present circumstance' (Foucault, 1982: 209, in Middleton, 1998: 1). She employs genealogy as a strategy to defamiliarize the rationality and commonsense of the present (Baker and Heyning, 2004: 28–33), and taking Foucault's lead, argues that research should not dwell on big questions such as, 'what is power?' or 'where does power come from?', but focus instead on 'the little question, 'What happens?'. This requires close attention to embodied practice and the minutiae of everyday and seemingly mundane events and interactions. For her, life history narratives offer a way of giving 'flesh' and voice to social abstractions and histories from above. 'When the stories of real people are positioned *inside* the educational and social theories we study in university courses, they offer an alternative to textbook presentations of these theories as typologies or flat maps' (p. 24).

Teachers are constructed as active participants in this history, not as recipients of imposed ideas but as authoritative and creative sources for translating, producing and enacting educational ideas. Life history thus provided a means for valuing teachers' viewpoints, and for telling a different story from the received chronologies and understandings of 'top down' educational history. While beginning from a different theoretical position, Middleton's methodological orientation echoes the rationales of early oral historians who sought to value the views of people 'on the ground' and to tell counter stories of political and social history.

Middleton's life history data encompass a large number of interviews with women secondary school teachers who recall their time as either teachers or students over the period from the 1920s to the mid-1990s (75 interviews conducted in the period 1984–95). With the aid of a qualitative data software package, she created textual snapshots of slices of time. Her book constitutes:

a textual collage of four slices of time and provide[s] access to their sequential and concurrent regimes of truth with respect to education and sexuality/the body, as my interviewees described their enactment in everyday disciplinary practices of the secondary schools that they attended as pupils and in which they taught. (pp. 2–3)

She begins with an analysis of current 'regimes of truth' regarding the disciplining of sexuality, organized according to three themes: 'the politics of clothing and appearance, questions of the allocations and deployment of school spaces for girls and boys, and contemporary technologies for the management of students' behaviours' (p. 9). In interviews, Middleton found, for example, many examples of surveillance and regulation – by students, by teachers, by parents – of heterosexuality, including denigration of feminists, binary constructions of women as good women or whores as well as instances of teachers resisting normative masculinity and femininity (pp. 21–4). She then considers regimes and practices from the 1920s to the mid-1980s, which represents the span of her participants' memories as either teacher or pupil. She does not present intensive analysis of biographical and memory processes or particular narratives, but extensively draws upon them to build up themes and patterns to inform a cultural history. Life histories are thus analysed as expressing cultural themes and resources for rethinking the present, rather than read in terms of intersubjective dynamics or the nuances of memory, myth and displacement, as discussed above.

Conventional histories of New Zealand education map four distinct policy phases during the 20th century but Middleton found that this chronology did not correspond to the periodization or themes emerging in her interviews (p. 26). For example, the period 1945 to the late 1960s is typically characterized in the 'policy story' as the time of an expansion of social democratic equal opportunity (p. 26). In interviews, however, the emphasized themes are the tension between the rhetoric of equality of opportunity and irreducible sexual difference, evident in the sexually-differentiated curriculum, such as girls compulsorily taking domestic science; the influence of progressive ideas in education and moves in school curriculum to include the 'biological facts of life'; 'moral panics' about young people's sexuality; and the policing of school uniforms and bodily appearance.

A key methodological challenge was whether to analyse the data chronologically or thematically, and Middleton's solution to this provides a distinctive cross-generational perspective on changing educational practices: 'Each cross-section, or slice, of chronological time is viewed from the perspectives found in the memories of multiple generations – of those who were children, adolescents, and adults of the time' (p. 27). This is not a 'what happened', linear account of educational change, but one that shifts across time, generation and interview-generated themes to capture different waves and regimes of truth to disrupt the commonsenses of the present and re-cast the past.

This example reveals the power of chronological narratives of social and personal change, and the potential to use oral and life history accounts in ways that disrupt this form. By organizing material thematically rather than chronologically, and by juxtaposing rather than narrating different temporal moments, Middleton's work suggests the significance of theoretical frames, strategies of analysis and modes of representation for how we understand the potential of this kind of data.

Conclusion

Oral history and life history bring an explicitly biographical focus to the task of researching social change. They offer ways into documenting and understanding how social change and circumstances are experienced at the level of the subject, and how the articulation of life stories and memories can itself effect personal and social change. Participant narratives and memories can be read as time travellers, constructed in the present, evoking and even transforming the past, and often told with a view towards the future, towards generational inheritance and a sense of other possibilities. From different perspectives, we have shown the value of examining the intersubjective dimensions of life history interviews, and of not reading the narrative as a simple mirror onto the past, or the present. Our discussion of memory, and the tricks of remembering and forgetting, revealed the interplay between psychological and cultural processes in, for example, the social production of memories or the political recognition of testimony.

In this chapter we have mapped some of the history and context for the emergence of oral and life history methods, in part to understand the form they take today and the methodological debates and developments that have constituted the field. It was also part of a larger argument about the need to situate the moment – the time and place – of social research methods and the different intellectual and socio-political moods that have animated them. The two case studies and the discussion of memory emerge from different philosophical and political positions, each offering different conceptual resources yet also showing some points of convergence. The discussion of the social production of memory connects with the notion of 'narrative accrual' and this, in turn, resonates with the Foucauldian notion of regimes of truth. Analysis of the intersubjective dynamic of interviews speaks to the psychoanalytically-informed readings of testimony; and the emancipatory and political agenda of early oral history echoes in the cultural and personal significance of Indigenous oral histories.

Oral and life history methods are not the province of any one tradition, even though they have been aligned with certain theories and politics at different times. The renaissance of oral history in the 1970s and 1980s is linked to the rise of socialist and feminist history, but these methods are also part of cultural studies and interdisciplinary memory studies; life history methods may be allied with psycho-social or psychoanalytical traditions, but they are also adopted in symbolic-interactionist studies (Plummer, 2001) as well as in Foucauldian 'histories of the present'. These diverse adoptions are united by their methodological orientation to working with biographical narratives, and to seeing these as both embedded in, and shedding light on, wider socio-cultural and historical processes.

For social researchers it can be difficult to work outside the representational and temporal logic of past–present–future (Harootunian, 2007). From the construction of autobiographical narratives to received folk wisdom and national histories, this ordering of time and history appears common sense and constitutive. Yet the biographical and historical methods discussed in this chapter point to some of the ways this linearity can be disturbed, showing how an emphasized focus on the past does not exclude the present and the future. The following chapters extend these themes through discussion of the temporal dimensions of different research methodologies.

Summary points

- Oral and life history are interdisciplinary approaches that take personal narratives and memories as a route into exploring social and historical processes.

- Interviews are the primary method of eliciting narrative, though these can be supplemented with other artefacts, such as texts or images – 'documents of life'.

- While the past is emphasized, understanding the relation between the past and the present is a feature of oral history work, such that the present is privileged to make sense of the past.

- There are several strands of work within oral and life history, including preservationist and recovery histories, and others with a pronounced emancipatory political agenda, in which the past is privileged to forge new stories, traditions and possibilities.

- Critiques of the empiricism of early oral history led to a greater focus on memory – on the social production of memory and individual memories.

- The interview is a site for the telling and production of narratives, and the intersubjective relation between the interviewer and interviewee is an integral part of this process.

- Life histories are a record for the future, an inheritance that can be passed on to future generations. As a form of testimony, life histories can offer restitution for the past, effect change in the present, and articulate a sense of other possible futures.

- Personal narratives and life stories are congruent with a contemporary culture of the self, in which narratives of the self are both incited and valued. But these narratives also have the potential to de-familiarize the present and offer perspectives for critiquing cultural commonsense.

- These biographical methods have been taken up by researchers working in diverse theoretical traditions, disciplines and political movements. They are methods that both document and have the potential to effect social and personal change.

Further resources

Samuel, R. and Thompson, P. (eds) (1990) *The Myths We Live By*. London: Routledge.
This book captured a mood of change in oral history, and showcased an engagement with the complexities of memory, myth and subjectivity in the telling of life narratives.

Rintoul, S. (1993) *The Wailing: A National Black Oral History*. Port Melbourne: William Heinemann.
This is a collection of oral history interviews with more than 70 Indigenous Australians, conducted by Rintoul in the late 1980s.

Chamberlayne, P., Bornat, J. and Wengraf, T. (eds) (2000) *The Turn to Biographical Methods: Comparative Issues and Examples*. London: Routledge.
Introduced with a history of biographical methods, this volume contains chapters on different examples of life history and biographical methods, which draw on and integrate psychological and socio-historical perspectives.

Cosslett, T., Lury, C. and Summerfield, P. (eds) (2000) *Feminism and Autobiography: Texts, Theories, Methods*. London: Routledge.
This volume canvasses feminist biographical and autobiographical research, including oral and life histories and historical biography.

Plummer, K. (2001) *Documents of Life 2: An Invitation to Critical Humanism*. London: Sage.
This is a substantially revised edition of Plummer's influential 1983 book. It outlines different approaches to biographical research and discusses the research process, including working with interviews, managing data and writing.

Perks, R. and Thomson, A. (eds) (2006) *The Oral History Reader* (2nd edn). Abingdon: Routledge.
A volume of classic and recent readings on oral history, with a comprehensive Introduction – it provides a useful overview and introduction to the field.

Hamilton, P. and Shopes, L. (eds) (2008) *Oral Histories and Public Memories*. Philadelphia, PA: Temple University Press.
This edited collection includes an informative overview of the relationships between oral history, memory scholarship and public history; the volume includes examples of research studies and oral history projects from many parts of the world that illuminate these relationships.

Notes

1 The description 'black armband' history had immediate popular resonance in Australia due to the widespread practice of Australian Rules footballers wearing black armbands at football games to honour recently deceased players or people associated with their club.

2   In June 2006, the Australian federal government sponsored a national summit of experts (his-
    torians, politicians, educators, community and business leaders) to investigate the teaching of
    Australian history in schools.
3   Working from within different disciplinary locations, Daniel Bertaux and Paul Thompson's
    shared commitment to the value of life history for understanding social and historical dynam-
    ics has led to collaborations on several influential projects, including a cross-generational study
    of families and social mobility, which we discuss in Chapter 6.
4   A selection of these stories can be found on the website of the Human Rights and Equal
    Opportunity Commission: www.humanrights.gov.au/social_justice/bth_report/about/personal_
    stories. html). See also the Bringing Them Home Oral History Project at the National
    Library of Australia: www.nla.gov.au/oh/bth/.

Acknowledgement

Passerini (2002) quote page 43: this paper is quoted with kind permission of Luisa
Passerini.

PART 2
Being With

4

Qualitative Longitudinal Research

Two compensations for growing old are worth putting on record as the condition asserts itself. The first is a vantage point gained for acquiring embellishments to narratives that have been unfolding for years besides one's own, trimmings that can appear to supply the conclusion of a given story, though finality is never certain, a dimension always possible to add. The other mild advantage endorses a keener perception for the authenticities of mythology ... poetry and the novel. (Anthony Powell, 1997: 560)

The business of representing human and social life is rarely afforded the luxury of operating at the pace of time as 'lived'. Anthony Powell's series of novels ' A Dance to the Music of Time' was written over the course of a long career and tells the story of a generation from the vantage point of an increasingly reflective and ageing author. Like the work of Proust that inspired him, these novels have become a resource for understanding the complexity of time as a subjective and lived experience. Another iconic representation of 'time as lived' is the '7 Up' television series, created by Michael Apted, which follows a gallery of 14 young Britons from the age of seven into middle age, interviewing them every seven years. This series continues to have an enormous impact on audiences across the world, inciting reflection on processes of ageing and the passage of time. Successive broadcasts have become collective events where millions vicariously encounter the forces of fate, chance and circumstance that are the stuff of all biographies. Begun as a social experiment to test the power of social class as a determinant of life chances, the series has become an increasingly existential and psychological project in which the ethics of voyeurism and representation are as much a focus as the theories of social reproduction that inspired it. Participants have withdrawn, returned and talked back to the director, who in turn has moved from his position behind the camera to become the visible and accountable character within the real-life drama.

In contemporary times reality television has become the genre through which this sense of life as lived (*durée*) is most obviously represented – programmes such as Big Brother and its countless spin-offs – produce the sense in the viewer that they are watching events unfold in 'real time'. Writing about a major exhibition on the art of the documentary shown at the Liverpool Tate Gallery in 2006, Mark Cousins suggests that this 'fly-on-the-wall' perspective, introduced by documentaries in the 1960's such as *'The Family'* made available a new aesthetic position in relation to the filming of reality where you 'let the real world direct you, yet you direct it too, gently shaping it, or semi-scripting it, or even restaging it' (Cousins, 2006: 46). It is the uncomfortable mediation of this boundary that has become the focus of the genre of 'reality tv' where 24-hour 'live' broadcasting gives the *impression* that we are seeing life as lived at the same time that debates over editing, staging and manipulation expose the constructedness of the 'real' that we seek to witness. For Cousins, documentary is an art form, which 'directs reality' yet is 'responsive to events in the real world', employing a 'socio-aesthetic palette' (Cousins, 2006: 46)

Researching in 'real time' – longitudinal approaches

Social research that follows the temporal rhythms of lived lives is also rare. Studies tend either to rely on retrospective accounts of the past (for example, life history approaches), or they seek to capture trends by repeating a survey with different groups of people. It is much less common for research to follow the same individuals or groups over extended periods. Those that exist fall into three main areas (although see Elliot et al., 2007, for a fuller discussion). First, a body of work within anthropology that has involved a tradition of studying a single small community over the course of a whole career (in some cases such studies have become intergenerational as anthropologists 'pass the mantle' to junior colleagues and research students). The important associated methodological literature on 'long-term fieldwork' explores a range of practical, ethical and epistemological issues (Foster et al., 1979; Kemper and Peterson Royce, 2002). Second, longitudinal studies (the most well known and well established studies of which are quantitative) involving panels of individuals researched at regular intervals.[1] In the same way that the 7 Up series returned to its subjects over time, these longitudinal cohort studies involve a series of 'sweeps' where data is collected from the panel. The scale, complexity and connectivity of the resulting data sets mean that the project of analysis is infinite, and the archiving and sharing of such data sets with a community of secondary analysts is a central element in realizing their potential and the investment made in them. While such studies are resource intensive, they offer a unique perspective on social change that promises the opportunity to disentangle generational effects from the individual's position within the life course.

The third is an area that we have chosen to focus on in this chapter: qualitative longitudinal studies that 'walk alongside' individuals or groups over time in such a way that privileges the present in which they are encountered (Corsaro and Molinari, 2000; Leisering and Walker, 1998). It is an approach that sits somewhere between the reflexive documentary approach of the 7 Up series and the large-scale academic enterprises of long-term ethnographies and cohort studies. Bren Neale and Jennifer Flowerdew (2003) develop a cinematic metaphor to distinguish the value of quantitative and qualitative approaches to longitudinal research, within which the former is portrayed as producing a series of still pictures, frozen moments in time, offering 'a bird's eye view of social life that is panoramic in scope but lacking in any detail'. Developing the metaphor, they argue that although quantitative longitudinal data has the capacity to sketch a 'grand narrative … it is a movie in which the intricacies of the plot and the fluid twists and turns of the individual story lines are hidden from view' (Neale and Flowerdew, 2003: 192). In contrast, a qualitative approach to longitudinal research is able to provide the 'close-up' shot of real lives, with a focus on plot, story line, turning points and defining moments.

Whether repeat interview studies escape the problem of presenting a series of snapshots (albeit of a qualitative character) is a challenge posed by the sociologist Liz Stanley (2007). Drawing on an established tradition of biographical studies, Stanley points to the inherent seriality of letters and correspondence, where one thing follows another by definition. Such data sources lend themselves to the exploration of temporal and associational processes in such a way that helps us to understand the space that lies between the individual and the social, the biographical and the historical. The use of data-generation techniques that are continuous (for example, written and visual diaries and ethnographic observation) as well as the collection of existing life documents from participants on an ongoing basis are an important part of a new generation of mixed method approaches to qualitative longitudinal research (Timescapes, 2007).

Qualitative longitudinal studies are not always intentional. Resourceful researchers have found ways to return to research subjects and/or sites over time, and such projects can reflect a lifetime of scholarship. It is the duration of such studies that is most revealing of the relationship between individual lives and wider social and historical processes. The longer the study the greater the insight, with outstanding examples including the impact of neo-liberalism on the formation of gender identities (Walkerdine et al., 2001), and the impact of educational reform on schooling identities (Pollard and Filer, 1996, 1999). Such research tends to recognize a two-way relationship between researcher and research subject and struggles with the pleasures and perils of an ever changing vantage point from which to tell its story (Andrews, 2007). By observing research subjects and inviting them to reflect on the past and to project themselves into the future, these studies can capture something of the process through which the self is made and remade over time, what McLeod has called the 'habitus-in-process' (McLeod, 2003) and Stanley describes as 'continued becomings' (Stanley, 2007). Grappling with this methodology for researching social and personal change has been at the heart of our own research collaboration and the genesis of this book. We begin this chapter by telling the story of how we discovered qualitative longitudinal research, attempting to locate the method within a cultural, historical and biographical context. By providing detailed accounts of our own two studies we hope to capture the way in which this approach can produce particular insights into the meaning of personal and social change, raising its own set of epistemological, ethical and practical challenges.

Why now? The (re)emergence of a methodology

Qualitative longitudinal research is coming into fashion as a social research method, due to a coincidence of a number of trends. Within the field of longitudinal studies there is a growing awareness of the need to supplement questionnaires with more in-depth methods. Within the qualitative research community there is a growing interest in dynamic processes and the potential of longitudinal methods. Repeat interview methods have emerged from government-funded evaluation studies as a flexible and responsive approach to understanding the longer-term and unintended impacts of interventions (Corden and Millar, 2007; Molloy et al., 2002). In social policy circles, qualitative longitudinal research (QLR hereafter) is being looked at to provide insights into the social and psychological processes that underpin behaviours that western governments are increasingly interested in influencing: social responsibility, risk-taking, resilience, etc., and other 'life-long' processes such as education, work and leisure (Halpern et al., 2004; Jones, 2005).

However, there is a more personal dimension to fashions in sociological thought. Although researchers generally work independently and with integrity, the collective and social nature of the academic enterprise means that we may arrive at the same place at the same moment, for our own reasons. The two of us both became involved in research that was both qualitative and longitudinal as a result of our frustration with one-off interviews, and our desire to go beyond the 'accounts' that individuals produced to discover what happens to them over time. Without knowing it, we both designed similar studies, at the same moment in time, yet on opposite sides of the world. Julie and her colleague Lyn Yates were interested in the process of schooling and created a study that would enable them to see what happened to 26 pupils in four contrasting high schools during their secondary education (McLeod and Yates, 2006). Rachel and her colleague Janet Holland shared similar interests and designed a study in which 100 young people living in five contrasting sites in the UK were followed over what was to become a 10-year period (Henderson et al., 2007).

Initially both research teams imagined themselves as pursuing a new kind of methodology and research design that raised challenges to their own habits and assumptions as social researchers. Before this we had limited experience of the continuous process of data collection and analysis demanded by the repeat interview format of our studies. We shared a desire to find others engaged in similar work and over the next few years we began meeting more and more people facing similar challenges. In 2002 we were part of a group that convened an international seminar in London to which we invited researchers involved in qualitative longitudinal research of various kinds. This included people working in education, in sex and drugs research, in family studies and youth studies. The editorial of the journal special issue that resulted from this event sketched the intellectual climate that made qualitative longitudinal methods increasingly attractive.

> The origins of this special issue lie in a combination of excitement and anxiety: excitement that we were working with a promising new methodology and anxiety that this was taking place without a relevant literature to inform and debate the epistemological or practical decisions we were making. For a variety of reasons, longitudinal qualitative research had entered our repertoires of study designs. Funders and policy makers were increasingly interested in a holistic understanding of the way diverse factors came together to determine behaviour. There has been an increasing interest in the temporal unfolding of behaviour and notions like 'career' in areas like drug use and sex work, with the sense that prospective data collection would be more revealing than retrospective accounts. And there were theoretical developments that gave a new zest to the structure/agency debate with propositions about the 'reflexive project of self' in an era argued to be one of detraditionalisation and individualisation. (Thomson et al., 2003: 185)

Others were also busy on similar projects. Later in that year a group of UK policy researchers published an important review of the literature on longitudinal qualitative methods in relation to evaluation studies (Molloy et al., 2002). In 2003 Johnny Saldana, a US-based theatre studies academic, published a detailed guide to QLR (Saldana, 2003). Since the publication of both there has been a rapid growth of excitement about the method. When in 2004 Janet Holland and colleagues were commissioned by the main UK academic research council (Economic and Social Research Council – ESRC) to undertake a literature review as part of a feasibility study for a major investment in QL research, they were to discover that far from being a 'new' methodology or research design, what was 'new' about QLR was the recognition that this method had the potential to produce the kinds of knowledge that might address some of the burning issues of the day: questions about process rather than outcome.

Defining Qualitative Longitudinal Research (QLR)

This literature review uncovered a significant body of studies that employed qualitative methods to explore phenomena over time (Holland et al., 2006). The review's key focus was on a particular kind of QLR, research that is planned, prospective, qualitative and longitudinal, and where the unit of analysis is usually but not always the individual. This kind of QL design is particularly useful when attempting to understand the interaction between temporal and geographical movement and between agency and structural determinants. For example, the study of *transitions*; how *pathways* are constituted; how *changes* and *adaptations* take place; the *impact* of key events and changing circumstances; the *evaluation* of specific policies, *developmental, incremental* and *cumulative* processes; and gaining a realistic grasp of *causality*. The areas in which these kinds of insights were most likely to apply were identified as: the study of the family and the life course; identity construction, processes such as ageing, disability, addiction, social mobility; the careers of key groups, organizational and community change and trends including changing values and attitudes and behaviour. Some essential characteristics of QLR emerged from the published literature:

- Ideally, QL research is open-ended and intentional (i.e. to keep on looking is the key concern).
- It relates to the number of waves rather than a period of time and to a dynamic research process, i.e. the separation between research design and research process decreases.
- One of the features of this kind of QLR is that the research process is historicized and comes within the frame of what is recorded and analysed.
- QLR also tends to be linked to personal/collective scholarship. In many cases it is driven by the intellectual projects and ongoing relationships between the researcher and the researched, and researchers have often had to struggle to draw together short-term funding solutions. The impetus towards maintaining funding and/or designing prospective studies from scratch brings with it a different set of politics and demands. (Holland et al., 2006)

As a way of illustrating the different ways in which these characteristics can be realized, we now consider the two QL studies that we have been involved in for a significant period of our research lives. Both studies address questions about young people's 'becoming', their transitions from childhood to adulthood, and their movement through the teenage years. While they are framed by distinct theoretical and cultural concerns, they nevertheless emerge from a set of interests in understanding young people in an era of social change and during a dynamic biographical period, and both explicitly draw on theorizations of identity.

The 12–18 project – Making Modern Lives

The 12–18 project was a study of subjectivity, schooling and social change funded by the Australian Research Council and carried out by Julie McLeod and Lyn Yates. Over a seven-year period (1993–2000) the researchers interviewed and videotaped 26 young Australians (14 girls and 12 boys) as they aged from 12–18 years. The young people came from diverse backgrounds, and attended four different types of schools. Interviews were undertaken twice annually over the high school years, and twice in the year afterwards. In the researchers' words:

> we listened to these students talk about their sense of self, their values, attitudes to the future, and their experiences of school. Their individual narratives illuminate

the uneven and differentiated impact of contemporary social and gender change, and the profound influence of school community and culture on the shaping of subjectivity. (McLeod and Yates, 2006: 2)

Central to the research design of the study was a focus on *school culture*, and the sample of 26 was carefully constructed to include young people from similar class backgrounds going to different schools, as well as those from a different class background in the same school – avoiding the conflation of the 'habitus' of school and family that characterizes so much educational research (Yates, 2003). So, although the study followed individuals over time, it was also a *comparative* study of institutional culture and the way that institutions shape subjectivities. The schools that provided the context for the research were as follows:

In a city:

- *City Academy*: an 'elite school … over-represent[ing] those from wealthy backgrounds' (p. 21)
- *Suburban High*: an ' "arty" informal school' in a 'middleclass suburb' (p. 22)

And in a regional town:

- *Regional High*: a school that attracts parents 'who want to send their children to a "good" school, but cannot afford the fees of a private school' (p. 19)
- *Regional Tech*: located on the edge of a public housing development, and also drew a number of students from some smaller, relatively poor rural towns' (p. 20)

Framing the study

McLeod and Yates locate their study at a crucial moment in the history of equity policy within Australian education. In terms of social inequalities, education policy had shifted away from the 'disadvantaged schools programme of the 1970s which targeted resources at schools in poorer areas, towards a focus on 'effective schooling' in the 1990s and the 'Schools of the Future' programme which economically rewarded 'schools who were seen to be winners' (McLeod and Yates, 2006: 30). Discourses around gender inequality were also on the move, with the attempts of feminists in the 1970s to identify sexism within the curriculum, giving way to a mainstreaming of gender reform in the 1990s and a growing concern with the underachievement of boys. McLeod and Yates were intrigued to understand how these changes in policy and discourse were manifest in different kinds of educational institutions, but also in the kinds of subjectivities of the young people growing up in these contexts. How exactly do class, gender and institutional cultures combine in this historical moment? Who are the winners and who are the losers in these 'contemporary times'?

The adoption of a qualitative and longitudinal methodology for the study was influenced in large part by the theoretical agendas that McLeod and Yates were engaged with at the outset of the research in the early 1990s. At this time they were feeling frustrated with approaches that emphasized the part played by discourses in the construction of the subject, creating 'a rather linear and flat picture of the individual life being made, a picture in which the person was a cipher of discourse, a one-dimensional figure on whom social messages were writ' (2006: 31). The researchers were part of a movement of feminist academics wanting to explore the emotional and psychological dimensions of how discourses turn into subjectivity (Bjerrum Nielsen, 1996; Hollway, 1994; Walkerdine et al., 2001). They were also interested in anchoring developmental discourses on gendered adolescence within particular historical and social circumstances. And it was in order to generate a sense of biographical *depth*, developmental *process* and social and historical *specificity* that they turned towards a research design that involved multiple interviews over time. In their words, a methodology that was 'longitudinal and recursive, to confront a flat linearity, but also sociologically framed, to keep difference and historical specificity in the foreground' (2006: 31).

The 12–18 study was designed carefully to enable the researchers to engage with questions about school type, education policy and social divisions as well as providing biographical portraits of how individuals are formed and transform over time. McLeod and Yates explain that they attempted to build two forms of temporality into the study: historical specificity – what they call 'contemporary times', and the timescape of the adolescent or high school years – what they call 'biographical life stage' (2006: 39). Through a qualitative longitudinal design they sought to bridge these two temporalities: showing the ways in which history is manifest in lives as well as demonstrating that the abstract and normative 'ages and stages' approach of developmental psychology is challenged by a recognition that nothing is inevitable in concrete times and places.

An intense research design

The 12–18 project is an example of an 'intense' research design, with relatively few cases over many waves. Lyn Yates has written about how their study was simultaneously small (based on only 26 cases) and large (350 interviews collected over eight years) and the consequences of this for methodological and substantive significance (Yates, 2003). The decision that the two principal researchers would do all interviews as well as analytic work was also consequential – for the quality of the research and for the speed and duration of the project. The intensity of this kind of research means that the biographical time of the researchers (always in play in any form of knowledge production) becomes explicit, as they acknowledge in the preface to their book:

> During the eight years of interviews we saw the participants change and grow, and we thought often about our own children and the world and the situations they face. Our project was concerned with schooling and identity, and with retrospective and prospective visions of that. Doing this research evoked emotions and memories for us of our own growing up, our own schooling, and the

support we had from teachers (in country high schools), our families, and especially our parents. (McLeod and Yates, 2006: xi)

The interviews themselves were recorded on video, allowing the researchers to capture the changing bodies and demeanours of the research subjects as well as the interpersonal dynamics of the interview encounters. In each interview participants were asked to describe themselves as well as imagine themselves in the future or recollect themselves when younger. The researchers used a range of other questions to prompt narratives about young people's present situation and asking them to reflect on school, family and friends. While keeping the initial request for a description of self as a standard part in every interview, the researchers also experimented: posing ethical dilemmas, asking students to make audio tape portraits of themselves and requesting that they bring a photograph that was significant to them to discuss in the interview. In the final year the researchers created compilation videos for each young person, drawing on excerpts from all their interviews, to be viewed in advance of the final research encounter. Commenting on the timeframe of the study, including the frequency of interviews and the use of visual methods, McLeod and Yates observe:

> Some changes can happen over a short period of time, especially during the 'teenage years' when things can shift quickly, and a seven to eight-year period is not essential for grasping this. Interviews conducted over a shorter period, and in quick succession, can capture elements of change and might also offer a more immediate 'as-it-is-happening' sense of change and development. However, the time frame we adopted allowed participants to experience some emotional distance from earlier events and recollections, and to have a sense of themselves in a long view. The length of secondary school in Australia – six years – also determined the time frame of the study, with interviews concluding in the year immediately after the end of school. (2006: 42)

In quantitative approaches to longitudinal research a great emphasis is placed on the importance of standardized questions that can be repeated in each wave of fieldwork, allowing comparisons of like with like to be made over time (Elliott et al., 2007; Leiserling and Walker, 1998). This is complicated by a changing research context in which new interests emerge demanding new questions to be posed, and by the way in which language evolves, with the same question subtly changing its meaning over time. McLeod and Yates endeavoured to have an element of standardization in their research design, with set themes – self, school, future – raised in each round of interviews. Importantly, there was a continuity of researcher and researched in each interview, supporting the incremental development of observations and interpretation. Second, the researchers insisted on repeating their request to each interviewee for a description of self and a projection of self into the future at every interview, however uncomfortable this made them both. Through this method they accumulated a body of responses that could eventually be read against each other, building up a picture 'of orientations and beliefs across different times, ages and moods' (2006: 43).

Analytic rhythms

The analysis of this data set was also developmental, and McLeod and Yates faced the challenge reported by others using QL methods of attempting to collect and analyse data simultaneously (see also Thomson and Holland, 2003). The problem of analytic closure – when is the right time to 'write' – is a characteristic feature of QL studies. Where fieldwork takes place over a period of years, it is important to find ways of interpreting and reporting on data on an ongoing basis. Yet to do so always raises the possibility of 'findings' being confounded by future events. McLeod has described this aspect of the QL research methodology as productive of 'perspectivism' and an aware-ness of our contingent temporal and social location as analysts (Andrews, 2007; McLeod, 2003). As time passes and more data is collected, we are always standing in a new place from where we can capture a new 'perspective'. This perspective not only involves the sequence of data that we apprehend but also the new intellectual resources that we bring to the process of analysis. Recognition of perspectivism within the QL research process not only cautions us against over-reading data, or overstating the significance of particulars, but it can also liberate us in our relation-ship with the theoretical and policy agendas that we orient ourselves to – recogniz-ing that they too are shaped within a wider historical process. This recognition of the mobile subjectivity of the researcher as well as the researched marks a shift in the terms through which reflexivity is generally attributed (Adkins, 2002b; Moore, 2005). It also echoes Anthony Powell's observations quoted at the beginning of this chapter, that for the ageing observer of other people's lives, 'finality is never certain, there is always a new dimension to add'.

The experience of conducting and living a qualitative longitudinal study results in a heightened awareness of the impossibility of separating the researcher from the researched, and of stepping outside the temporal flow that encompasses the whole research enterprise – from the power relations that shape policy agendas and fund-ing decisions, and the ebbs and flows of fashion for social theory, through the biographies of researchers and their subjects through to the sequence of labour that constitutes the research process. The method proceeds by capturing fragments of the 'present' – in this case in the form of videoed interview encounters. These fragments are then brought together within new contexts, and interpretations and accounts are forged. These accounts are themselves fixed in times and places and may be revisited with hindsight. The nature of QL research processes demands that we understand the endeavour as socially and temporally located *and* as mobile, and this has conse-quences for our claims about the kind of knowledge that we produce. This kind of insight can be very productive; as McLeod and Yates observe: 'refusing the possibil-ity of full truth does not cancel meaning, does not remove the possibility of learn-ing something new, of gaining insight while being mindful of the construction and limits of the research encounter' (2006: 83).

Brett's story

We draw this example to a close by illustrating how QL methodologies can cap-ture the changes, continuities, 'motifs', 'repetitions' and 'reiterations' that are part and parcel of the process of becoming. Here McLeod and Yates offer the story of Brett, whose self description remained consistent yet 'resonated differently in changing circumstances' (2006: 81).

> When Brett was in grade 6 (end of elementary school), he looked directly at us, smiled, and told us that he sees himself as a good friend, a kind and cheerful boy. This remains a vivid memory for us, one somewhat poignant in retrospect. He was sweet-faced, and slightly serious, excited about going to secondary school, which was one that had a poor reputation in the town and was known by other students as 'Tip Tech', a 'dirty school', where there were lots of fights. In the middle years of secondary school, he tells us again that he hopes his friends know that 'I'd do anything for them'. In his final year he is impatient with school and longs for the adult world of work, where he can be with his mates and be treated by others as an adult. At each of these stages, being close to his friends is important for Brett, and central to how he sees himself. But 'having mates' takes on different meanings as Brett gets older, and he becomes more obviously embittered with the rest of the world around him. As he moves through high school, the commitment to his friends is no longer voiced as a gentle expression of concern for them, which we had found quite touching. Soon it becomes part of a litany of grievances he voices about the school and the uncaring teachers and about bullies and his readiness to fight. The relationships with friends are a refuge rather than a more intense reflection of how he relates to others, as it appeared in the earlier interview. Brett leaves school without completing his year 12 qualification, hoping to get work in the manufacturing and construction industries: it is likely that he will have limited opportunities for full-time work in the future. Doing things with his mates, being seen as a good friend becomes particularly important; signifying entry to adulthood against the child's world of school and providing a focus for activity against, simultaneously, the dull routine of school where he is labelled as a bad boy/a poor student and unreliable, and the likely prospect of unemployment. (McLeod and Yates, 2006: 81)

The 12–18 project is a good example of the essential characteristics of QL research. The demand to 'keep looking' is central to the aims of the research to explore the process of becoming and the formation of educational subjectivities. The comparative design provides a conceptual framework through which these biographies 'make sense'. Researchers maintain their engagement over the span of the young people's high school education, through 14 waves of data collection over seven years. The dynamic research process is much in evidence. McLeod and Yates not only recognize that their methodology plays a part in the phenomena that they are studying, but they also self-consciously locate themselves and their changing theoretical frameworks within the problematic of what needs to be accounted for. The personal character of the research enterprise is evidenced not only by the responsibility that the authors took for conducting all the fieldwork and analysis themselves – and the expansion of the project way beyond the funded period of activity – but also in the ways in which they show that the research and its questions about school choice and social mobility are part of their own biographies and those of their children.

Inventing Adulthoods: making and sharing the long view

The Inventing Adulthoods study took place between 1996 and 2006. Its most recent phase has involved a digitalization project and the creation of a partial online archive. It did not begin life as a longitudinal study, but became one over time, being funded in four distinct phases by the UK Economic and Social Research Council. The original study from which it grew was a multi-method investigation of children's moral landscapes. This research was undertaken through secondary schools located in five contrasting sites in the UK, and involved questionnaires (1800), focus groups (62) and interviews (57). The UK is a diverse and unequal society, and these locations were chosen to capture a range of economic, social, cultural and environmental conditions within which young people in the UK grow up. The sites were as follows:

- An isolated rural area in the east of England.
- An inner city area: economically disadvantaged, ethnically diverse, close to the centre of a major city in the south of England.
- A leafy suburb: affluent commuter area near a commuter belt town in the south of England.
- A disadvantaged estate: economically marginalized, ethnically homogeneous (predominantly white), located on the outskirts of a large city in the north of England.
- A city in Northern Ireland.

These five sites then became an enduring element of what turned into a 10-year study, in which researchers followed the lives of approximately 100 young people. Volunteer participants were recruited from mixed ability classes in nine secondary schools in the original study locations. At the beginning of the study (in 1996) these young people ranged in age between 11 and 17 and at the end of data collection between 21 and 27. The primary method employed to collect data was the individual interview. For most participants, at least six interviews were conducted over this period. Many also took part in focus groups and created 'memory books' (a kind of reflective diary) which gave the research team a way of capturing representations of self over time outside of the interview context (Thomson and Holland, 2005). The final data set comprises almost 500 individual interviews, 68 focus groups and a range of other data.

The Inventing Adulthoods project was larger in scale and scope, but less intensive in fieldwork terms than the 12–18 project. For all these reasons it demanded a larger research team. The core of the team (Rachel Thomson, Janet Holland, Sheena McGrellis, Sue Sharpe and Sheila Henderson) were consistently involved throughout the 10 years of the research. At an early stage the team established the importance of continuity in research relationships and most of the interviewing was undertaken by just three members, each of whom took responsibility for their own research sites and maintaining their research relationships with individual research participants (Henderson et al., 2004). Although fieldwork was effectively 'decentralized', the administration of the study and the organization of the data set were highly centralized, ensuring consistency of transcription styles, coding and analysis. These data management practices became important as the team recognized the potential for transforming the data set into an archive.

Although the Inventing Adulthoods study began as a school-based research project, its focus was less on school culture and more on the ways in which opportunities and resources are shaped by a range of factors (class, gender, ethnicity and family resources) which are themselves mediated by locality. Over the course of the study a detailed understanding was built up of the 'economies' of each of the localities: not simply in terms of the labour market or housing costs, but also in terms of what 'counted' and was 'valued' in local terms (Henderson et al., 2007; Thomson, 2000). The research focused on the ways in which school culture, family values and youth cultures combined with material resources and personal resourcefulness to shape very different transitions to adulthood. The relatively large scale of the study enabled researchers to think in terms both of the ways in which transitions are shaped within places and how certain patterns and responses transcend such particularities. QL studies have the capacity to create holistic (or de-centred) understandings of why people act as they do (Neale, et al., 2003). The Inventing Adulthoods study set out to replace the problem-centred approach to young people within youth studies (where attention has traditionally divided young people's lives into different policy problems: 'drugs', 'unemployment', 'school failure', 'risk taking', etc.) with a holistic biographical perspective (Henderson et al., 2007).

A biographical approach

The research team were also interested in using QL methods to engage in critical conversation with late modern theories concerning detraditionalization and individualization, which point to the significance of demographic changes in family life and the re-negotiation of familial roles, duties and expectations. Within youth studies this involved imagining the process of becoming an adult as open, undetermined and without an intergenerational blueprint. The starting point for the research was Anthony Giddens' idea of the 'reflexive project of self … whereby self-identity is constituted by the reflexive ordering of self narratives' (1991: 244). The researchers imagined a methodology that would enable them to capture individual projects of self as they evolve and change over time, and to explore how the different contexts within which individuals grow up shape these changing accounts. In that sense the researchers were interested in two interlocking forms of change: first, a set of macro or historical changes that provide the conditions for the emergence of a new generation, whose experience differs significantly from that of their parents and grandparents. Second, the process through which an individual forges a story of their life, a self-identity, a story of who they are, where they come from and where they are going. In engaging with late modern theory the researchers were also aware of the many critical voices that had challenged the work of theorists such as Giddens and Beck, including those who suggest that such theories simply incite us to focus on accounts of agency and to ignore more complex processes and practices through which privilege and inequality are forged

(Adkins 2002a; Heaphy, 2007; Skeggs, 2004). Throughout the research the team employed the reflexive project of self as a vehicle through which to empirically document how individuals create identities for themselves and others. These empirical accounts provide a starting point for thinking about the kinds of claims that late modern theorists make about the relationship between social and personal change.

Interviews were wide ranging, and young people were asked about all areas of their lives: education, work, family, romance, health, fun and well-being. At each interview researchers 'caught up' on events since their last encounter and looked into the future with the young people mapping what they expected to come next. In two interviews young people were asked to complete life lines in which they predicted the shape of their lives in three years' time, and at the ages of 25 and 35, enabling researchers to compare shifts, continuities and contradictions in their life plans (Thomson et al., 2002). Interviewers kept structured field notes after each encounter, recording both details about the interaction and their own emotional responses, but also condensing the content of the interview itself. Over time these developed into 'case profiles' – incremental records summarizing researchers' perceptions of the participants' lives at each wave of fieldwork, making it possible to trace changes in the individual over time through successive time horizons. These summaries were an essential means of making the data set manageable as it was evolving, enabling researchers to make provisional interpretations explicit.

Analytic directions

The management and organization of data is always a challenge in longitudinal studies. Conventional approaches to the storage and analysis of qualitative data privilege comparison across cases in fixed moments of time. Thus we tend to look across cases coding data around common themes, either by hand or using computer-assisted qualitative analysis packages. This is exactly how the Inventing Adulthood team began the process of analysing their data set, coding all the interviews within a single wave using a common coding frame. However, the labour of simultaneously collecting new data and coding becomes increasingly problematic and it can be hard to keep analysis ahead of fieldwork. As the number of waves conducted increases, there is a growing need to find ways of privileging longitudinal analyses, following individuals or groups of individuals over time.

The Inventing Adulthood research has given rise to insights about the challenge of QL data management and analysis, including the double burden of analysing data in two directions: cross-sectional (synchronic) and longitudinal (diachronic) (Thomson and Holland, 2003). Cross-sectional analysis is likely to be most intensive at the beginning of a study when it is the only way in which the data can be interrogated and enables the breadth of the data to be mapped. Longitudinal analysis becomes increasingly attractive as a data set matures and it is possible to draw on a significant run of data. The integration of cross-sectional and longitudinal analyses continues to be the most challenging aspect of QL research design, particularly with large-scale studies. Researchers are experimenting with ways of displaying and articulating the different dimensions of the case, the themes (as represented by a coding frame) and temporality. For example, Jane Lewis has described how she and colleagues have adapted a framework analysis approach to include multiple waves of data (Lewis, 2007).

The Inventing Adulthoods study was a large-scale undertaking, comprising 1500 hours of recorded interview. Now that the process of data collection has ended, the team are beginning the task of relating the longitudinal parts to the cross-sectional whole. The researchers are now working more closely with transcripts, re-imagining the data in terms of individual archives to which they can return, and from which it is possible to forge case histories (R. Thomson, 2007). The data archive for one individual appears as follows. This example is taken from the digital archive www.lsbu.ac.uk/inventingadulthoods.

inventing ADULTHOODS

Keith

Click in one of the themes below to read an excerpt of the interviewa:

COSMOPOLITAN	AVHIEVER	THE BASICS	
NETWORKER	WORK ETHIC	Sex:	Male
CREATIVE ARTS	CLASS CONSCIOUS	Location:	Rural
CLOSE FAMILY	EARLY LOVE	Interview age:	15-20
		Class:	MC
		Ethnicity:	White Caucasian

HOME

BIOQRAPHICAL TIME

KEITH

MAISIE

PATRICK

EMER

KHATTAB

SU

GLEN

CYNTHIA

SAM

NEVILLE

In the context of a tight-knit school and inward-looking rural community, Keith adopted a cosmopolitan, internationalist and independent-thinking indentity from an early age, experiencing a far greater range of other lifestyles and cultures than his peers through travel. An all-rounder, he maintained a balance between a number of different social worlds and associated identitties. With a strong sense of self-sufficiency, Keith drew on all resources – networks that guaranteed him paid employment in the creative arts on leaving university. At university, he gained a more acute sense of class, noting how the majority of his fellow students were richer and much more work-shy than he. His family was a central, emotional, cultural and, to a lesser degree, material resouce. Carring for his mother (who had a long-term illness) with his father and sister also brought early responsibility and maturity and he found leaving home to live with his girlfriend a difficult transition. Meeting 'the one' at 17 complicated his plan for the future but the 'take-it-as-it-comes' approach to life he adopted as a result of becoming aware of the precarious nature of life from a young age enabled him to adjust accordingly.

DATA ANONYMISATION	INTERVIEWS (transcript, audio tape, mp3 file)		
Keith's interview data have undergone an anonymisation process. His case profile will be anonymised next. The rest of his data has yet to be digitized and anonymised and is stored separately with that of other people: Lifelines, Memorybooks, Questionnaires and Focus Groups. For more information on the anonymisation process, click here	. Date	Age	Interviewer
	1. 22/06/98	15	SH
	2. 16/07/99	16	SH
	3. 29/03/00	16	SH
	4. 26/04/01	18	SH
	5. 19/11/02	19	SH
	6. 07/04/04	20	SH

OTHER DATA	
Case profile	Questionnaire 1 hard copy
Focus group 28/11/97 transcript, audio tape	
Emergent Focus group 08/12/00 transcript, audiotape	

The ethical dimensions of QL research

In both of the studies described, researchers have nurtured the research relationship. At the most pragmatic level, longitudinal studies are highly vulnerable to the withdrawal of participants (attrition). Maintaining contact and communication with participants is then a vital part of the research process, and can be time consuming in itself. The studies have employed a range of tools to assist in this process, including sending Christmas and birthday cards, newsletters and reports and developing interactive websites for participants. One of the ethical dilemmas involved in QL research concerns the ongoing negotiation of informed consent. While participants may agree to each interview, it is unlikely that they have a sense of the cumulative power of the data set and what it may reveal about them.

In both the 12–18 study and the Inventing Adulthoods study, data was returned to the participants. In the 12–18 study the edited video both enabled the researchers to share the perspective that they were forging for the individual and provided the participants with the opportunity to respond to this. In the Inventing Adulthoods project the researchers offered all participants copies of their tapes at their third interview. Some, but not all, took up the offer, and not all of these reported listening to them. Subsequently, researchers offered all the young people involved in the study a copy of the final book, as well as negotiating with individuals around more in-depth and revealing case histories. In sharing representations with research subjects we open ourselves up to conflict over interpretation and representation. A useful resource in developing reciprocal relationships can be found in the methodological reflections of long-term anthropological fieldworkers who conceptualize the researcher as located on a continuum from observer to active partner to advocate (Peterson Royce and Kemper, 2002). For Peterson Royce and Kemper, ethical issues in long-term research are 'like the challenges of family life. The more intimate the relationships and the mutual knowledge, the greater the potential for disagreement. At the same time, such intimacy allows more opportunities and more avenues for resolving conflicts' (2002: xx).

A QL data set is more than the sum of its parts. Contradictions between accounts over time, repetitions, silences and recurrent motifs all provide insights that go beyond what is possible with one-off qualitative research. The biographical 'depth' sought by McLeod and Yates is certainly a dividend of the method. Taking care of the research relationship is therefore a serious responsibility, involving not only attentiveness to confidentiality but a recognition of the potential for invading privacy (R. Thomson, 2007). It is inevitable that research that involves the repeat use of in-depth interviews will have some effect on participants. In most cases and most of the time these effects will be neutral or even positive, but there will also be times and cases where being involved in this kind of study is uncomfortable and difficult. (For a cautionary tale and an honest and provocative discussion of ethics in qualitative longitudinal research see Woolcott, 2002.) A willingness to involve participants and to share the results of the research is not a simple solution to this complex situation. People may not like the way in which they are represented, or may feel exposed through the representation. This could be framed in the language of psycho-social methods as the unwillingness of the 'defended subject' to recognize themselves within a research account (Hollway and Jefferson, 2000), yet it could as easily be framed in terms of the 'defended researchers' (Lucey et al., 2003) who are invested in particular interpretations and readings of the data. One of the Inventing Adulthoods research subjects felt that she had been made to 'look stupid' in the book – though this was not the researchers' intention nor their evaluation of the case. The following quote is from a young woman involved in the Inventing Adulthood study who had read an extended case history based on her interviews, and it suggests some of the complexities for both parties involved.

A: It was kind of cringe-worthy reading it. But at the same time I know every-
      thing I told you, you are just kind of passing it back now. You didn't just pick
      things out of nowhere, so nothing shocked me.
Q: Do you feel that it is an accurate feedback?
A: Yeah. There were some things 'Ah, I knew that already' and then there were
      other things 'Oh really? I'll have to think about that'. But yeah.
Q: So what kinds of things surprised you?
A: I was surprised by the whole, ahm [laughs] that I should 'try and transgress
      conventional modes of femininity'. I didn't know I did that! But then, when
      I think about it, aye, I did. But I wouldn't have noticed that myself. ... You

didn't come up with anything shocking. I told you something, you thought about it and then told it back to me in your ways.

Q: It's quite an unusual thing, for anybody involved in research to actually receive that back again.

A: Yeah. I think that it would have been much easier for me not to have got this. See, if you are ever doing this again, don't bother. I don't think that anybody needs to [laughs].

Q: You think it would have been better not to have it?

A: I might be more wary about talking to you. 'Cos I never know what you're going to think about me now.

There is an established tradition of archiving and secondary analysis of quantitative longitudinal data sets, reflected in the effective separation of the processes of data collection and data analysis, and the development of communities of secondary users growing up around each data set. The archiving of qualitative data is a developing practice, with a number of centres of excellence including the Murray Centre at Harvard University (James and Sorensen, 2000), the Special Collaborative Centre 186 'Status Passages and Risks in the Life Course' at the University of Bremen, Germany (Kluge and Opitz, 2000) and Qualidata at the University of Essex in the UK (Corti, 2000; Corti and Thompson, 2003) (see Chapter 7). Paradoxically, QL studies may be both especially suitable for archiving and secondary analysis (because of their scale and their unrealized potential) and especially unsuitable (because of the problem of delegating or sharing the duty of care to participants held by the original researchers). One of the main obstacles to the secondary analysis of qualitative data has been the difficulty of recording/recapturing the context of the original research (including the subjectivity or original researcher) (Hammersley, 1997; Heaton, 2004; Mauthner et al., 1998). These questions have been the subject of sustained discussion, with what was once a relatively polarized debate moving towards an interest in how archiving might enable us to bring questions of temporality and context into focus in new productive ways (Bornat, 2005; Gillies and Edwards, 2005; Moore, 2005). Studies such as the Inventing Adulthoods project are finding ways of documenting and sharing detailed accounts of that research context, distinguishing between the biographical time that is captured in data, the research time of the methodology and the historical time that encompasses the whole enterprise (Henderson et al., 2006).

Qualitative longitudinal studies do not necessarily raise new ethical problems but they do amplify existing ones. The creation of archives of interview and other material for an individual over a period of years not only represents a rich source of data but a uniquely revealing one (Bishop, 2005). Within the social sciences it has been accepted practice to promise interviewees confidentiality and anonymity. This is not an accepted practice within the oral history community, for whom such accounts are part of the historic record (Bornat, 2003, 2005; Parry and Mauthner, 2004). The creation of data archives that draw on both traditions and which assume an interdisciplinary (even popular) user group must balance competing demands and standards.

Conclusion

In this chapter we have attempted to locate the current enthusiasm for qualitative longitudinal research in context – shaped by cultural, theoretical and technical trends. We have suggested that qualitative studies that follow individuals over time have a particular quality that undermines distinctions between the documented life of the research subjects and the subjectivity of the researcher. As researcher and researched walk alongside each other, they come to share a common timescape and grapple with issues of synchronization and differential tempos (Adam, 2004). The project takes on aesthetic, moral and sociological aspects, which become heightened at the point of analytic closure and when we share the resulting representations, thereby fixing both researcher and researched. Whereas the 'audience' is integral to the project of the novelist or the documentary filmmaker, the social scientist has traditionally imagined a highly circumscribed and specialist audience for their work. Yet with developments in information technology and growing demands to disseminate findings and to archive and share data, those conducting these kinds of studies are engaging in increasingly open and iterative relationships with research subjects and audiences. Qualitative longitudinal research enables us to capture personal processes that are socially situated, capturing psychological depth and emotional poignancy. The way in which these processes are framed and presented is inevitably partial, contingent and open to account.

We have shared our experiences of engaging with QLR, showing how and why we arrived at our research designs, and what we did with them. In presenting and sharing our qualitative longitudinal data we have embraced an epistemological stance that demands that we make our claims to knowledge explicit. This is realized in a range of ways: a detailed documentation of research context (Henderson et al., 2006), revealing the unfolding character of analysis (Thomson, forthcoming 2009) and charting the influence of our reading on our 'findings' (McLeod, 2003). A central lesson of researching over time in this way has been how the data always exceeds any of the theoretical frameworks that we bring to it, encouraging us to treat theories as necessary yet blunt tools in the impossible endeavour of representing the complexity of lived lives.

Summary points

- Qualitative longitudinal research methods have been used in many fields and disciplines, yet they are ideally suited to documenting the meanings involved in processual phenomena and transitions.

- Qualitative longitudinal research is well established in a number of disciplines, yet is currently attracting interest from researchers and funders because its facility to address processes is in tune with a growing interest in fluidity and dynamism that can be found in social theory, social policy and popular culture.

- A characteristic of QL research is that the researcher and the research process form part of the data.

- QL studies have the potential to enable an understanding of the interplay of historical, biographical and research time.

- The format of the repeat interview that lies at the heart of much QL research contributes to the representation of a psychologically complex, embodied and mobile research subject constituted in relation to others and within a changing social context.

- By designing comparison into the study it is possible to see beyond the individual as a unit of analysis, towards an understanding of how communities and institutions play out over time and in relation to each other.

- The open-ended character of QLR is associated with a lack of analytic closure. The changing vantage point from which data are apprehended gives rise to a form of 'perspectivism' that acknowledges the contingency of interpretation and the specificity of data and analysis to the situation in which they were generated.

- The ethical complexity of QL amplifies over time, especially in relation to issues of representation, consent and privacy.

Further resources

Pollard, A. and Filer, A. (1999) *The Social World of Pupil Career: Strategic Biographies through Primary School.* London: Continuum.
One of a series of books reporting the findings of the Identity and Learning Programme that followed the educational careers of 17 children between the ages of 4 and 16, using ethnographic methods. Yields insight into the complex processes through which learning takes place, and provides a unique document of the impact of educational reform over a 12-year period.

Walkerdine, V., Lucey, H. and Melody, J. (2001) *Growing Up Girl: Psychosocial Explorations of Gender and Class.* London: Palgrave: Macmillan.
This book reports on over 20 years of research with a group of young women who participated in a series of studies. Drawing on a psycho-social framework, the authors explore their changing perceptions of the young women engaged in projects of social mobility within a period of rapid social change.

Kemper, R. and Peterson Royce, A. (eds) (2002) *Chronicling Cultures: Long-Term Field Research in Anthropology.* Walnut Creek, CA: AltaMira Press.
Drawing on the established practice of long-term fieldwork in anthropology, this book provides methodological insight (especially in relation to research ethics and relationships) as well as examples of studies that span whole careers or which link generations of researchers.

Saldana, J. (2003) *Longitudinal Qualitative Research: Analyzing Change through Time.* Walnut Creek, CA: AltaMira Press.
A thorough guide to all aspects of QL research design and analysis, based on the author's own research in theatre studies.

There are two special issues of journals focusing on QLR:

The International Journal of Social Research Methodology 6 (3)

This includes a series of papers exploring QLR, research notes detailing insights and lessons and an editorial outlining the emergent field.

Social Policy and Society 6 (4)

This special 'section' includes several papers exploring the value of QLR to social policy research, a bibliography on archiving and an editorial.

Websites

www.lsbu.ac.uk/inventingadulthoods

Website providing an overview of the Inventing Adulthoods study, including access to a digital showcase archive.

www.timescapes.leeds.ac.uk

Website for a major new qualitative longitudinal study, bringing together seven empirical investigations of different stages in the lifecourse. The website will also provide a gateway into the 'live' timescapes archive.

Note

1 For example, the British birth cohorts which have followed nationally representative panels of around 13,000 individuals born in a single week in 1946 (The National Child Development Study), 1958, 1970 (Ferri et al., 2003) and, most recently, a millennium cohort which follows babies born in the UK in 2000. In Australia, influential longitudinal studies include the Longitudinal Survey of Australian Youth (Lamb and McKenzie, 2000) and the Life Patterns Longitudinal Study (Dwyer and Wyn, 2001).

5

Ethnography

Cultural analysis is intrinsically incomplete. And, worse than that, the more deeply it goes, the less complete it is. ... To commit oneself to a semiotic concept of culture and interpretive approach to the study of it is to commit oneself to a view of ethnographic assertion as, to borrow W.B. Gallie's by now famous phrase, 'essentially contestable'. (Clifford Geertz, 1973: 29)

Problematizing the temporal: a break with the trope of history in realist ethnography. The break is not with historical consciousness, or a pervasive sense of the past in any site or set of sites probed by ethnography, but rather with historical determination as the primary context for any ethnographic present. ... The past that is in any site is built up from memory, the fundamental medium of ethnohistory. (George Marcus, 1992: 316, emphasis in original)

Ethnographic enquiry seeks to document and understand the everyday worlds of social groups and communities. It aims to illuminate the detail and significance of social practices, rituals and interactions as these happen and unfold in the lived time of the present (Atkinson et al., 2002; Eisenhart, 2001). Its 'distinctive features revolve around the notions of people as *meaning*-makers, around an emphasis on understanding how people *interpret* their worlds, and the need to understand the particular cultural worlds in which people live and which they both construct and utilise' (Goldbart and Hustler, 2005: 16). In the detail of cultural life, ethnographers look to see the meaning of the cultural whole. Yet, as Geertz (1973) notes above, inevitably cultural analysis is 'intrinsically incomplete' and 'essentially contestable'. Ethnographies are conventionally conducted within specific bounded spaces, such as a village, or school, or workplace, in locations that may be unfamiliar or familiar to the researcher. When conducting 'fieldwork', ethnographers employ a cluster of methods to build descriptive accounts, including participant observations, interviews, and analysis of documents and material artefacts. Typically, the research design is relatively open-ended, and while an ethnographer usually begins with some '"foreshadowed problems", their orientation is an exploratory one' (Hammersley and Atkinson, 2007: 3, 20–4).

Ethnography captures cultural processes and events as they happen, privileging the here and now of the present; yet the focus of this chapter is upon what ethnographic enquiry offers for researching change. Ethnography's orientation to the 'here and now' perhaps inhibits thinking about change over extended periods of time, as the focus is more firmly and typically oriented to practices and meaning-making over shorter periods of time and in particular places. Qualitative longitudinal research is effective for documenting change over time, for charting shifts in cohorts – either groups or individuals – and has an explicit temporal agenda built into its methodology. In contrast, ethnographic methods appear to be particularly suited for observing routines and noticing disruptions to those routines, and for capturing change as it emerges and evolves. Its inclusive gaze allows attention to the unexpected, to micro-level interactions and dynamics in which social changes are felt and articulated, and to the coexistence of the biographical time of the researcher and researched. And, as our opening quotation from Marcus suggests, enthnographic enquiry is embedded in understandings about the relationship of the past to the present, and with how memories of the past inform the ethnographic present.

Much recent debate about theoretical and methodological innovation within ethnography privileges writing and spatial relations, and in this chapter we consider what this work offers for rethinking relations between time and place and for researching change. We argue that ethnographic approaches allow distinctive insight into change processes precisely because they foster close-up analysis of phenomena over and in a distinct period of time, even if the temporality of that endeavour is not made explicit. Following a brief review of influential methodological debates within ethnography, we examine two case studies – the first conducted in the late 1960s and the second in the 1990s. Both address gender relations and generational change and both are informed by feminism; in combination, they capture some revealing moments and shifts in feminist theory and in ethnographic enquiry.

Disciplinary travels

The history of ethnography is caught up in the history of a number of disciplines, notably anthropology, but also urban sociology – the Chicago School, community studies and subcultural studies (Gelder, 2007) – and popular knowledge forms, such as travel writing (Hammersley, 1998). Ethnography was taken up by anthropologists in the late 19th century to record the lives of 'exotic others' (for example, and famously, Malinowski and his research in 1915–18 on the Trobriand Islanders of New Guinea), for whom no library-based research existed. Methods to observe life as it was happening were the basis for generating knowledge about other cultures (see Burke, 1992). By the second half of the 20th century, such studies were increasingly regarded as having been harnessed to colonial projects of dominating, surveying and cataloguing the other. Yet, interest in ethnographic approaches continued to flourish, taken up by sociologists and cultural studies practitioners to study facets of their own society, embraced by anthropologists and others to look afresh at 'western societies', to study what seemed ordinary – to make 'the familiar strange and the quotidian exotic' (Clifford and Marcus, 1986: 2). Clifford characterizes this as the rise of the 'indigenous ethnographer' – 'insiders studying their own cultures' (1986: 9). Our first case study is an example of an anthropologist (Diana Leonard) investigating marriage and courtship practices in a local community in Wales; and the second case study is an example of a school-based ethnography conducted by a researcher (Mary Jane Kehily) embedded in cultural studies and feminist traditions.

A once common image of the ethnographer, largely derived from the idea of the intrepid anthropologist, was of a serious-minded and curious scholar, with well-worn book of field notes in hand, scribbling away under all manner of difficult circumstances. This image has perhaps been overtaken by that of the modern fieldworker, not necessarily working in exotic locations or villages, who juggles digital equipment so as to generate a multi-layered visual, textual and aural montage of field notes that are reflexively and even nervously offered as a partial and incomplete representation of an event, which is itself understood as shaped indelibly by the presence of the fieldworker. The textual and cultural turns in the social sciences and humanities have also had a strong influence on ethnographic practice, but before turning to this, let us consider what is meant by an 'ethnographic stance'.

An ethnographic stance

Ethnography usually 'begins with description of settings, objects, and the behaviour and classifications of individuals and groups, and ends with an analysis of the structural relationships among the elements of the group' (Harper, 1992: 149). As we have noted, ethnographic methods are not confined to the conduct of fieldwork away from 'home' and are embraced in a wide range of disciplines – what unites these disparate and different inflections? In contemporary research practice, the 'ethnographic stance', Ortner suggests, 'is as much an intellectual (and moral) positionality – a constructive and interpretive mode – as it is a bodily process in time and space' (Ortner, 2006: 42; see also Willis, 2000: viii–xx). This stance can inform textual interpretations, be one element of a case study, a strategy for contextualizing research interviews, or adopted by historians to reconstruct a sense of time and place for which direct observations in the traditional sense are not possible. There are, moreover, different strands within the broad descriptor of ethnographic research, such as institutional ethnography (Smith, 2005), performance ethnography (Alexander, 2005) and feminist, critical, historical or postcolonial ethnography (Comaroff and Comaroff, 1992; Skeggs, 1997; Willis, 2000).

For Ortner, the distinguishing and unifying aspect of an ethnographic stance is that it involves 'first and foremost a commitment to what Geertz has called "thickness", to producing understanding through richness, texture, and detail' (2006: 43), often leading to exhaustive documentation. Subsequently, thickness came 'to be synonymous with holism, the idea that the object under study was a "highly integrated culture" and that it was possible to describe the entire system or at least fully grasp the principles underlying it' (Ortner, 2006: 43). A persuasive critique of holism is its failure to acknowledge the gaps, fragmentations and contradictions within cultures, and its hubris in imagining that 'the other' can be known so comprehensively by a researcher (Crang and Cook, 2007: 7–13). Earlier hopes for ethnographic holism are now undercut by reflections on the inevitable partiality of any account and a self-conscious analysis of the role of the ethnographer in shaping what is shown and seen. Even so, Ortner suggests that a commitment to 'thick description' remains 'at the heart of the ethnographic stance' (Ortner, 2006: 43).

Persistent tensions

Ethnography encompasses a range of research practices, but has minimally 'always meant the attempt to understand another life world using the self – as much of it as possible – as the instrument of knowing' (Ortner, 2006: 42). This idea is common to qualitative approaches, but takes a heightened form in ethnographic enquiry through the practice of fieldwork, in which the immersion of the 'whole self physically and in every other way' (p. 42) enters into other life worlds. An enduring tension within ethnography has been how researchers navigate their relationship with the field, and the ambiguous position of the participant observer, a description that encapsulates a tension between distance and immersion, objectivity and subjectivity (Coffey, 1999; Crang and Cook, 2007; Tamboukou and Ball, 2003). The anthropologist Ruth Behar describes this as a 'deeply paradoxical' intellectual mission, which requires one to 'get the "native point of view" … without actually "going native"' (Behar, 1996: 5).

As with oral and life history, and most forms of qualitative enquiry, an ongoing challenge is navigating the relation between the particular and a larger collective or entity (whether that be nationality, class, gender, identity or (sub)culture). This dilemma has an urgency in ethnographic work because so many of its claims to methodological and epistemological significance rest on its capacity to elucidate and render the local which, in turn, illuminates a larger or wider issue or relation or culture. The particular is thus seen as an instance of a larger whole, which the close-up observations of ethnography illuminate. Clifford Geertz's (1973) much-quoted essay on the Balinese cockfight, for example, illustrates the power of 'thick description' to interpret the meaning of specific events. Yet, his semiotic analysis of this particular episode has met with criticism from those who see it as a problematic basis for generating an account of 'Balinese culture' (which Balinese? whose culture?), or of being able to explain how particular cultural texts relate to each other, or of showing how separate, in-depth analyses can be synthesized to speak to the cultural 'whole' (Biersak, 1989).

Time in the field

Ethnographic study involves a considerable commitment from the researcher, traditionally requiring intensive and extensive time in the research site (Hammersley and Atkinson, 2007). One major benefit of long-term and in-depth engagement is that it assists the researcher to distinguish between the routine and the exceptional (Nayak and Kehily, 2008). Some ethnographies are conducted over many years, other researchers may regularly return to their field sites and have a long-term relationship with their informants and community (Kemper and Peterson Royce, 2002); yet other ethnographic texts may be 'written up' some years after the completion of fieldwork (Hey, 1997). And yet others may be essentially 'one-off' observations – intense but comparatively short-term. This form of ethnographic enquiry appears to be becoming more common, aggravated by the speeding up of academic life. In the social sciences (but not necessarily in anthropology), one is now more likely to hear of people *employing* ethnographic methods than undertaking full-scale ethnographies that require long-term engagement and participant observations. This could be a consequence of funding and difficulties in securing support for such research, particularly during a time of intensification of academic work. It is also likely connected to an intellectual suspicion of what constitutes ethnography as a research method and set of knowledge claims, as we elaborate below. However, a counter mood, exemplified by Law's (2004) call for 'slow methods', might open the way for a rethinking of the time of fieldwork, and the kind of knowledge that can be generated by slow, long-term involvement in the field.

The extended nature of ethnographic work, and the kinds of relationships and reflections that this makes possible, have typically formed the foundation of what is distinctive about the ethnographic method. Ethnographies can be conducted over varying periods of time and have different interests in the passage of time and how it impacts upon their research site and informants. Time may not be considered directly relevant to their questions; it may be central to the design, as in long-term or return fieldwork; it may become important retrospectively, as in follow-up ethnographies, which we discuss in Chapter 7; it may arise in implicit comparisons with earlier generations, as suggested in both our case studies; or it may simply be a consequence of the length of time involved in researching and writing, as evident in our first case study. These otherwise diverse negotiations of time and research design share a methodological interest in researching and 'writing culture'.

Time, tense and the ethnographic present

With its commitment to immersion in the field and an inductive method, ethnographic research typically produces massive amounts of data that require substantial time to analyse (Hammersley and Atkinson, 2007). Field notes are vital for making sense of events and observations as they happen, but they also need to be revisited, often some time after, examined as another research artefact on which the final ethnographic writing draws. This poses particular challenges for the ethnographer who in some respects is working against the passage of time, constantly trying to capture and write about a fleeting present. Ethnographic writing thus involves a kind of sleight of hand, the trick of trying to represent the unfolding of events when there is always a time lag – the writing is inevitably a representation of a present that has already passed.

The idea of the 'ethnographic present' is partly a matter of grammatical tense – the use of the simple or continuous present tense that evokes an ongoing action or truth, or event, and which has been a characteristic mode of ethnographic writing. Methodologically, it refers to the 'practice of developing analyses and generalizations from ethnographic research as if they represent a timeless description of the people being studied' (Davies, 2008: 193). Yet, as Charlotte Aull Davies observes, this view 'implicitly denies the historicity of these people':

> The data on which such analyses are based are acquired in an historically located encounter between an ethnographer and some individuals from among the people so described. Yet, whereas the ethnographer moves on, temporally, spatially and developmentally, the people he or she studied are presented as if suspended in an unchanging and virtually timeless state, as if the ethnographer's description provides all that is important, or possible, to know about their past and future. (Davies, 2008: 193)

The stylistic form of the ethnographic present reflects the complicated relationship between anthropological fieldwork, colonial domination and the desire to 'capture' what were constructed as disappearing and timeless cultures. Not surprisingly, the idea of the 'ethnographic present' has been subject to critique from many quarters and, Davies notes, has become more important for the 'criticisms it generates than its actual application' (p. 193). It is criticized for conveying a sense of culture and practices frozen in time and for refusing to 'admit either competing chronologies or even to recognize itself as a normative construct' (Britzman, 2000: 34). More dynamic accounts of temporality in ethnographic research are emerging, as 'ethnographers have become more concerned with emergence, practice, and performance'. This has brought 'history and the diachronic back into ethnography, and makes culture less a superstructural object hanging over subjects than something which emerges in the local production of discourse and practice' (Brown, 2003: 72).

History and ethnography

Indeed, the relationship of history to ethnography, and of the past to the ethnographic present, is somewhat vexed, echoing dilemmas raised in our discussion of the past/present relation in oral histories. As the opening epigraph from George Marcus indicates, gestures to historical determinism to explain the present no longer suffice. One of the challenges for ethnography is to problematize the temporal relations implicit within ethnography, to 'break with the trope of history' and the idea that the present is both the realization of and produced in the past. Disrupting this linear account of temporal relations demands a reconsideration of the 'ethnographic present'. This would be to imagine a very different present, one that has been largely ignored in 'classic functionalist anthropology. ... This is a present that is defined not by historical narrative either, but by memory, its own distinctive narratives and traces' (Marcus, 1992: 317). Davies offers a different take but still returns to the significance of memory. She suggests that 'historians are more likely to treat the past as behind us and as productive of the present [whereas] anthropologists frequently challenge both of these perspectives':

> First many adopt what has been called a memorial approach to the past, which emphasizes that as 'memory it [the past] remains very much with us: in our bodies, in our dispositions and sensibilities, and in our skills of perception and action'. ... [O]n the second point, the formal remembering of events that have passed can be seen as a process of making them explicable in terms of the present, virtually the present producing the past (altered by knowledge of what has come since) rather than the reverse. (Davies, 2008: 196)

A further view is to see ethnography as 'current history', which requires an expanded understanding of the ethnographic present, one which consciously locates ethnography 'with regard to the past' and 'situates both subjects and ethnographer in time and space'. This view must also 'give attention to the likely future that is being produced' and this, in turn, works against the 'structuralist tendency to overlook heterogeneity and change' (Davies, 2008: 197). (There is, as well, a strong tradition of 'ethnographic history', but it is not possible to elaborate this work here, other than to note the influence of cultural and semiotic ethnography on historical enquiry; Comaroff and Comaroff, 1992; Hunt, 1989.)

For others, including those working in structuralist traditions, ethnography works to expose the arbitrariness and historicity of the present. For example, Pierre Bourdieu in *Masculine Domination* (2001) revisits his earlier ethnographic study of Kabyle society in Algeria, analysing the structure of gender relations and the historical production and re-production of the seemingly natural principle and practice of masculine domination. This principle, Bourdieu argues, has the appearance of an eternal or natural state of affairs, whereas it is in fact a cultural arbitrary whose effects and status must be historicized, in part by demonstrating the ways in which it operates as natural. Further, the ongoing creation of an aura of eternality itself warrants historical and sociological interrogation. In this view, the role of the ethnographer is to show how history becomes nature, and how the practical and ideological processes of 'de-historicization' function (Bourdieu, 2001: viii, 102–3).

To summarize, ethnographic method emerged in a particular historical moment, and facilitated a way of apprehending cultures, communities and practices that emphasized immediacy. Subsequently, ethnography has travelled in time and place, becoming part of a number of academic traditions. While the emphasized temporal register of ethnography is the present, the past and the future are also invoked. These aspects are not necessarily responded to explicitly or uniformly. But working through how researching in the present tense (time and place) presumes, or interrogates, or recasts the past, and anticipates a future is part of the ethnographic endeavour and shapes – directly and indirectly – methodological choices and interpretations. And, as with the other methodologies discussed in this book, the history of ethnography reveals something about how it is employed as a research and writing practice in the present.

Local time

The challenge of negotiating the relationship between the particular and the larger 'whole' is increasingly played out via the local/global problematic associated with globalization (Nayak and Kehily, 2008). This has given rise to concerns about the 'unboundedness' of the local and the blurry and reconfiguring relations between global, national and local space (Appadurai, 2001; Burawoy, 2000; Dale, 2006). Under such circumstances, what is the role of ethnography? The 'task of ethnography now becomes the unravelling of a conundrum: what is the nature of locality as lived experience in a globalized deterritorialized world?' (Appadurai, 1996: 52, cited in Kenway et al., 2006: 44–5).

Such arguments arise in the context of postcolonial critiques of ethnography's heritage of constructing the other, but they equally apply to any construction of so-called local culture (Crang and Cook, 2007: 12). Colonialism and associated desires to study the disappearing local were part of the birth of ethnography, but mapping global connections has become part of its present and future project. Critiques of holism and the local/global relation are part of a series of lively debates over the last few decades, coming from diverse disciplinary and theoretical vantage points, regarding the methodological, epistemological and ethico-political purposes of ethnography (Atkinson et al., 2002; Britzman, 2000; Clifford, 2003; Eisenhart, 2001; Tamboukou and Ball, 2003). A volume edited by Clifford and Marcus (1986), *Writing Culture: The Poetics and Politics of Ethnography,* remains a landmark collection of essays that articulated the mood of change, and many of the challenges it raises remain salient today. Before turning to our case studies, we briefly discuss two of these challenges that are pertinent to our interests.

A (productive) crisis of representation

Writing is central to ethnographic research; ethnography 'literally means writing about people' (Goldbart and Hustler, 2005: 16). Ethnographic writing encompasses the writing of field notes, a relatively private practice of documentation and reflection that is defining of the ethnographer's craft, and the translation of those notes into a commentary or account of the research that then circulates in publicly available articles and books (Hammersley and Atkinson, 2007). Even when ethnographic writing is supplemented with visual, aural and digital media (Crang and Cook, 2007), questions of representation remain.

The 'crisis of representation' is shorthand for a crisis of faith in the possibility of capturing and conveying the full truth of the object under ethnographic gaze: 'representation cannot deliver what it promises, unmediated access to the real' (Britzman, 2000: 35). Representation is seen as an act of construction, not a simple reflection of an 'out-there-and-waiting-to-be-documented' empirical reality, but a productive act of invention. Messiness, partiality and provisionality replace ordered systems of meaning, core truths and rescued realities (Law, 2004). There is also an element of suspicion, with writing and other forms of representation regarded as both dangerous and seductive – dangerous because of what is inevitably excluded, and seductive because representations can entrance readers as truth. Such concerns extend to ethical questions about how to represent the 'voices' and stories of research participants; to what extent can ethnographic accounts silence, distort or enable voices, or hinder or help the capacity and agency of participants (Britzman, 2000)?

Clifford describes the current mood among ethnographers as one that assumes 'the poetic and the political are inseparable, that science is in, not above, historical and linguistic processes' (Clifford, 1986: 2). The textual turn in ethnography, with its focus on text making (both field notes and research report) and rhetoric, 'serves to highlight the constructed, artificial nature of cultural accounts. It undermines overly transparent modes of authority, and it draws attention to the historical predicament of ethnography, the fact that it is always caught up in the invention, not the representation of cultures' (p. 2). Clifford argues that ethnographic texts are a form of a literary writing in that they employ literary processes such as 'metaphor, figuration, narrative' (p. 4). Paul Willis similarly describes the 'ethnographic imagination' as attuned to the nuances of figurative–metaphoric language and its local inflections (Willis, 2000: 11).

Literary borrowings are also at play in claims that 'ethnographic writings can properly be called fictions', not with connotations of falsehood, but in recognition of the 'partiality of cultural and historical truths' and in the sense of 'something made or fashioned', of making, and of making up (acts of invention) (Clifford, 1986: 6). Ethnographic writing attempts to tell a story about other worlds, aiming, variously, to render intelligible, to make strange, to seek to understand through new lenses. For both researcher and researched, 'all constructed truths are made possible by powerful "lies" of exclusion and rhetoric. Even the best ethnographic texts – serious true fictions – are systems, economies, of truth. Power and history work through them, in ways their authors cannot fully control' (Clifford, 1986: 7).

Looking at writing in these ways destabilizes the idea of the ethnographer as someone who comprehensively captures and faithfully records a culture. It also produces a more unstable and troubling ethnographic present, because in underlining the inventive and figurative dimensions of ethnographic writing it works against a view of culture as either fixed in time or timeless, waiting to be documented.

Autobiographical turns

What did the postmodern ethnographer say to the informant?
'Enough about you, now what about me?'

Classically, the 'ethnographer's personal experiences, especially those of participation and empathy, are recognized as central to the research process, but they are firmly restrained by the impersonal standards of observation and "objective" distance' (Clifford, 1986: 13). The notion of 'fieldwork', a core activity of ethnographers, is historically connected to the 'idea of culture as cultivation and the practice of going into the field as the place where one finds culture' (Rabinow, 2003: 84). Other terms are needed to capture the changing practices of ethnography, yet few are available. A possible alternative descriptor, 'participant observation', is a 'purposively oxymoronic term' (p. 84), one that Rabinow suggests has also 'served its times, done its historical duty in anthropology'. Moreover, it can be misleading 'as the observation pole implies more distance than is appropriate, as well as an exterior spatial location; the participation pole misleadingly implies that one engages in some mimicry of the natives' practices' (p. 84).

A position of detachment for the field worker is now widely regarded as neither desirable nor possible. The presence of the embodied researcher is, minimally, regarded as influencing the research setting and what is seen; in stronger formulations it addresses the biographical and cultural context of the ethnographer's gaze, and the ethnographer's own responses and feelings as an important trope – the ethnographic encounter becomes as much a journey of self-discovery as a discovery of the 'other'.

The reflexive turn in qualitative methodologies manifests in ethnography in two seemingly contradictory impulses – a questioning of the authority of the ethnographer and a concern with autobiographical positioning of the ethnographer. Britzman identifies a questioning of three types of ethnographic authority: 'the authority of empiricism; the authority of language; and the authority of reading or understanding' (Britzman, 2000: 28). On the one hand, this has produced a 'more tentative' and reflexive form of ethnographic theorizing and, on the other, it has fostered an intense self-consciousness and introspective gaze on the part of the researcher.

Autoethnography, in which the ethnographic gaze is turned inwards onto the 'personal and its relationship to culture' (Ellis, 2004: 37), is one, increasingly popular, manifestation of the autobiographical impulse in ethnography which also seeks to connect the biographical time of the researcher and the researched (Okley and Callaway, 1992). 'Autoethnography is both a method and a text of diverse interdisciplinary praxes … situating the sociopolitically inscribed body as a central site of meaning making' (Spry, 2001: 710). Consequently, some autoethnographies are represented as performances, enacted by the researcher, who is understood 'as the epistemological and ontological nexus upon which the research process turns' (Spry, 2001: 711).

Vulnerable observers

Attention to the emotional connections and close relationships that may arise (or appear to arise) between ethnographer and participant is also part of the person-alizing turn (Coffey, 1999). Ruth Behar's (1996) notion of the anthropologist as a 'vulnerable observer' is one influential response. In making sense of the messy intersections of her professional and personal life, Behar decided to make 'my emotions part of my ethnography', expressing 'a desire to embed a diary of my life within the accounts of the lives of others that I was required to produce as an anthropologist' (p. 19). She historicizes the autobiographical turn within anthro-pology, noting the tradition of personal narratives within the field, the influences of life history, and feminist and minority writers and politics. Despite the sceptics of autobiographical writing, Behar insists that vulnerability 'is here to stay' (Behar, 1996: 32).

Researcher and researched are always located in time and space, and analysing this can bring a dynamic temporality to any study. But the tricky issue is the degree to which the researcher's location and subjectivity become the prominent point of reference. The self-consciously autobiographical voice can be commodified, for-mulaic and inhibit thinking about social processes beyond one's narcissistic reaction to them (Fine and Weis, 1998; McLeod and Yates, 2006). At the same time, the auto-biographical turn is significant in the history of ethnographic methods and, at its best, provides methodological resources for enabling analysis of social *and* bio-graphical change and for illuminating the intersection between them.

Selecting the case studies

The following two case studies bring the researcher into the writing, but do so in quite different ways. The first, a study of wedding and courtship conducted by Diana Leonard, adopts a more anthropological frame, and the second, a study of gender rela-tions and schooling by Mary Jane Kehily, is informed more by cultural studies. The first case study, published in 1980, was chosen in part because it is on the cusp of sig-nificant social, theoretical and methodological changes, and the second and more recent study shows the marks of the methodological innovations we have been dis-cussing. Both are shaped by feminism, and both explore questions of social change and gender relations, yet with different conceptual and methodological languages.

Deciding on the selection of case studies for this chapter was difficult, with the final choice representing two moments in 'feminist' ethnography of intimate life that reflect the times in which they were created. The first study develops a critical problematization of the gendered divisions of labour within marriage and family life; in this respect it is also an example of the kind of de-naturalizing of the seemingly natural that Bourdieu's work advocated. In Leonard's case, this is articulated against and in opposition to a theoretical backdrop of anthropolog-ical functionalism – a framework which itself bears many of the traces of the ethnographic/theoretical present (that is, showing how the 'system' or the present works, but not critiquing it). The second case study emerges in a 'post-feminist' moment in which the making of gender is problematized, and the fragility and resilience of that process is acknowledged, alongside agency and a sense of possibility. Interestingly both studies focus on 'performance', with Leonard taking up anthropologically-influenced ideas of ritual and attempting to locate them historically and culturally, and Kehily realizing the potential of the theoretical shifts regarding the performance of gender that feminist work such as Leonard's helped make possible. In combination, these two British studies provide a fascinating view of shifts in gender relations in the second half of the 20th century, from the second wave to girl-power feminism, and a glimpse of trajectories in recent ethnographic and feminist research.

Getting married: South Wales in the 1960s

Our first case study is located within a community studies tradition, and discusses an ethnographic study conducted by Diana Leonard in the late 1960s of practices and attitudes concerning courtship and marriage in Swansea, a provincial town in Wales – *Sex and Generation: A Study of Courtship and Weddings* (1980). Against the backdrop of a social history of the region and community, courtship and wedding practices are documented in rich descriptive detail, and their significance examined in light of emerging feminist and materialist theories about the family and gender ideologies.

The topic itself, and much of the tone of the writing, is framed as an anthropological investigation of the rituals of everyday, urban community and familial life. These rituals are judged to be inherently significant for understanding how that society works, so that 'by looking at the rituals of a given society – i.e. at its largely expressive, symbolic, formalized acts – we can get profound insights into its values and institutions. Rituals "say things which are difficult to think" (Beattie 1966)' (Leonard, 1980: 2). An ethnographic account of a ritual, such as marriage, overtly attends to its symbolic form, functions and meaning in the present. But, if we want to explain the 'continuance of a particular custom – such as the bride wearing a white dress for the wedding – anthropologists would argue that we have to provide a historic account of its development and see what meaning it has for present-day performances' (Leonard, 1980: 2). This description captures the tension inherent in the 'ethnographic present', where the present is paradoxically both timeless yet embedded in a history that gives cultural practices their significance. An historical account of present-day practices is allied to an understanding that such rituals are neither static, unchanging practices, repeated across generations, nor 'meaningless charades continued through force of habit' (p. 2).

> They [the rituals] are repeated to reiterate their message, and the rituals associated with the rites of passage from one social status to another are repeated for each individual in that society. Each repetition allows the accommodation of new developments and new interpretations, or builds up pressure for reform if

change requires legal enactment. Participants may modify or manipulate or change some parts to express major or minor changes in the message they wish to give; or those involved may try to introduce new customs for extrinsic reasons (e.g. people in trades catering for weddings attempt innovations in order to sell new products). Change therefore not only *occurs* in rituals, it is endemic. (Leonard, 1980: 2)

Researching rituals thus goes hand in hand with understanding cultural innovation. Rituals are not traditions cemented in time, and ethnographic enquiry requires an approach attuned to the relationship between what has meaning in the present and what has happened in the past.

Leonard interviewed brides or couples, most both before and after their wedding and, for many of the couples, interviews were also held with their immediate families. Her sample comprised 34 couples planning a church wedding (predominantly Anglican) and 20 couples marrying in a Registry office (Leonard, 1980: 29–31; 274–86). Conducting interviews in their homes, she asked informants to talk about 'courtship', the lead up to the wedding, the wedding itself and the period of early married life, as well as gift giving, preparation for the wedding reception, organizing the new marital home, managing in-laws, who to place on the invitation list, what a period of 'engagement' signifies and so forth. She combined interviews with participant observations, attending weddings, 'hen nights' and receptions, and conducting interviews in family homes. Having herself recently moved to Swansea as newly married and the mother of a young child, she was also able to draw on more informal observations and interactions.

Leonard's interest in studying weddings was motivated by an 'anthropological concern with describing the scale and assessing the significance of what I knew to be a major ceremonial cycle within my own society' (1980: 2). It was also informed by an interest in understanding 'the nature of relationships between the sexes and generations', and the study of weddings allowed special opportunities for this. She also reasoned that as a young, recently married woman herself it was likely people would be more willing to talk about weddings than if she asked them to talk about other matters of family life. Additionally, weddings provided many occasions for her to participate in, observe and discuss family events. She planned then 'to use the study of ritual both directly and indirectly as a means of "opening a window onto opaque urban social processes"' (p. 3).

The researcher's time

The research was conducted in the late 1960s, the study written up during the 1970s and published as a book in 1980. This lengthy process illustrates the complicated temporal layering in ethnographic research. Although it is a method that seemingly privileges the present, the demands of fieldwork to obtain intensive and extensive familiarity with the site and informants means that gathering and recording material is time consuming, often taking place over many years, even when a longitudinal focus is not an intended part of the design. In this case, fieldwork was from autumn 1968 to autumn 1969, with plans for the study and recruitment beginning a year earlier in 1967. Leonard describes her methodical process for writing field notes, both immediately after and during an interview or observation. The thorough documentation of her research procedures reveals the time-intensive and practical aspects of ethnographic fieldwork.

The personal circumstances of the researcher also have a bearing on the extended nature of the research. For Leonard, the lapses of time between field work, writing and publication arose in part from her own family circumstances, raising three young children, securing an academic job, and moving away from Swansea, on top of the time necessary for processing and analysing the vast amounts of material and observations generated by such a study. Explaining the protracted process, Leonard reflects that it was partly 'because I lacked an adequate theoretical framework, partly because it was necessary for me to be moved out of the field in order to distance myself from the material; but it was also because I had to get away from what is conventionally involved in being a wife and mother in our culture to have the time and motivation to finish' (p. 38).

Leonard inserts into the text her situated presence as a researcher, describing how her identity – as a young mother, living in Swansea, but not as a complete insider – shaped the topics she was able to raise and created possibilities for access to informants. Her struggles to work out the framework for analysing the material are noted, as are her own practical struggles to complete the writing. In comparison with much of the researcher reflexivity that populates research writing today, Leonard's reflections may seem – refreshingly – modest and cautious, but they are purposefully directed to a methodological or interpretive point.

For example, after describing delays in her writing, Leonard observes that the passage of time from fieldwork to writing and publication is not always negative or a limitation on the relevance of the insights. While acknowledging some minor changes, she observes at the time of writing the book that the material was not dated and that overall little had changed; 'further … what I have to say about Swansea still applies to many areas of the country and across the middle and working classes. The wisdom derived from being somewhat geographically and temporally removed from the field suggests the generality of my findings, rather than their specificity' (p. 39). Moreover, distance from the field allowed her to reframe her analysis, a shift that, in turn, reflects the influence of feminism and something of the broader changing intellectual and political climate in which Leonard was immersed and to which her own work contributed. When she began the research, Leonard was interested 'in showing what the associated ceremonial was saying about structures and implicit values'. Yet with the experience of and distance from fieldwork she came 'to analyse the material in terms of inter-sex and intergenerational relations in a particular socio-historical context' (p. 286).

Challenging accounts of gender and family relations

Throughout, Leonard comments on her evolving theoretical position and rejection of the then dominant functionalist accounts of the family. She came to see the marital relation as an economic relation, with family life made up not simply of affective relations of kin but of material relationships between husband and wife, and parents and children (see Chapters 5, 6 and the Conclusion). Materialist and feminist critiques of the ideology of family life were gaining ground and Leonard's analysis is part of this movement. Marriage, she argued, 'is a particular form of labour relationship between men and women, whereby a woman pledges for life (with limited rights to quit) her labour, sexuality, and reproductive capacity and receives "protection", upkeep and certain rights to children' (p. 5). Most sociology of the family and marriage – whether functionalist or phenomenological – confined itself, Leonard argued, to the emotional relationships and to its meaning for spouses. But this 'totally ignores the work the two sexes do – the different ways in which they make a living – and the consequent disparity, and indeed antagonism, of their life situations' (p. 261).

In discussing how couples started married life, Leonard draws out how such disparities between the sexes are connected to intergenerational relations. A clear division of domestic labour existed within families and among the newly married couples, with women of both the parent and child generation responsible for the 'maintenance of kin ties' (p. 251).

> Not only does the wife-mother take the brunt of the labour and cost of the children when young and when as young adults they live at home, but it is mainly she who continues to work for the new couple gratis or to maintain contact via letters or visits when they move to live some distance away. The return on this – the status from being a successful parent (and grandparent) and pleasure from the company of children (and grandchildren), together with the assurance of care in old age – accrues to both the husband and the wife of the older couple, though perhaps rather more to the wife. (It is certainly more important to her since she has fewer other sources of prestige or companionship, and she is likely to live longer.) (Leonard, 1980: 251)

Changes in the position of women are acknowledged, such as improvements in the status of married women, but this 'is not to say that the sexes are now equal' (p. 276). Leonard concludes: 'the essence of the labour relationship of marriage is unchanged, and the ceremonial associated with courtship and wedding affirms this' (p. 268).

A stated aim of her account was to bring to the forefront the specificity of the time and place in which her research was located. Too many studies of family life, she argued, tended to abstract the family from its social setting and to treat it as a contained unit of analysis, with little attention to either the social relations that surrounded it or the gender relations that underpinned family organization. In contrast, Leonard draws out the specific socio-historical context of her informants, wanting 'to explore critically the relationship between the *institution* of the family ... the local *and* the wider society' (p. 273). The opening chapters of the book provide detailed descriptions of the socio-economic and demographic profile of Swansea, its labour and cultural history, religious mores and strong sense of community identity. What her informants tell her, and how we read about them, is thus filtered through a longer story about Wales (and not England) and about values, community expectations and sense of belonging.

Shifting theoretical frames

Leonard critiques and explicitly rejects anthropological functionalism, and she makes a convincing argument for attending to the specificity of time and place. This argument is allied with a broadly structuralist framework and a materialist–feminist analysis of gender and family relations, in which patriarchy is positioned as a relatively coherent (if fundamentally irrational) system of social organization that underpins repeated gendered divisions and inequalities. This represents an interesting moment in the history of feminist theory, and in the ongoing dilemma of how ethnography navigates the relationship between the local and the cultural 'whole'. The analysis stands between the functionalist traditions it repudiates and feminist theories that are grappling with structuralism and the challenges of locating particular gender struggles and inequalities in relation to wider patterns, while not succumbing to either structural determinism or individual voluntarism.

Leonard's reflective account of her approach brings to the fore certain methodological dilemmas that have been at the heart of ethnography for some time. Current calls for 'global ethnographies' or for research methods that respond to the reconfiguring relations between the local and global emphasize what is new and distinctive about the present, but can tend to gloss the history of these dilemmas in ethnographic writing. Indeed, returning to Leonard's study, more than 30 years since it was completed, we are struck by several themes and methodological challenges – although expressed in a different theoretical lexicon – that are typically associated with more recent ethnographic writing. It is important to acknowledge the history of such struggles if we are to avoid a kind of scholarly amnesia or selective remembering. We are not saying that 'there is nothing new under the sun'; but we are arguing for the value of returning to earlier studies in order to understand and learn from how obdurate tensions have been previously named and navigated.

This ethnography examined wedding and courtship rituals in Swansea in the late 1960s, seeing rituals as events of cultural repetition as well as innovation. Through detailed documentation of the everyday it exposed how rituals work and have significance for families and communities and, as Leonard convincingly argues, for broader social relations and structures. As an account of social change, Leonard's analysis of her fieldwork reveals the changing theoretical and political terrain wrought by feminism, and the re-viewing of relations between the sexes and generations that it made possible. She describes a situation that is 'ripe for change'. Our next case study continues the thematic focus on understanding gender relations, beginning from a different 'post-feminist' historical time and theoretical frame, in which some of the changes anticipated by Leonard have happened, not necessarily with desired outcomes. It is a study more concerned with subjectivity – of the researcher and research participants – and this frames the research questions and methodological and conceptual framework.

Sex–gender identities and school cultures: British Midlands in the 1990s

Sexuality, Gender and Schooling (Kehily, 2002) explores young people's (aged 11–16) negotiation of gender identity and sexuality through a focus on peer group interactions and popular and informal school cultures. Mary Jane Kehily's experiences as a former secondary school English and social education teacher prompted her to explore schools as sites for the working out of identity, sexuality and gender. Kehily also wanted to understand how the significant social and economic changes of the late 20th century impacted upon the lives of young women and men in school and asks: 'What are the implications for versions of masculinity and femininity? Is there a new, emergent sex–gender order?' (p. 5). These questions are explored from the perspective of young people themselves, who are regarded as active producers – not simply acted-upon recipients – of cultural practices and meanings. The study is also underpinned by an acknowledgement that the 'cultural specificity of the school as a local space … exists in complex interaction with wider global processes relating to migration, the economy and culture' (p. 4).

Located in two school communities in the British Midlands, the study began in the early 1990s, with a period of fieldwork in schools in 1991 and another in 1995 and 1996. Both schools were co-educational and served 'a largely working-class local community'. One school, Oakwood, was non-denominational with an ethnically-mixed school population and many students from Asian and African-Caribbean backgrounds. In contrast, Clarke School was a Church of England school with a predominantly white student population (p. 3). (At Clarke School Kehily developed a particularly close research relationship with groups of girls aged 15 to 16, and in order to gain more of a sense of boys' perspectives she 'supplemented the fieldwork with focus group discussions at an all-boys secondary school in a large city in the south-east of England' (p. 3). The location of the fieldwork in the Midlands is significant in terms of understanding the impact of global changes on local communities and for seeing how these then form part of the backdrop to the negotiation of sex-gender identity in particular school communities. As Kehily observes, the Midlands region 'has witnessed widespread de-industrialization' alongside the emergence of the competitive 'global economy'; in the postwar period, there has also been significant migration and settlement of communities from the 'New Commonwealth' countries as well as from Pakistan and Ireland (p. 4). 'At the local level the very fabric of the Midlands region seems to speak of an industrial heritage that can no longer be realized, functioning as a symbol of post-industrial alienation' (p. 4).

Even though there were different phases of fieldwork, the research was designed with an emphasized focus on the unfolding of the present and not set up, as were the studies discussed in Chapter 4, as a longitudinal study to examine change between or over the two research phases. Nevertheless, questions of change and continuity were pivotal. The locus of change was not, however, the different waves of research, but conceived as manifest in responses to wider socio-economic and cultural change, as well as in a more diffuse sense of generational change, of young people's difference from and points of affiliation with dominant social norms, including the cultural expectations of the generation embodied in their families and teachers. While Kehily observed some changes, there were also marked points of continuity. She found that: 'In many respects the sex–gender identities of young men and women in the area appear strongly traditional and deeply embedded in older forms of social and cultural practice' (p. 5).

Autobiography, feminism and cultural studies

Chapters in the book address topics on the production of heterosexuality in schools, the teaching of sex education, teenage magazines, masculinities, and the emotional and classroom work of teachers of sex education. In researching these topics, the study combined different research methods, including participant observations – of classes, of informal interactions and of talk outside of classrooms – the writing and ongoing reflection on field notes, life history interviews with teachers, group and individual or paired interviews with students, discourse analysis of interviews and texts, analysis of documents of popular culture, such as teen magazines, and memory-work practices.

Kehily introduces the study with memories of her early teaching experiences, which are deliberately and evocatively employed to show the psychic, emotional and political connections between research questions, biographical experiences and personal investments (pp. 10–32). This strategy, Kehily reflects, is 'indebted to contemporary feminist analyses which embrace auto/biographical modes of social research and stress the importance of self-reflexivity to the process of fieldwork and analysis' (p. 10).

The study's methodological and conceptual framing emerges out of a British Cultural Studies tradition associated with the work of the Birmingham Centre for Contemporary Cultural Studies [BCCCS], and while it has some affiliations to critical approaches, it is more strongly shaped by feminist and psychoanalytic theory and studies of popular and school cultures. Kehily names three methodological approaches to which her research is indebted: ethnography, feminist theory and auto/biography. The core understandings taken from this combination are 'an abiding concern with issues of reflexivity and experience that value research subjects as producers of knowledge' (p. 6). The study design and analysis exemplifies the benefits that can flow from the autobiographical turn in ethnographic (and other qualitative) research. It also illustrates some of the productive methodological insights generated in the alliances between feminism, with its attention to the 'personal', and cultural theory in its elaboration of the significance of subjectivity for understanding social processes.

Two further powerful influences on the study are the work of Valerie Walkderdine, whose research on class, gender and identity is also informed by the confluence of psychoanalysis, feminist and poststructural theory, and Michel Foucault's genealogical analyses of sexuality, biopower and the regulation of populations. Interestingly, Kehily reflects on the power of these influences in terms of their political and emotional resonance for her, and employs, for example, the language of psychoanalysis to explain her attraction to Walkerdine's work: 'I viewed

Walkerdine's body of work as politically informed writing and thinking which was generative in its analysis and innovative in its method: as such it provided me with inspiration and desire' (p. 46). Central to this appeal was Walkerdine's 'compelling mode of reflexivity, creatively employed in the interweaving of autobiographical reflections and social research' (p. 46) – a style of ethnographic writing that Kehily also effectively adopts in this book. The influence of Foucaultian ideas is evident in her analysis of 'discursive strategies' to do with sexuality and identity, and the 'ways in which discursive formations produce sexual identities within school settings', and particularly the inscription of sexualities as 'normatively heterosexual' (p. 53).

Illuminating moments

In keeping with this orientation, the study does not to aim to generate a systematic framework for classifying gender relations, nor does it advance a grand theory to explain the historical and cross-cultural persistence of certain principles of gender power and domination. Kehily seeks to illuminate moments and contexts that might, in their evocation of everyday practices, point to or capture how social and symbolic processes are given meaning and negotiated – perhaps transformed, or recontextualized or even sustained. There is a deliberate focus on the subjectivity of the participants, as complex agents, with contradictory desires and powerful emotional investments, who are working out shifting gender dynamics in their everyday social practices and interpersonal relationships.

In order to tease out these negotiations, Kehily adapts methods from literary and textual studies to identify and 'read' particular 'moments' as distillations or illuminations of wider processes. She deliberately did not attempt to 'recreate the reality-effect of field relations produced in a just-like-being-there linear narrative' and instead follows Liz Stanley's notion of '*moments* of truth and writing' (p. 7). Kehily looked for '*moments* in the transcripts that provide a commentary on the relationship between the domain of the sexual and the domain of the school', regarding them as '*discursive clusters* – instances where ideas and relations are condensed in particular ways' (p. 7). These clusters became the focus of analysis, treated as 'literary texts'; drawing on her own background in literary studies, Kehily interpreted them with 'close attention to linguistic features and devices, particular words and phrases and, occasionally, the absences too' (p. 7). Interweaving aspects of the researcher's autobiographical experiences helps situate methodological choices and subsequent modes of analysis.

Kehily's approach eschews the pursuit of ethnographic holism and associated attempts to catalogue and fix a culture in time, and explores the emergence and performance of dynamic cultural forms and identities through close analysis or 'thick description' of particular key moments and exchanges. Brown (2003) described (above) such an orientation as allowing history back into ethnography, as it works against the petrifying impulse of the ethnographic present by focusing on cultural processes of invention, repetition and interruption. A parallel argument in Kehily's study is the 'importance of the activity and agency of student cultures in the regulation and performance of gendered heterosexualities. Through exchanges in school, young men and women engage in elaborate forms of social learning whereby they learn about sex and *do* gender' (p. 206).

A formal and informal exchange

Let us turn now to an example from one of Kehily's research scenarios to see how she 'puts to work' these methodological and conceptual principles. We discuss here an example drawn from a discussion of how schools produce normative hetero-sexuality that was based upon observations of formal and informal learning in a Personal and Social Education (PSE) class. Kehily focuses on how students receive the formal curriculum of PSE and the 'social meanings that pupils ascribe to events and the ways in which these meanings contrast and overlap with sexual learning in formal spaces such as PSE lessons' (p. 65). Informal exchanges and relationships among adolescents 'form part of a sexual economy where features such as physical attractiveness, desirability and status are commodified and played out in rituals of dating and dumping ... same-sex peer groups play an important part in the medi-ation of ideas and exchanges which constitute these processes' (p. 66).

Kehily describes in detail the exchange among a group of year 10 girls, as they respond to a quiz sheet on different forms of contraception; she is sitting at the same table as the girls, able to listen and observe the different levels and types of communication. The formal classroom work of responding to the quiz is done in a 'haphazard fashion' while the more compelling topic of 'Naomi's' relationship with 'Nathan' occupies centre-stage; immediately prior to the quiz, Nathan had been asking Naomi a series of questions, verbally and via notes, about 'going out'. The informal discussion among her same-sex peers turns on how Naomi is treat-ing Nathan and advice on what she should do. Kehily describes and unpacks the meaning of the two different agendas operating in the classroom – the contracep-tive quiz and the dialogue between and about Nathan and Naomi (p. 67). We see here how the inclusive and exploratory gaze of ethnographic methods enables both incidents, and the interaction between them, to be apprehended. This capacity to capture coexistence is a distinctive feature of participant observation.

> The exchange illustrates the ways in which two contrasting approaches to the power–knowledge couplet are being deployed and negotiated within the same educative space. The official classroom task sees sex education in terms of tech-nical knowledge, details of biology and sexual health to be learned and accumu-lated, while pupil interactions stress the importance of the experiential and the instrumental role of the peer group in key aspects of learning. The 'dialogue' between Naomi and Nathan indicates that, for them, negotiating the sexual is strongly gendered. Asking to go out with someone and agreeing to go out with someone entails engagement with normative sex–gender categories that in turn involve identity work and imperatives to act. ... In this exchange Nathan appears to be enacting boy-who-wants-girl while Naomi's responses involve her in a per-formance of the opposite, girl-being-chased-by-boy. ... There is a strong sense of

Naomi and Nathan's 'business' being public property. This sense of collective ownership and negotiation in relation to male–female relationships contrasts with the construction of sex in PSE classes as 'private', involving two people in matters of personal choice, intimate relations and medical knowledge. The activities of the peer group indicate that sexual relations offer a sphere for the negotiation and regulation of gender appropriate behaviour in school. (p. 67)

This analysis of a peer group exchange during a seemingly uneventful and regular class captures the subtle ways that gendered interactions are actively worked out by young people in the context of (but not rigidly determined by) influential social and personal gender norms. Throughout (and in an implicit argument against social reproduction theories), Kehily locates students 'as active subjects who produce sex–gender identities through specific discursive strategies ... pupil agency in the domain of the sexual operates as a counter-point to discourses of sexuality in the official curriculum and classroom practice' (p. 202). Methodologically, this reading shows the value of close attention to the everyday and ordinary perspectives of participants while remaining in reflective dialogue with wider socio-cultural frames and theoretical and political discussions.

Questions of change and continuity in relation to sex–gender identities are prominent themes, and in her conclusion Kehily remarks that her study provides 'many points of continuity with earlier ethnographic studies that have focussed on sexuality, gender and schooling' (p. 206). These include the 'pervasive presence of homophobia' and the 'naturalisation of heterosexuality' within school sites (p. 206). While public representations may suggest that there have been significant changes in these arenas, the young people in her study 'remain preoccupied with the less radical and often more reactionary aspects of sexuality and gender and utilize them to style their own forms of social learning that can be both agentic and regulatory' (p. 206). Kehily argues that the key to this disjunction lies in student peer group cultures in which 'issues of gender and sexuality take on a logic and momentum that makes sense to the young people involved' (p. 207). These cultures are sites away from the regulation of schools and families and allow space for young people to express 'autonomy and agency'. Further, the collective negotiations and social learning of the group stand in contrast to the 'individualising culture of contemporary education practice' (p. 207).

Conclusion

In this chapter we have examined recent theoretical and methodological debates within ethnography, in particular the autobiographical and reflexive turns, and questions about representation and writing. We have also shown, via two case studies, how different theoretical positions inform and shape the meanings made from ethnographic observations and, in turn, how different theoretical traditions offer ways of historically locating ethnographic research. The kind of ethnography undertaken, the type of questions posed and interpretive frameworks adopted shed light on the substantive topic as well as on the history of ethnographic methods and on social and cultural theory and – in our two case studies – on trajectories and tensions in recent feminist theory.

What makes ethnography an attractive approach for many researchers is its potential to yield compelling accounts of cultural life. Through close and detailed observations derived from in-depth and extended immersion in the field, the researcher, traditionally working as a participant observer, can generate powerful insights into how cultures or communities 'work' and how 'social actors' make and derive meaning from their practices. The researcher occupies the same time and place as the informant and, as with longitudinal studies, biographical and research time coincide. In the case of some ethnographies, as with our first case study, the passage of time becomes a feature of the interpretation and writing of the study in a way that was not intended at the outset. A feature of all ethnographies, however, is a complicated relation to researching in the present time, when the researcher is in the awkward position of trying to write about a present or a setting that no longer exists, or is in the process of inexorably changing. The notion of the ethnographic present is equally paradoxical in that the present is dynamic and cultures elude fixing, despite representational claims to do otherwise.

Questions concerning place and locale are central to ethnographic practice: Where is the study located? Is it strange or familiar? How will it be explicated? What is the 'boundedness' of the field site? Yet we have argued that questions of temporality are equally important, if not always brought to the fore. This encompasses the experience of long-term immersion in the field, the passing of time from research to writing, returning to field sites as well as the relationship between present, past and memory as it is played out and apprehended in the research site – by participants and by the researcher. In describing her study, Diana Leonard argued that change is endemic to rituals. An ethnographic approach illuminates the meanings a ritual has but, depending on the timeframe, we might not always see how it has changed or whether it is undergoing change. We might only know that retrospectively. Follow-up and revisiting studies – discussed in Chapter 7 – are showing how returning to ethnographic studies offers exciting possibilities for researching social and generational change, providing an expanded sense of how researching in the present tense can also allow for comparison in the long view.

Summary points

- Ethnography aims to document and understand events and interactions as they are happening from the perspective of participants. In the detail of cultural life, it aims to see the meaning of the cultural whole.

- Its origins are in anthropology but its methods and orientations are now taken up across a range of disciplines that seek in-depth understanding of cultural phenomena.

- Ethnographic methods developed in the context of colonialism and the desire to capture disappearing cultures and in the move from library to field-based research.

- The conventional method of enquiry is participant observation in which the ethnographer immerses themself in the field for an extended period of time. The duration of fieldwork assists the ethnographer to distinguish between routine and exceptional practices and beliefs.

- *Ethnography*, derived from the Greek, means 'writing culture', and the form and quality of the ethnographer's writing, in field notes and published accounts, is an essential part of the ethnographic endeavour.

- Ethnographic methods are suited to researching interactions and rituals in the present, and for observing change as it happens. These processes are always located in particular times, places and histories, and the documentation of the present happens in the flow of time.

- The 'ethnographic present' is both grammatical and epistemological, invoking immediacy but also a false sense of cultural holism and timelessness.

- The 'ethnographic present' also belies the manner in which ethnographic insight is linked to history and memory and to how people make sense of the past in the present, and vice versa.

- A concern with representation and reflexivity reflects the partial and situated nature of ethnographic research, and the researcher's paradoxical role as participant observer.

- Because of the detail afforded by its methods, ethnographic accounts become valuable histories of social life, enabling comparison across generations and time, and insight into what has changed or remained familiar.

Further resources

Geertz, C. (1973) *The Interpretation of Cultures; Selected Essays.* New York: Basic Books.
This is an influential collection of essays that critiqued the orthodoxy of functionalist anthropology and outlined a semiotic analysis of culture and the method of thick description.

Clifford, J. and Marcus, G. (eds) (1986) *Writing Culture: The Poetics and Politics of Ethnography.* Berkeley: University of California Press.
This has become a 'classic' in the field, capturing the discursive and postmodern turn and its impact on ethnographic approaches across a range of studies and disciplines.

Skeggs, B. (1997) *Formations of Gender and Class: Becoming Respectable.* London: Sage.
This is an ethnographic study of working-class women in the north of England and their negotiations of class and gender, interpreted through feminist and cultural reproduction theories.

Atkinson, P., Coffey, A., Delamont, S., Lofland, J. and Lofland, L. (eds) (2002) *Handbook of Ethnography*. Thousand Oaks, CA: Sage.
This is a major and useful collection of essays that combines examples of ethnographic studies in different settings as well as from different theoretical frameworks.

Back, L. (2007) *The Art of Listening*. Oxford: Berg.
Written by an anthropologist, it reviews a range of methodologies, including visual methods, and presents a strong case for paying close attention to the ethical connection at the heart of ethnography.

Davies, C.A. (2008) *Reflexive Ethnography: A Guide to Researching Selves and Others* (2nd edn). London: Routledge.
Combines analysis of the impact of reflexivity on ethnography methodology with examples of research practices and insights from a range of different methods, e.g. interviewing, visual, online research, life history, surveys.

PART 3
Inheriting

6

Generation

There was something else about Umfraville that struck me, a characteristic I had noticed in other people his age. He seemed still young, a person like oneself; and yet at the same time his appearance and manner proclaimed that he had time to live at least a few years of his grown-up life before the outbreak of war in 1914. Once I had thought of those who had known the epoch of my own childhood as 'older people'. Then I found there existed people like Umfraville who seemed somehow to span the gap. They partook of both eras, specially forming the tone of the post war years; much more so indeed than the younger people. Most of them, like Umfraville, were melancholy; perhaps from the strain of living simultaneously in two different historical periods. That was his category certainly. (Anthony Powell, 2000: 665)

Dear Mother, when my child is born, you may perhaps forgive me and we will be close again. Or is this wishful thinking? Between you and I, I am scared. Your labour pains have got mixed up with mine. (Edna O'Brien, 2006: 134)

These two fragments, the first taken from Anthony Powell's epic account of the lives of a social circle over the backdrop of the 20th century, the second from Edna O'Brien's meditations on the mother/daughter relationship, provide a taste of how we experience generation in everyday life. Powell's comments are about a common generational location, which can provide the potential of identification between members of an age cohort, but also for distinctions be drawn between their own experiences and those of others. Generational affiliations are as much a case of culture and class as they are of age. Individuals may identify with the values, tastes and cultural products of those older than them, the same age, or younger. Generation is both an objective fact and a cultural expression of the way in which influence and power are mediated over time. O'Brien's comments concern generation as expressed in kinship relations. Here we grasp the inevitability of inheritance, both conscious and unconscious, and glimpse the dynamism of such relations where the arrival of a new generation forces a reconfiguration of identifications – themes that have been productive in feminist explorations of the negotiation of desire, expectations and achievement between women of different ages (Lawler, 2000; Reay, 2005; Steedman, 1986).

In Chapter 4 we explored the way in which qualitative longitudinal methods can enable us to follow a cohort of individuals who share a generational location over time – capturing the ways in which peers experience the same historical events from distinct social positions. In this chapter we will look at generations as both cohort and as kin (Pilcher, 1995). We begin by employing generation as an analytic lens for understanding processes of social change. We then explore generation methodologically, focusing on cross-generational research as a way of looking more closely at the forms of relationship, communication and transmission that exist *between* generations. Our aim in doing so is to develop an awareness of the interplay between the two dimensions of generation, tying us horizontally to our contemporaries and vertically into 'continuous' intergenerational chains of belonging (Hagestad, 1985).

Conceptualizing generation

In periods of significant change (economic, technological and political) it is likely that questions of generation will come to the fore. One commentator goes so far as to suggest that 'The conflict between classes has been increasingly replaced by the turnover of generations as the prime mover of history. This temporalization of social structure is reflected by a new public sensitivity for generational differences' (Geisen, 2004: 37). Drawing on the work of Maurice Halbwachs, Geisen argues that generations are structured by different temporal horizons and 'the unity of a generation and of its collective memory is constructed by a fundamental common experience that devalues the experience of a previous generation' (Geisen, 2004: 33). Certainly, many contemporary accounts of generation emphasize their relative economic marginalization in relation to the Baby Boomers who came before and continue to dominate in terms of economic, social and cultural influence. The precise character of generational tension varies according to country and culture and will frequently characterize a particular socio-economic group. For example, Australian Ryan Heath, who was born in 1980, describes the iGeneration of which he is part as 'income-rich and asset poor, immersed in a culture of debt' (Heath, 2006: xvi). In less affluent economies generational divisions are also evident, but may be shaped by distinct forces such as the politics and economics of post-colonialism (Harootunian, 2007).

The articulation of generational tensions may also vary, depending on the arena within which it is played out. Martin Kohli explains that 'The conditions for continuity or conflict between generations – and this for social reproduction or change – vary according to the field on which the generational process occurs; demarcation and conflict between generations can shift from one field to another. Conflicts in one field can be offset by transfers in another field, but conflicts can intensify each other'

(1996: 18). In a similar vein, the sociologist Pierre Bourdieu points to the importance of education in the process through which the idea of a 'generation' becomes meaningful; 'in many cases, conflicts that are experienced as conflicts of generations are in fact acted out through persons or age-groups based on different relations to the educational system ... the mere fact that they have encountered different states of the educational system means that they will always get less out of their qualifications than the previous generation would have got' (Bourdieu, 1993: 100–1). Within Bourdieu's conceptual schema, the habitus that we occupy is generationally specific, yet tied to intergenerational processes through which cultural and material assets are transferred and secured.

The sociology of generations

Karl Mannheim's essay on generations is generally seen as 'the classic sociological account', the potential of which has not yet been exhausted (Kohli, 1996). The essay on generations was published in English translation in 1952, at which point Mannheim was living in London, having escaped from Berlin before the outbreak of the Second World War. The essay was an attempt to make sense of the generational politics that gave rise to the fall of the Austro-Hungarian empire, making possible the Nazi Party sweep to power in 1933. Mannheim begins his essay by posing the problem of generations in terms of finding a way between positivist approaches that simply seek to document generations in descriptive terms (employing a linear and external conception of time) and the Romantic approaches that employed a subjective understanding of time, experienced qualitatively, seeking to capture the *zeitgeist* of a particular generation – a German iteration of the distinction between objective *temps* and subjective *durée* coined by Bergson. Mannheim's aim was to harness the best of both traditions: acknowledging the subjective experience of the generation but also imposing an empirical discipline on the process of how particular generational voices are formed, expressed and gain ascendancy. He was critical of the overly generalizing approach of the Romantics, who through the concepts of *zeitgeist* and *gestalt* attributed agency and purpose to history itself. For Mannheim, things were more complicated. Developing a musical metaphor, he suggested that the *zeitgeist* of a period is not a single sound, but instead can be understood as a combination of sounds, 'an accidental chord' (1952: 284). This chord is comprised of the distinct notes that express the *units* that exist within a generation. As with melody, the combination of these notes is subtly changing over time.

Drawing on the positivist tradition, Mannheim begins with the idea of a generation as simply and descriptively constituted 'by a similarity of location of a number of individuals within a social whole' (1952: 290). As such, the transition from generation to generation is a continuous process (p. 293), with the emergence of new participants and the continuous withdrawal of previous participants (p. 294). Mannheim devotes some attention to the social and familial mechanisms through which a continuity of culture is secured in the context of such basic flux and renewal. As a sociologist of knowledge, Mannheim is concerned with how continuity of culture is achieved, and he distinguished between conscious mechanisms through which past experience is captured and transmitted in 'models' and the less conscious processes through which knowledge is transmitted in a form that is 'condensed', merely 'implicit', or 'virtual' patterns' (p. 296). Members of any one generation can only participate in a temporally limited selection of historical flow. And depending on the speed and intensity of historical change, the form in which transmission takes place may have to change. Periods of slow social change may be characterized by a kind of 'piety', where young people look to their elders, possibly adopting their dress and values. During periods of fast social change the old will be more receptive to the young, sometimes even more so that the intermediate generation between them who may experience themselves as being more 'stuck'.

For Mannheim, generations are in a state of constant *interaction*, focused on the negotiation of the present. In order to achieve what Mannheim calls an 'uninterrupted generation series', the kinds of communications that take place between generations are not simply one way, from older to younger. Mannheim points to the 'necessity for constant transmission of cultural change' (p. 299), observing that:

> The 'up-to-dateness' of youth … consists of their being closer to the present problems … and in the fact that they are dramatically aware of a process of de-stabilization and take sides on it. All this while the older generation cling to the re-orientation that had been the drama of their youth … not only does the teacher educate his pupil, but his pupils educate the teacher too. (p. 301)

Mannheim gives particular weight to the influence of the formative years of childhood and youth for establishing common generational identities. Yet he is also keen to observe the 'stratification of experience' that exists within a generation. Although members of an historical cohort may experience the same events, these experiences will not impinge on them in the same way, and it is here that Mannheim's theory makes space for diversity and agency on the part of individuals and groups.

> Youth experiencing the same concrete historical problems may be said to be part of the same actual generation. While those groups within the same actual generation, which work up the same materials of their common experiences in different specific ways, constitute separate generation units. (p. 304)

Generation units can be identified qualitatively, using the language of the romantic tradition, by their common *gestalt* or 'affinity of responses' (p. 306). To qualify, in Mannheim's terms, as a generation in itself (in actuality), a cohort must participate in 'a common destiny' (p. 303) and the *gestalt* of a generation unit must find 'satisfying expression in the prevailing historical configuration' (p. 307). There is nothing inevitable about the formation of a generation as actuality. Mannheim observes that where the tempo of change is too fast or too slow, generations may become inert, simply orienting towards those who come before or after. Rather, generational expression is the outcome of a complex and contingent relationship between timing, conditions and resources. In Mannheim's words: 'The generation location always exists as a potentiality seeking realization – the medium of such realization, however, is not a unitary Zeitgeist but rather one or the other of the concrete trends prevailing at a given time' (p. 319).

An example of how Mannheim's approach has been taken up in recent years is provided by a study of the 1960s generation conducted by June Edmunds and Bryan Turner, who draw on his idea of 'generational units' in order to identify the way in which a particular political and cultural avant garde came to dominate an era. Edmunds and Turner (2002) combine Mannheim's understanding of how a generation becomes actualized, or 'active', with Bourdieu's understanding of how particular social groups succeed in turning their social, cultural and economic resources into symbolic capital, i.e. having authority beyond the social location in which it originated. Their account focuses on the particular conditions that made this possible: the shared distress of the Second World War and Vietnam, mentors, sacred places, and a coincidence with demographic change (the Baby Boom). Thus it is that the 'habitus' of this 'strategic generation' continues to be recognized and accommodated by subsequent 'passive' generations – who, for example, may still be listening to the Beatles. Edmunds and Turner (2002) suggest that the 'cultural lag' that is evident in the continuing domination of the culture of the Baby Boomers is a reflection of their strategic power vis-à-vis other cohorts, pointing to an oscillation between active and passive generations over time. Consonant with Mannheim's appreciation of the heterogeneity of those with a common generational location, and the equivocal character of its expression, they point to the slow yet dynamic process through which historical potentialities are played out in conversations between generations over long periods of time.

Mannheim's approach to understanding intergenerational processes was influenced by psychoanalysis, both in terms of the importance he attributes to the formation of a common generational disposition in childhood and youth and in terms of the less than conscious processes that play out between generations (Kohli, 1996). The psychic and cultural expression of intergenerational dynamics also lies at the centre of work that arose from the Birmingham CCCS, in particular the ideas associated with the book *Resistance through Rituals* (Hall and Jefferson, 1976). In this volume, Phil Cohen suggests that a particular youth subculture can be understood as a 'magical solution' that seeks to converse with (or symbolically resolve) contradictions within the parent culture. Cohen's research was with working-class young people growing up in the 'regenerated' communities of the 1970s' East End of London. Urban planning effectively ruptured the continuity of face-to-face culture and transmission of traditional working-class traditions. He argues that in the formation of skinhead youth subcultures young people sought both to mourn the loss of community and to recreate it symbolically through styles of dress, attitude and behaviour. In their introduction to the volume, John Clarke and Stuart Hall propose a way of thinking about culture as a historical formation in which there is a coexistence of cultural forms, what they term a 'double articulation' in which the past and the present coexist in dynamic and expressive conversation. Drawing on the work of Gramsci rather than Mannheim, Clarke and Hall suggest that the character of intergenerational processes and generational consciousness differs according to social class, with the middle classes giving rise to countercultures and the working classes giving rise to subcultures, reflecting their marginalization. Jon Savage provides a vivid example of this psychologically inflected approach to understanding the situated complicities that are involved in cultural expression when he reflects on his own teenage investments in the light of the experience of his parents:

> Each generation has its own task. To try to abrogate another generation's experience is pointless, and potentially dangerous. Having experienced the storms and stresses of a 1960s and 1970s teenage, I came to realize that part of my cohort's task was to help deal with our parents' war damage. The unresolved horror of that period, as well as the huge existential question posed by the fact of the H-bomb, informed the extreme manifestations of youth culture within which I thoroughly immersed myself. (Savage, 2008: xvii)

These examples of the sociology of generations are all concerned with capturing and understanding how social changes and continuities are secured by collectivities, and the resulting form of their cultural and political expression. Their analytic focus is on the horizontal (or synchronic) connections that individuals make with others on the basis of age in the process of building and articulating a generational voice. The examples explored here include the peer group (Cohen) and a cultural and political elite (Edmunds and Turner). But as the quote from Jon Savage suggests, it is also possible to explore generations vertically (diachronically), as chains of individuals and meaning that cut through historical time. One of the fields in which this approach is most developed is that of the sociology of the family and the life history tradition.

The life history tradition

One of our tasks in writing this book has been to collect together examples of research and conceptual development which may or may not be in conversation with each other. Although we have constructed the parts of the book according to different temporal registers, it is evident that there are many links between the sections, not least through the work of scholars who have taken several different methodological approaches to understanding the operations of continuity and change over and through time. In Chapter 3 we encountered the work of British oral historian Paul Thompson whose reflections on the role of memory in oral history (Thompson, 1988) have been influential and generative (see Popular Memory Group, 1982). Through collaborations with several colleagues, most notably French sociologist Daniel Bertaux, Thompson has been involved in the production of a number of edited collections that bring together examples of empirical work and progressively build a conceptual framework for the understanding of intergenerational processes operating within families (Bertaux and Thompson, 1993/2005, 1997/2003; Samuel and Thompson, 1990). Bertaux and Thompson draw on their collaborative Anglo/French research on families as well as studies of intergenerational processes conducted with colleagues in France, Russia and the UK. In a series of introductions and methodological essays, Bertaux, Thompson and Isabelle Bertaux-Wiame map out a conceptual agenda for intergenerational studies that we summarize here.

The authors draw on a range of theoretical sources to build their framework. Thompson cites the particular influence on his work of psychotherapeutic perspectives in the form of the family systems approach of John Byng-Hall (1995). This clinical framework conceptualizes the family in terms of a continuous contractual relationship across time, where unresolved emotional dynamics can be transmitted through the 'symbolic coinage' of family stories, within which motifs, patterns and difficulties are repeated and the 'very phrases echo down the generations' (Thompson, 1993/2005: 30). Bertaux draws more heavily on the work of Pierre Bourdieu and the concept of the 'habitus' that captures the 'condensation of experiences' that takes place within families over generations. Influenced by Bourdieu's observations that the transformation of capital includes the preparation or production of the receiver (1997/2003: 19), Bertaux and Thompson emphasize the dynamism and 'openness' of transmission, where an 'offer only becomes a transmission when it is received' and the 'form of what is passed down can be transformed in the transmission' (Bertaux-Wiame, 1993/2005: 47). Individuals may choose both to accept and reject their transgenerational inheritance (Thompson, 1993/2005: 15), and families may be more or less successful in 'calling back' children into family traditions (Bertaux-Wiame, 1993/2005).

What most distinguishes this approach is its capacity to capture the simultaneous and symbiotic operations of social reproduction and innovation, which connect the intimate operations of family life to the social and economic landscape within which they are situated. Continuity and change do not exist simply in opposition. Rather they show that in order to maintain some continuity over generations, innovation is always necessary – in intergenerational terms, you have to run in order to stay still. In conceiving of families as open-ended systems involved in the circulation of economic, social and psychological 'gifts', they draw attention to the way in which families are a central medium through which time is experienced and, to some extent, mortality is transcended. Referring to the work of Pierre Legrende they observe:

> His final conclusion 'that the object of transmission, is to transmit' may seem at first glance merely tautological, but it is indeed important that for most transmissions between generations the significance of the particular content is, for the participants, much less than the fact that transmission to children in itself constitutes a relationship transcending the limitations of human mortality. (Bertaux and Thompson, 1993/2005: 7)

Bertaux and Thompson share a methodological commitment to using life stories as the raw material of social history. These life stories may also operate as personal self-analyses and examples of oral literature (Thompson, 1993/2005: 36), yet their interest is not so much with the form of these narratives or the terms of their cultural production. Instead they adopt a realist approach committed to reading *through* these accounts to the social history beneath. Bertaux and Bertaux-Wiame demonstrate this approach in their defence of the interpretative value of case histories that are the result of their research. They describe a single case history of a French farming family over five generations, mapping life stories against the transformation of the agricultural economy during this period. In describing what happened against the range of 'possible destinies' that open up at different points in time, they point to the complex condensation of experience that takes place within families and how 'unachieved possibilities are an effective part of reality' (1997/2003: 82). The case history provides insight into what they call the 'dialectics of external/internal' and of 'objective/subjective' (p. 82). Taking the whole family as the unit of analysis, it is possible to see the interdependency of destinies, as the options for one sibling close down (for example, when they are 'caught' as an heir) while the options of others open up. Where social science traditionally forms generalizations through the process of abstraction, they argue that it is largely through the complex interaction between psychological and social factors, over time, that destinies are shaped. In preserving detail, the case history approach makes different things visible in analysis – in the case of social mobility, that 'resources not constraints may determine behaviour more' (p. 87). Bertaux and Bertaux-Wiame suggest a generative understanding of social change in which agency, timing and the ghosts of possible destinies are all very much in play:

> The idea … that a life trajectory may be determined – or rather, conditioned – much more easily by the supply of resource than by the imposition of a constraint lends an entirely new context to the concept of determination: one that includes both the socio-structural dimension and praxis. (Bertaux and Bertaux-Wiame, 1997/2003: 95)

These ghostly lives, destinies that could have been but do not come to pass, are not simply the subject of the life historian but form part of the way individuals narrate their own lives. The Italian oral historian Alessandro Portelli borrows the term 'uchronia' from literary studies to characterize the telling of hypothetical events that he discovered in the life histories of Italian Communist Party members – things that *could* have happened. He suggests that the telling of such stories reveals the individual's understanding of the relationship between the contingency of their choices and the wider forces that shape their lives. In Portelli's words, uchronia 'saves the precious awareness of the injustice of the existing world, but supplies the means of resignation and reconciliation. While it fans the flames of discontent by uncovering the contradiction of reality and desire, it helps keep this contradiction from breaking out as an open conflict' (1990: 157). This kind of work on life histories suggests the potential for working with narratives in order to capture the complex psychodynamic processes that mediate meaning and concrete outcomes over time.

Working and caring over the 20th century

One study that has been influenced by the life history tradition and the work of Mannheim is an investigation of work and caring in four-generation families conducted by Julia Brannen, Peter Moss and Ann Mooney. In this project Brannen and colleagues identified 12 'bean pole families' in which four generations were living. Up to eight individuals were interviewed in each family. With one exception, the family members only include those in relationships with the persons they had children with. Families were accessed through the middle 'grandparents' generation', and were selected on the basis of a purposive sample to represent a range of working situations in this generation. An explicit aim of this study was to explore the interplay of biography and history in the tradition of C. Wright Mills, drawing together both realist and interpretivist traditions. As with most qualitative research, this study relies on depth rather than breadth in its contribution to knowledge. As with the qualitative longitudinal research discussed in Chapter 4, the study is both small (12 case studies) and large (71 interviews), with a strategic choice of cases providing 'a strong foundation on which both to generate and examine theoretical questions' (Brannen et al., 2004: 5).

A generational design

The researchers define their generations historically, drawing on overviews of 20th-century British history that categorize generations in relation to political events (Hobsbawm, 1994) and phases in the evolution of welfare provision and discourse (Rose, 1999). Thus we are presented with three adult generations, identified in terms of their respective positions vis-à-vis each other from the perspective of the middle 'access' generation:

- The great grandparents, born between 1911 and 1921, living through what Eric Hobsbawm calls the 'age of catastrophe', including two world wars and the Depression – a time both of disruption and the 'emergent social state' (Rose, 1999).
- The grandparents, born between 1940 and 1948, a postwar generation living through a 'golden age of growth and transformation' (Hobsbawm, 1994) and enjoying the 'full flowering of the social state' (Rose, 1999).
- The parents, born between 1965 and 1975, living through the 'decomposition and crisis' brought about by the policies and Thatcherism and witnessing the impact of economic and political liberalism (Hobsbawm, 1994).

The primary research technique employed in the study was the interview. In pursuit of a way to explore the interconnections between historical time and biographical time, the research team adapted the Biographic–Interpretive Narrative Interviewing and Analysis approach (Wengraf, 2001) that provides techniques for distinguishing and relating the 'told story' (biography) from the 'lived life' (the chronology and historical context) (see Chapter 3 for further discussion). The interview style employed by the research team was tailored to this method (although it did not include repeat interviews as encouraged by proponents). The interview took place in three sections: an initial invitation to provide an uninterrupted life story prompted by themes of work and care; a subsequent invitation from the researcher to elaborate on issues introduced in this initial narrative (approached in the order that they were revealed); and a third semi-structured section involving questions and vignettes. The interviews took around three hours. The idea of the first uninterrupted narrative was that it would provide a sense of the *gestalt* of the individual's life, and that in following the order of this narrative in the second part of the interview schedule, the structure of this *gestalt* would be preserved and elaborated.

A layered approach to analysis

Methods of analysis also sought to distinguish biographical and historical 'facts' from subjective experience and interpretation, involving the abstraction of historical timetables and individual life histories for each individual. The researchers describe three distinct stages or levels in their approach to analysis.

- The first stage involved the analysis of individuals. This entailed writing field notes after interviews as well as extended summaries and preliminary analyses of individual cases once full transcriptions of the interviews were available. These preliminary analyses would relate key research questions to aspects of the text.
- The second stage involved the analysis of whole families, focusing in particular on tracing continuities and changes across generations.
- The third level of analysis involved looking across the 12 families and comparing themes. This would involve reading across generations as well as developing typologies of patterns of family dynamics. This level of analysis formed the basis for the chapters of the book that resulted from the study.

The authors explain that it is not possible to simply read history from this kind of data, produced as it is in the here and now. As with any life history account, narratives are produced in the present:

> The method generates retrospective accounts of decisions, actions and events, often in distant parts of life courses, and in the contexts of particular situations, relationships and moral judgements pertaining to those times. Not only may recall falter, but the evaluations of those decisions and events are made with reference to present time frames, even though informants seek to recall the past and how they thought and felt then. It is, in practice, impossible for a raconteur to stand outside the present when considering the past. (Brannen et al., 2004: 84)

Having lived through periods of significant social change, members of the older generations in particular were aware of more than one possible evaluative framework for questions as to the best way to parent, to balance work and care as pursued by the researchers. Rather than identify different generations with different sets of values, Brannen and colleagues draw on a conceptual framework that emphasizes the extent to which families must *negotiate* family responsibilities (Finch and Mason, 1993). The way in which they do this is always rooted in concrete circumstances, and will vary according to time and place. As such, intergenerational family relationships tend not to be characterized by judgement, but rather by *ambivalence*:

> Tensions between these beliefs, judgments and actions … involve carefully differentiated positions, each negotiated in relation to a particular time, place and reference group. Older generations of women might still espouse certain beliefs or standards that were normative when they themselves were mothers of young children (most commonly, that mothers should not work); but these do not have to cloud their contemporary evaluations of how their own daughters and grandchildren should live their lives in the present context or their current decisions about what support to offer them. (Brannen et al., 2004: 82)

Fatherhood as a dynamic inheritance

We only have space here to discuss one example of the kind of insights and analysis that this study gave rise to, though we would encourage readers to follow up the publications from the study.

In their analysis of fatherhood, Brannen and colleagues show how the different elements of their approach come together, enabling them to comment on how fatherhood has changed over generations as well as to comment on processes of intergenerational 'transmission'. They begin by exploring the timetabling of fatherhood in different generations, drawing primarily on their analysis of 'the life as lived'. Although there is an overall linear trend towards later parenthood and smaller families, Brannen and colleagues suggest that their data set suggests a picture of uneven change. The transitions to adulthood of the great-grandparents' generation were disrupted by war and economic displacement. For the men this often meant a delay in becoming economically independent and relatively late parenthood. In contrast, the next generation (growing up in the postwar years) tended to have rapid and intense transitions, with very few years coming between entry into work, marriage and parenthood. The younger generation of parents reached adulthood during a period of economic insecurity. Unlike the previous generations, the men of the 'parent' generation mostly cohabited with partners before marriage and/or parenthood. Securing housing in advance of parenthood was also a priority for this generation, reflecting important shifts in the economy brought about by economic restructuring. Consequently, this generation of men tended to become fathers later than earlier generations within their family, and experienced significantly different circumstances than their own fathers in particular.

The next layer of the analysis focuses more on the way in which the different generations of men *talk* about fatherhood, in particular the different discourses that they draw on. The researchers take as their starting point longitudinal/attitudinal data that suggest a trend towards increasingly egalitarian attitudes towards the gendered division of labour. Although they find distinct generational discourses about what constitutes a 'good father' emerging when individuals talk about their own experiences of parenting, positions are more ambivalent when talking about other generations, with individuals recognizing the significance of changes that have taken place. Men do not stop being fathers when their children become adults, and the way that the older men talk suggests that they may be engaging with different values in their grandparenting and their parenting of adult children than suggested by their accounts of parenting in the past. There is a complex relationship between the way in which individuals talk and the historical landscape against which such talk must be contextualized. For example, individuals may not mention what are important 'facts' (for example, the 'hands-on' father who presents his version of parenting in terms of a journey of personal discovery, not mentioning that it is made possible by extensive state support), highlighting the need for the researcher to have a good knowledge of the relevant historical and policy context for each generation. And those accounts that individuals do produce may themselves reflect the historical formation that they are part of – for example, the tendency for the father's generation to present the division of labour within the family as a result of the woman's 'choice'.

In comparing the families, the researchers develop typologies of fatherhood which they map against relevant axes.

Main/sole breadwinner

Strong fatherhood involvement	Weak fatherhood involvement
B–*Family men and child-oriented fathers* Two great-grandfathers Four grandfathers Three fathers	A–*Work-focused fathers (career men and provider fathers)* Two great-grandfathers Six grandfathers Four fathers
C–*Hands-on fathers* Four fathers	D–*Non-employed fathers with a weak investment in fatherhood* No cases

Not main/sole breadwinner

(Brannen et al., 2004: 128)

In categories A and B it is possible to see continuity over time, with men of three generations repeating a pattern of acting as a main breadwinner and, to differing extents, being involved with their children. Other categories suggest emergent practices of fathering, for example category C, which at least in this study was only evident in the newest generation and depended on a particular pattern of welfare provision and/or female employment. The researchers suggest that the reason that the study had no examples of category D is not so much that these kinds of fathers do not exist in the current generation but that they were excluded by their sampling strategy.

The intergenerational case studies make it possible to see the interplay of the historical and the biographical dimensions described above, revealing *how* change and continuity take place within real families. In one extended case study the researchers discuss the three generations of the working-class Prentice family, and the emergence in the most recent generation of a new kind of hands-on full-time fathering where child-care is shared, concluding:

> There are strong similarities in the occupational status and life chances of all three generations of Prentice men. At the same time important structural shifts have taken place, in particular the decline in low skill employment, which had weakened the work ethic of the current generation of fathers. Normative and structural changes in family life had also weakened fatherhood as an institution based on family breadwinning. In this context, Andrew [the youngest father] used the decline in traditional resources available to men of his social class as an opportunity to take advantage of new cultural resources which give legitimacy to men being actively and equally involved with their children. For Andrew has made fatherhood in the first years of his children's life a meaningful and rewarding occupation in the absence of paid employment. Moreover, in the future, he and his wife intended to share breadwinning. (Brannen et al., 2004: 145)

This brief discussion of the 'working and caring' project suggests the value of this kind of intergenerational research design for gaining an understanding of how a changing social landscape is mediated subjectively by a family. Brannen (2005) is careful to point out that this kind of methodology provides a mediated perspective on the past and on processes of change and continuity. It is important that researchers are aware of the silences in the accounts of respondents and, in particular, how they take resources for granted (see Chapter 3 for further discussion of challenges of using personal narratives as historical sources). She also alerts us to a sensitivity towards shifting discourses on the agentic self and the historical specificity of ideas of 'duty' and 'care'. Respondents themselves are likely to move between discursive frameworks, depending on whether they are describing their own experiences in the past or commenting on the experiences of choices of others in the present. It is not possible to simply trace changes in 'care' over time when the meaning of 'care' itself is dependent on historical context (Brannen and Nilsen, 2006).

Three generations of Norwegian girls

The second example of intergenerational research comes from Norway and the work of Harriet Bjerrum Nielsen and Monica Rudberg (1994, 2000; Bjerrum

Nielsen, 2003). In this project 22 intergenerational chains of women were interviewed in 1990–1 about their lives as children and young girls. Fourteen of these
chains included three generations (grandmothers, mothers and daughters), the
other eight consisting of the two youngest generations.

- The oldest generation (born between 1910 and 1927) went through their adolescence during the decade 1925–35.
- The mothers' generation (mostly born between 1940 and 1948) went through
  adolescence in the decade 1955–65.
- The daughters, born in 1971/2, experienced adolescence between 1985–95, the
  period during which fieldwork was taking place.

The chains were accessed through the daughters' generation, with volunteers sought
from two high schools in Oslo – one 'with a very good academic reputation' where
'students come from mainly middle-class families where parents have higher education' (Bjerrum Nielsen, 2003: 25), and another 'more ordinary suburban school with
students from lower-middle-class, working class, and small self-employed families'
(2003: 25). The study also involved ethnographic research in these two school settings,
and the female generational chains form part of a wider sample of life history interviews collected as part of a study.

Interrogating theories of social change

Although the research of Bjerrum Nielsen and Rudberg has different conceptual
roots to that undertaken by Brannen and colleagues, their investigation is also theoretically generative and provides a test of existing theory. The study was designed
as an explicit means of engaging empirically with the influential late modern theories of Ulrich Beck and colleagues that point towards a process of individualization, a progressive freeing of agency from structure and a shift from ascribed
differences (such as gender and social class) and traditionally shaped 'normal biographies' towards 'choice biographies' where individuals are increasingly responsible
for managing their own destinies.

Bjerrum Nielsen and Rudberg were concerned to explore two themes: first, how
the process of individualization had impacted on the lives of women and their relationship with each other, and, second, to show the importance of the psychological
and the emotional domain, not simply as a reflection of the shifts in material and
social processes but as a force and medium of change in its own right. The study was
designed both to 'test' out a theoretical claim about change and as a means to generate conceptual and empirical insights that could enrich such theoretical approaches.
In researching their three-generation chains of women they sought to document and
relate three aspects: historical embeddedness, cultural norms and subjectivities.

These researchers employ a psychologically nuanced approach in order to capture
the interplay of these dimensions. For example, they distinguish between *gender
identity* (the gender I have – I am a woman and therefore act in this particular way),
gender subjectivity (the gender I am – I am me, and therefore I act in this particular
way, laid down in childhood and unconsciously influenced by the gendered

subjectivity of their parents) and cultural and social possibilities offered by the society at any time (Bjerrum Nielsen and Rudberg, 1994: 92). They explain that at the point of adolescence there is always a lack of 'contemporaneity' or 'fit' between these dimensions. The character of this configuration is particular for each generation. For example, girls growing up in the 1960s and 1970s experienced contradictions between a modernized gender identity and an 'old-fashioned gendered subjectivity (development of autonomy through relationships with men)' (1994: 109). For their mothers, who were girls in the 1940s and 1950s, the contradiction was between a modern gender identity and restricted cultural possibilities. For girls in the 1980s and 1990s the contradiction was between gendered subjectivity and cultural and social possibilities. So the modern girl may not 'acknowledge her sex as a limitation – she wants everything and believes she can do anything. But is that possible?' (1994: 111).

Bjerrum Nielsen and Rudberg show that individual 'characters' are the result of diverse influences and contradictions, echoing Mannheim's portrayal of the character of a generation as formed by the diversity of an age cohort. They describe their project as seeking to combine the insights of psychology, psychoanalysis and sociology in order to create 'psycho-biographies', citing the influence of the Frankfurt School's project of delineating 'social characters'.

In making sense of the interview material generated from their three-generational chains, the authors tend to begin with the historical, using the analysis of the 'generation' as a means to capture something of their particularity. They explain that the discourses of the grandmothers tend to be highly pragmatic, featuring descriptions of actions and facts rather than interpretations. These narratives are infused by norms of modesty and a focus on the material conditions of life. Grandmothers tend not to position themselves as individuals but as part of family teams, a typical comment being 'we didn't have so many problems in those times'. In contrast, the discourse of the mothers' generation is much more psychological in character. Their accounts are evaluative and interpretative, motives are problematized and parents frequently blamed. The discourse that characterizes the daughter generation has similarities with that of the mothers, in that it is also highly psychological. Yet where their mothers' accounts are blaming, the daughters' accounts tended towards irony and performativity. They describe the daughters as being like 'stand-up comedians' who perform and quote the accounts of others. The generational styles of narratives are likened to the distinctive voices of different academic disciplines, with grandmothers talking like sociologists emphasizing structural constraints, mothers talking like psychologists emphasizing subjective experience and motivation, and daughters speaking in the playful and ironic style of cultural studies (Bjerrum Nielsen and Rudberg, 2000).

Bjerrum Nielsen and Rudberg are also careful to avoid a literal reading of history from these accounts. They recognize that using interviews as a method for the creation of data means that in one sense they are always researching the 'now' (the interviews all being 'remnants of 1991'). Yet the very different discourses employed by the different generations when talking about their childhoods make it possible to view them 'as small pockets of history, preserved in the individual' (Bjerrum Nielsen, 2003: 18). Although the researchers asked all the interviewees about their childhood, they recognize that in comparing these accounts they are not comparing like with like. Not only are these women at different stages of their lives, but they are viewing their childhoods through different lenses. For the grandmothers there is a powerful cultural narrative through which their memories are mediated, one that stresses a progressive improvement in standards of living and a liberalizing of morality. For the mothers' generation, memories of childhood are mediated through a generational story of enlightenment and gender equality. In the current generation they observe how women frequently slip between accounts of self and wider generalizations about women like themselves, a sign perhaps of the actualization of this generation in Mannheim's terms.

Constructing the 'housewife'

A fascinating example of the way in which generational identity may shape memory is provided in a discussion of how the middle generation construct the figure of the 'housewife'. When the researchers compared the accounts of the grandmothers and the mothers they found that the middle generation tended to describe their mothers as having been 'housewives' during their childhoods. This is the case even though many of these grandmothers provided accounts of themselves as working, often in family and/or agricultural work. Bjerrum Nielsen suggests that the figure of the housewife operates as a symbolic dividing line for the women growing up in the 1950s and 1960s – the 'Other' of the liberated women. There is some evidence that this is a shared intergenerational discourse, with the mothers attributing bitterness and frustration to the grandmothers, and the grandmothers expressing regret themselves. Yet significantly, the regret expressed by the grandmothers is not for a lack of work, but for their lack of travel and education. Bjerrum Nielsen describes the 'housewife' as a '1970 construction of the 1950's, exaggerated ... to support the self constructions of the adult daughters' (2003: 23). It is not the absence of work per se that defines the housewife, but the absence of paid work in the public sphere. And it is paid work that also provides the focus for the youngest generation's attempts to distinguish themselves from their mothers, asserting an unwillingness to commit so fully to paid work and career.

So although the shifts identified by the analysis of discourse suggest change over time, there is also evidence of conversation, transaction and continuity along the conduit of the generational chain. History, culture and subjectivity operate within and through each other, in Bjerrum Nielsen's words, 'here we have a case of these complex relations between a structural change in women's lives and a cultural change of norms of femininity, and a specific pattern of inner mother–me relations' (2003: 24). This is a process that should not be reduced to either the economic or the emotional; rather, it shows the serendipity of a process in which the 'readiness' for change is conditioned, 'culture triggers new psychology, and new psychology triggers new culture' (2003: 24).

Conclusion

Reflecting on her own empirical studies of the lifecourse, British anthropologist Jenny Hockey observes that people tend to emphasize intergenerational rupture when asserting connections with their age cohort and intergenerational continuity when talking in terms of family relationships (Hockey, 2008). Continuity and change are *perspectives* and are produced by the direction of our gaze and identifications. The ways in which we forge identifications are shaped by generation.

In this chapter we have explored the concept of 'generation', considering both 'inter' and 'intra' generational dynamics. The chapter began with an exploration of two academic traditions that have influenced this research agenda, the sociology of generations and the life history tradition. Within the sociology of generations we concentrated on the work of Karl Mannheim, whose distinction between a generation 'in itself' and 'for itself' has been influential. We also considered the dual nature of Mannheim's vision of generation as having both objective and subjective as well as conscious and unconscious dimensions. Another of Mannheim's contributions was an awareness of the irreducible complexity of generation, that is always heterogeneous and dynamic. It is this internal diversity that contributes to the particular character of a generation or the climate of an era.

Mannheim was primarily concerned with generations as collectivities that simultaneously create and express the spirit of the age. Life history approaches have helped to develop understandings of how generations within individual families operate as a microcosm of wider social relationships. Seen from the perspective of a family, it is possible to see generations as a continuous flow in which objective and subjective resources are entangled. It is a productive approach, in which the focus is not on restraint but on agency, resources, potential and readiness. From this perspective change and continuity are understood as necessary partners. Innovation is always part of changing social and economic conditions, yet continuity is the inevitable outcome of transmission. The nature of intergenerational communication can be indirect and elusive, haunted by the ghosts of unrealized possibilities.

Through two empirical examples we gained insight into what can be achieved by research that focuses on the relationships *between* generations. Both studies were theoretically productive as well as offering a test of theories concerning the nature of social and historical change. They were also analytically demanding, requiring data to be analysed and collated in several different ways in order to reveal individuals, families and generations. These studies demonstrate the interplay between the personal, the social and the historical in such a way that the integrity of each is maintained. Where the sociology of generations conceptualizes individuals as the bearers of historical processes, these intergenerational accounts tend to portray individuals and families as making history, driven by interpersonal dynamics that themselves are shaped, though not determined, by wider forces.

Summary points

- Generations can be understood as active or passive. This relates to the historical circumstances in which the generation is formed and the intensity of changes between generations.

- Generations can be understood horizontally (relationships within a generation) and vertically (relationships between generations).

- Continuity and change are not mutually exclusive terms but have to be understood in and through each other, realized through iterative processes.

- The specificity and depth of the kind of descriptions that characterize intergenerational research, and the strategic contrast of cases, can provide a foundation for the generation and testing of theory.

- The discourses that individuals employ exhibit traces of the historical era of their origin as well as the contemporary conditions of their performance and their social location.

- Intergenerational research confounds distinctions of past, present and future, showing the ways in which existence always includes both past and future.

Further resources

Bertaux, D. and Thompson, P. (eds) (1993/2005) *Between Generations: Family Models, Myths and Memories*. London: Transaction Books.
International collection of life history research focusing on transmission within families.

Bertaux, D. and Thompson, P. (eds) (1997/2003) *Pathways to Social Class: A Qualitative Approach to Social Mobility*. Oxford: Clarendon Press.
International collection of papers drawing on life history methods to explore intergenerational processes within families.

Bjerrum Nielsen, H. and Rudberg, M. (1994) *Psychological Gender and Modernity*. Oslo: Scandinavian University Press.
First of a series of publications based on a three-generation study of gender in Norway. Includes extended theoretical discussion.

Rosenthal, G. (1998) *The Holocaust in Three Generations: Families of Victims and Perpetrators of the Nazi Regime*. London: Cassells.
A powerful example of social history that employs clinical and narrative models in an exploration of intergenerational family processes and employs juxtaposition as a mechanism for understanding the complexity of historical moments.

Brannen, J., Moss, P. and Mooney, A. (2004) *Working and Caring over the Twentieth Century: Change and Continuity in Four-Generation Families*. Basingstoke: Palgrave Macmillan.
Empirical study of four-generation families in the UK.

7

Revisiting

The whole *of anything is never told. (Henry James, emphasis in original)*

Qualitative research demands thorough documentation and careful attention to how and in what circumstances research data is produced. Reflexive methodologies in particular invite sustained reflection on the research process itself. Whatever its methodology, timeframe or topic, qualitative research consequently generates a mass of research artefacts – field notes, transcripts, video and audio recordings, photographs, mementoes, rough drafts, working papers, case summaries, documentary sources, contemporary readings, and final published papers, books and reports. The value of this documentation is generally judged in terms of what it offers for the planning, analysis and writing of the study in the 'research time' of the project. Yet, from another angle, it offers a remarkable opportunity to see how research practices develop and researchers work. It can provide a 'behind the scenes' picture of how research methodologies are realized, in the messy and uncertain time that may precede, and even accompany, the crafted published papers. Depending on when and where they are reviewed, research artefacts can be reframed as providing a lens onto another historical period, and the questions and puzzles that animated researchers working then. They can also become sources for subsequent study and re-use by others, or by the original researcher, working in a different time and place, bringing new questions to the original study. 'The *whole* of anything is never told', observed Henry James (1981: 18). And the richness and value of qualitative studies is not exhausted or fully captured in one reading or telling, or in one time.

In this chapter, we consider two types of revisiting research – follow-up studies and the archiving and re-analysis of research studies – and consider benefits and dilemmas arising from them. Follow-up studies include those where the original researcher reviews a previously completed study through a different temporal and conceptual lens, or extends the original study with another wave of research, or subsequently returns to a research site or follows up participants – we discuss an example of the latter in our first case study. Follow-up studies share some characteristics of longitudinal research in that they generate comparison between different times, but may not have been set up originally to track changes over time. The points of return to the research group are therefore likely to be fewer and the observed changes between the research phases possibly more dramatic. The second strand, the archiving and re-use of data, includes the re-interpretation of a study by a researcher/s (secondary analyst) who did not participate in the original research study and who may be using the data for purposes different from those that motivated the original study. Secondary analysis is 'best known as a methodology for doing research using pre-existing statistical data' (Heaton, 2004: 1). Since the mid-1990s, there has been a growing interest in re-using data from qualitative studies, accompanied by increasingly polarized debates regarding the ethical and methodological challenges of secondary analysis (Moore, 2007; Temple et al., 2006). We examine these debates in reference to our second case study, a secondary analysis of interview data on people's views of social class. With both follow-up studies and secondary analysis, how materials from the initial study are archived has a significant bearing on what meaning can subsequently be made from them.

Why revisit or archive qualitative studies?

A flourishing interest in revisiting research studies some time after they were first conducted is motivated by both historical and comparative questions. How is what was studied then different now? How might returning to studies assist in understanding the distinctiveness of the present; what patterns of historical and social change do they reveal? There are also methodological interests: how do we read and re-interpret studies completed at different times and in different places, and even with different purposes (Bornat, 2005; Thompson, 2000)? The prospect of revisiting a study or following up a cohort of research participants may be part of the original design, and shape how one plans the phases of research and conceptualizes the research questions and methodology.

Whether planned in advance or decided after completion of the initial study, revisiting qualitative studies offers many benefits to researchers working in the present. When archived, such studies are immensely valuable resources for empirical and historical investigation of social change. This is so even when questions of change were not an explicit focus of the original study. Returning to studies after a lapse of time brings comparison to the fore. Material archived from a particular study – its field notes, interviews, analyses, aims and so forth – represents a record of that project and inevitably, even when only implicit, a record of the initial study's social and historical context. Returning to earlier studies sheds comparative and historical light on contemporary topics and on the type of questions and concerns that frame studies (e.g. Gillies, 2008). Additionally, it offers insights into changing research practices and shifting agendas in theory (Savage, 2005, 2007a; Thompson, 2000) and assists with building more historicized accounts of the development and use of qualitative methodologies.

Themes explored in this chapter reconnect with our earlier discussions of memory and history. Archiving practices are implicated in the social production of collective and individual memory and the organization of the past. Inevitably, returning to studies provokes reflection on the processes and criteria for selecting and creating an archive and the methods that initially generated the research materials. It also encourages reviewing the type of interpretations made from the original study, and how both the research material and interpretations of it are constructed as 'evidence' or 'stories' from an otherwise lost time. And, as Mike Savag (2005) suggests, returning to archived studies invites reflection upon the research process itself and on how researchers employ methodologies and build knowledge.

Archiving a research study, as with archiving artefacts and documents more generally, is undertaken in the present with a view to preserving records for future use and with an eye to transforming the present into the past. Questions about what is kept, excluded or designated as peripheral, how materials are organized, coded and transferred (from oral recording to written text), stored (digitally or in 'hard copy'), the type of things archived (sound, images, written text) and the conditions for access are, at one level, practical matters. They are also profoundly linked to the making of history and the stories that will, in the future, be possible to tell about the present. As Paul Ricoeur admonishes, echoing Pierre Nora, 'Archive as much as you like: something will always be left out' (2004: 169).

As social spaces and institutions for the storage and organization of materials, archives retain a powerful role in the creation and mediation of historical knowledge, framing how the past enters the present and vice versa (Ricoeur, 2004: 167–8). Archives manage more than records for future use; they work to foreclose and make possible some stories rather than others. There is a tension for archivists in wanting to archive as much as possible and the knowledge of inevitable gaps and omissions. Researchers might want some stories or materials preserved rather than others, and the marks of such decisions and attendant exclusions and inclusions may not be immediately evident or may be erased from the archival record. Additionally, archives bear the biographical traces of the original researcher. These traces may be obscured, faint or palpable, evident in the type of questions asked, the choice of methodology, and the style of analysis. But there is also the matter of the original researcher's emotional investments – their ambivalences, their vulnerabilities and uncertainties, and questions about how or whether these can be captured in archived material. How one incorporates this intersubjective aspect of research into re-analysis of a study is an ongoing dilemma for re-use, as it is for researchers whose studies are archived and re-analysed by others: what will archiving and re-analysis expose about the original researcher? We return to these issues below.

Follow-up studies

Follow-up studies provide especially striking insight into social processes at different points in time. Curiosity and 'human interest' guide desires to find out what has happened to people since they were last studied, or the social circumstances they inhabited, or the framing questions that informed the study: what's different; what's the same? Comparative questions are built into cross-generational studies which allow the researcher to view generational change as it is being enacted, rather than retrospectively. With ethnographies, and especially those conducted and written up over an extended period of time, as we saw in our case study of wedding rituals, questions about what has changed since the time of fieldwork can nag at the edges of the analysis. But the temporal frame of the approach is geared to observing the lived time of the research encounter – that of the informants and the researcher – and observations regarding changes since the completion of the ethnography are usually beyond or in addition to the initial fieldwork. Yet ethnographies, precisely because they give detailed observations of what was happening in a particular time and place, temporarily 'freezing' that present, offer valuable opportunities for revisiting.

When follow-up studies are conducted by the original researcher/s, questions about the context of the original study, which beset secondary analysis and re-use of data, are of a different order. Indeed, elaborating the different contexts of the various waves of research is likely to be part of the focus of the study. For example, Howard Williamson's *The Milltown Boys Revisited* (2004) is a follow-up study of a group of boys living in troubled circumstances in a housing estate of an industrial British city with whom the author first conducted ethnographic research in the mid-1970s. Williamson revisits these young men 25 years later, conducting further fieldwork in the same community and with a significant number of the original boys. Williamson charts in rich detail the circumstances of the boys' lives at the different periods, describing it as an 'unashamedly empirical study, a wholehearted exercise in "grounded theory"' (p. 23). The lapse of time between the two periods of fieldwork, and the deliberate focusing on how things unfolded over an extended period of time, 'implicitly challenges (though in other respects, it also confirms) the marginalisation and exclusion theses advanced by youth researchers, for it is as much a testimony to the resilience of many of the Boys (against the odds) as it is an affirmation that youth disadvantage translates, *for ever*, into social and economic marginality' (p. 8, emphasis in original).

Other follow-up studies do not strictly return to an earlier study, but revisit a cohort or generation of which, as in the case of Sherry Ortner's (2003) *New Jersey Dreaming: Capital, Culture and the Class of '58*, the author was a member. Ortner was curious to see what had happened to her classmates from the graduating class of 1958, Weequahic High School, New Jersey. As an experienced anthropologist, Ortner decided to turn her ethnographic gaze upon her own society and peers, to track their life journeys, from high school through to mid-life. She wanted to understand the social changes that had accompanied the lives of her classmates, and the wider cultural and historical significance of their biographical experiences, particularly their class positioning. Ortner surveyed and interviewed her classmates, playing off 'her informants' memories against a larger world that they embodied, enacted or in some cases resisted' (Ortner, 2003: 8). She argued that the class of '58 represented an unusually successful and upwardly mobile generational group. While not discounting the effect of individual agency, she analyses this class movement as directly connected to the impact of major social and identity movements during the latter half of the 20th century, notably the civil rights movement, campaigns against anti-Semitism, and feminism.

Our first case study, Lois Weis' (2004) *Class Reunion*, is a follow-up ethnographic study, set in the US and similarly concerned with shifts in class positioning. This discussion also builds on methodological themes raised in our earlier chapter on ethnographic enquiry.

Revisiting the American white working class: 1985 to 2000

In 2000–1 Lois Weis returned to a group of white men and women living in Freeway, a rapidly de-industrializing town in the northeast of the US, that she had first researched 15 years previously in 1985, when the participants were teens in the third year of high school. That first study was a 'full-scale ethnographic investigation of a white working-class high school' (2004: 1) in which Weis explored 'identity formation among American white working-class male and female students in relation to the school, economy, and family of origin'. She found that 'young women exhibit what I call a "glimmer of critique" regarding traditional gender roles in the white working-class family, and that young men are ripe for New Right consciousness, given their strident racism and male-dominant stance in an economy that offers them little' (p. 3). From that original study, Weis located a group of former students, now adults in their 30s, most still living in or connected to the Freeway community, and re-interviewed them about their life since leaving school, looking particularly at work, family life, aspirations and values. The book provides a substantive insight into contemporary class relations as well as methodological and conceptual strategies for researching the complex and contradictory processes of social change (pp. 185–92).

From the 41 white student participants in the 1985 study, Weis re-interviewed 31 and conducted relatively incidental participant observations – at participants' homes or workplaces, local bars or cafés where meetings took place. In both the 1985 and 2000 study, Weis interviewed a small number of people of colour, but those interviews are not the focus of this book, though the presence of 'others' permeates the interviews and the self-constructions of the white male and female participants. As prompts for the 2000 interviews, Weis brought a copy of the participants' high school yearbook and a transcript of their interview from 1985. She conducted all interviews herself, 'as I quickly concluded that part of the "magic" of the interview lay in the fact that I had worked with them fifteen years earlier' (pp. 187–8).

Weis provides instructive 'nuts and bolts' details on how she moved from data collection to analysis. Interviews were tape-recorded, transcribed and then coded using a qualitative software program. Coding categories were established after Weis read about one-quarter of the transcripts across gender, and these categories became 'labels through which the data could be chunked and analyzed' (p. 188). These 'empirically developed coding categories were added to theoretically driven codes' and included topics such as 'Family When Growing Up', 'Race Relations', 'Desire for Future', 'Marriage' (p. 188). After this initial process of classification the various categories were 'recombined' in dialogue with other research and theoretical literature to produce the final text. As with Diana Leonard's explanation of her methods for recruiting and interviewing informants in her ethnographic study (discussed in Chapter 5), such procedural descriptions show the steps by which research is done, and the attention to detail required to scaffold interpretations.

The first two chapters present a descriptive synthesis of findings from the initial study, drawing on material from a large number of participants. These serve as a background to the arguments developed out of the follow-up study and contextualize the comparative insights. The chapters drawing on the 2000 study (Chapters 3–6) employ a different technique, using 'thick data' from 'individuals whom I see as *emblematic* of key trends'. The later chapters more explicitly take up 'heavy theorizing' regarding 'whiteness, masculinity, femininity and the new economy' (p. 16).

The study was intended to be more than the story of 31 individuals: it is 'an exploration, empirically and longitudinally, of the re-making of the American white working class in the latter quarter of the twentieth century' (p. 2). A framing argument is that 'identities are constructed over time and in relation to the constructed identities of others, as well as dialectically in relation to the broader economy and culture' (p. 190). Against claims that the working class has been eclipsed, Weis argues that the white working class has 're-articulated itself as a distinct class fraction' in relation to 'massive changes in the global economy' and in interaction with constructions of gender and of racial and cultural 'others' (p. 3). Weis adopts a double focus, first by examining formations in two different periods, and moving back and forward between the two to build an analysis of change based on ethnographic comparison; and, second, by adopting a kind of 'methodological "diptych" that enables me to shift between larger social forces and lives "on the ground"' (p. 15).

Weis describes her methodology as '*ethnographic longitudinality*' (p. 2), an approach that tracks 'interactions and relationships over time, causing us to shift our eye from pieces drawn at one point in time to those drawn at another' (p. 190). It is also a method established over time, constituted retrospectively. As the longitudinal element of the study was not planned at the time of the original ethnography, a methodological template and rationale were subsequently developed to accommodate the way the study evolved. This repositions the significance of the initial ethnography. It acquires an explicit temporality that recasts its findings in a different and inevitably comparative light, indicating how methods evolve in response to emerging research practices.

Weis further characterizes her approach as an example of a 'compositional study' (pp. 14–15; 189–90), which Weis and her frequent collaborator, Michelle Fine, define as a 'theory of method in which analyses of public and private institutions, groups, and lives are lodged in relation to key social and economic structures' (p. 14). Influenced by the conceptual language of visual arts, this methodological orientation gives attention to both the 'positive' (main referent) and 'negative' spaces of a composition and the borders between them. 'Like the artist, I explicitly explore the negative bridging spaces within the composition, intentionally probing the relations between "negative" and "positive" spaces, understanding at all times that no "positive" exists except in relation to the "negative"' (p. 14). Ethnographic longitudinality enacts this approach with particular force, Weis suggests, because it allows one to examine two points in time in detail and to trace connections and disconnections over time. It allows one to see how 'global and national formations and relational interactions seep through the lives, identities and communities of youth and adults, ultimately refracting back on the larger social formations that gave rise to them to begin with' (pp. 189–90). Ethnographic longitudinality has the potential to illuminate shifts and stalemates over time in individuals, as well as in the local/global settings they inhabit (e.g. pp. 163–5).

Race, class and gender – changes and continuities

The overall conception of the study bears the legacy of feminist, critical and anti-racist traditions, with elements of participatory action and advocacy research (see especially Chapter 7 and pp. 179–84). It straddles structure/agency debates by exposing persistent patterns of exploitation while showing how these might shift and reconfigure over time and how individuals and communities participate in complicated ways in this process of remaking: 'While class may bear the same long-term imprint, it will not necessarily do so in the same way' (p. 8).

We draw out two significant shifts that occurred between the two studies. First, in the 1985 study Weis found that 'white working-class modal male and female identities were on a collision path, with boys loudly affirming male-dominant relations in the home, and girls exhibiting a challenge to these relations in key ways' (p. 69). Girls were imagining a future life of greater autonomy, a future not immediately defined by marriage. In the 2000 study, the women remain 'ener-gized by the possibility of a life markedly different from that of their mothers or grandmothers' (p. 114), and many of the interviewed women had achieved some of the symbols of freedom that they longed for as teenagers – further study, a qual-ification, a degree of economic independence. Yet these stories of independence and change, artefacts of feminism and restructured economies, coexist with some persistent dangers and vulnerabilities. In their private lives these same 'successful' women had not escaped the patriarchal power of symbolic and physical violence, usually from husbands or boyfriends. Gender relations continued to be policed in terribly familiar ways. Weis concludes that for these women 'the lived-out moment of critique has not been able to wholly challenge all that goes on in the private sphere' (p. 134).

Second, in the 1985 study, while white working-class males insistently con-structed their identity in relation to and against racially different 'others', this was not a common strategy among their white female peers. In the 2000 study, white working-class males still 'draw upon their collective youth identity so as to con-tinue to patrol racial borders and assert their own superiority in relation to all those who are not white' (p. 163). Further, in an 'ever-fragile economy' in which they are increasingly vulnerable to unemployment and economic marginalization, these white men assume a 'symbolic dominance' by asserting an older 'racial and gender hierarchy' that is itself under challenge and unstable (p. 74). Most strikingly, however, white working-class women in 2000 articulate similar claims to white superiority and the need to maintain boundaries between racial groups. The women reflect:

> There's beginning to be a lot of Arabians. They seem to be taking over the whole United States. They're taking over everywhere ... Arabians are now living on this side of town. On the corner, on the other street ... they're all over now. ... Just like they took over in the First Ward [a part of the suburb]. (Sandy, p. 158)

> And there are all the blacks and the Arabians. It's totally out of control. ... Why do they all congregate? ... There's too many, you know, racial relationships. It's a mess. The black students are all dating white girls. (Chris, p. 159)

How does 'ethnographic longitudinality' help us to understand these shifts in identification and racial boundary work? Weis suggests that it is partly explained by life course trajectories, which her follow-up study captures at key points of change. At the point of adulthood and anticipated home ownership and children, white working-class women join forces with their white male counterparts (p. 162). This further embeds an 'us and them' mentality and embodies the indissoluble character of class, gender and race relations, even as these re-articulate in dramatically changing social and economic circumstances. Thus, class '*reconverges around race*', and 'the wages of whiteness', Weis argues, 'enable these men and women to construct and hold on to a new white working-class fraction in spite of the potentially destabilizing effects of the rearticulation of gender roles and relations within this class fraction, as well as the fundamental challenge of the restructured world economy' (p. 164).

In our earlier discussion of ethnographic methods, we noted challenges to the 'ethnographic present'. Thick descriptions of the present can evoke a sense of a culture or event frozen in time, captured once and for all in ethnographic representation. Revisiting an ethnographic study brings the question of time and tense to the fore. In revisiting and adding a further wave of research, Weis attempted to 'engage both myself and the reader in movement over time', and in doing so 'to blast open the "freezing" so characteristic of ethnographies conducted at one point in time' (p. 190). However, despite criticisms of the limitations of the 'ethnographic present', in follow-up studies such as Weis', the very 'thickness' of the initial ethnographic account of a particular present (now past) provides the groundwork for building comparisons. In this case, it was the starting point for researching social relations in transition, and the follow-up study drew out its potential to illuminate movement and shifts over time.

Other kinds of data 'revisiting' are possible, as when the researcher was not involved in the original study. The quality and depth of re-engagement depends as well on how thoroughly the original study was documented, the decisions made about what was to be preserved and how it was archived. Archiving materials from qualitative studies enables them to be returned to and re-interpreted by researchers working in different times and places.

Archiving qualitative research – ethics, practices and new possibilities

Interest in archiving and re-using qualitative studies comes from funding bodies, international research agencies and researchers themselves. Funding organizations wish to maximize their investment in research, to ensure that findings and research materials circulate more widely. In the UK, the Economic and Social Research Council (ESRC) now requires projects it funds to make the research study available for archiving and funds an Economic and Social Data Service (ESDS), Qualidata, to support this (www.esds.ac.uk/qualidata/). Writing in 2000, the social historian Paul Thompson reflected that qualitative researchers have typically been reluctant to share their data with other researchers, and that 'among qualitative sociologists – in contrast to social historians – there has been much less of a turn towards the re-use of data' (Thompson, 2000: 2). This is possibly because social researchers feel their material would not make sense to people who had not been involved in its collection, and equally researchers themselves may feel ambivalent about re-analysing a study someone else has conducted. However, there is now a momentum of interest in following up and reviewing earlier studies and in archiving records for future and secondary analysis. This opens up new research opportunities for comparative and historical study, and ensures that rich qualitative data are not underutilized or forgotten (Heaton, 2004; Thompson, 2000). Anecdotally, qualitative researchers often wryly reflect on the problem of generating more research data than they have the time to systematically analyse, and in serious vein, of having boxes and files of data that warrant further attention or could be helpful sources for someone else.

Archived qualitative studies encompass an array of material – transcripts and recordings of research interviews, such as oral and life history interviews; interviews on specific topics to do with work, or health, or education; sound recordings, images, digital records. It can also include project artefacts such as the researcher's notes, field notes, methodological jottings, correspondence, interview schedules and published and unpublished interpretations (Fielding, 2004: 98–101). The capacity for digitalization expands the possibilities for archiving, enhancing accessibility and usability of material (Hodgson and Clark, 2007). There is scope for creative representation of research, away from file-after-file of transcripts towards the incorporation of a mix of easily cross-referenced resources including video, sound and text. Preparation of the study for a website introduces a new phase in the project, fostering a level of meta-reflection on the project itself, even involving participants in this process. This is illustrated in our earlier discussion (Chapter 4) of the digital archiving of the Inventing Adulthoods qualitative longitudinal project (Henderson et al., 2006).

Deciding what belongs in the archive from any research project is a major organizational and interpretive task. What might seem incidental to the primary researcher could be regarded as essential by subsequent researchers, or indeed by the participants themselves. In most cases, material will already have undergone many stages of selection, transcription, sorting, culling, prioritizing in the process of 'doing the research', and before it is further categorized for archiving (Bishop, 2005; Fielding, 2004: 103–4). At each stage, choices are made about what matters and why. Numerous guidelines are available to assist researchers prepare materials for archiving (Qualidata: www.esds.ac.uk/qualidata/). Such practical and procedural matters are not, however, easily separated from methodological, ethical and epistemological challenges; and technical guidelines alone do not adequately address them (Parry and Mauthner, 2004). Even the apparently simple task of anonymizing transcripts is not straightforward, because removing names does not mean that people and places cannot be identified (Bishop, 2005; Parry and Mauthner, 2005). The very richness and specificity of qualitative research risks exposing participants, even when overt identifiers are removed. Other strategies such as disguising, removing or falsifying some contextual details are also awkward solutions because so much of the value of qualitative data, and its potential value for re-use, lies precisely in this detail. Added to these concerns is the blurry nature of participant consent, particularly when archived data may end up being used for purposes that differ from those stated in the original project. Parry and Mauthner (2004: 147) question whether participants can fully understand the implications of consent, once the data set of which they were a part is handed over to an archive.

Further dilemmas arise from the current trend towards inclusive and prospective archiving. Conventionally, materials have been archived retrospectively, guided by hindsight, with agencies determining after a period of time that certain materials or collections represented 'important studies', or they were archived as part of a significant individual's papers, usually when they were older or after they had died. The move to archive qualitative projects once they are completed, as is the case in the UK, where archiving is linked to funding, introduces some uncertainty about whether all projects warrant preservation. There are considerable costs involved as well, even with the availability of digital technologies. And for qualitative researchers, the knowledge that their materials – their notes, schedules, interview transcripts – will be archived is likely to incite a certain self-censorship, and possibly modifications to the research project, in the anticipation of an unknown and imaginary future audience. Finally, there are real questions to consider about whether or the extent to which vast amounts of archived data will actually be utilized, and whether decisions about what deserves preservation will or should take place after, rather than before, the labour of archiving.

These are significant practical, ethical and epistemological matters, but in our view the benefits to be gained from archiving and the potential it offers for re-analysis warrant a continued wrestling with them. Consent and ownership, for example, have added dimensions when archiving, but are currently negotiated at many stages in the qualitative research process. Additionally, it might well be that not all qualitative data are equally appropriate for archiving and re-analysis. Paul Thompson suggests that the most 'valuable qualitative datasets for future re-analysis are likely to have three qualities: firstly, interviewees have been chosen on a convincing sample basis; secondly, the interviews are free-flowing but follow a life story form, rather than focussing narrowly on the researcher's immediate themes; and thirdly, when practicable, re-contact [with participants] is not ruled out' (Thompson, 2000: 41).

Constructing meaning when working with archived qualitative research

An extensive range of national and international archived quantitative data sets exists and some lessons can be learnt from their protocols (Fielding, 2004; Heaton, 2004). Yet distinct methodological, ethical and epistemological issues arise when archiving qualitative compared to quantitative studies. Transposing archiving practices from the latter to the former may not be helpful (Bornat, 2005; Parry and Mauthner, 2004). At the heart of this matter is the relationship between the original researcher and research study, and the context-specific data typically elicited in qualitative projects. Contextual knowledge is typically understood as 'only derived from involvement in the research at the time of its collection' and 'in this view "being there" is all important, and the lack of being able to engage in reflexive interpretation is a barrier to secondary analysis' (Temple et al., 2006: para 44; see also Blaxter, 2007: para 1.3; Hammersley, 1997). 'Context' encompasses local, national and global levels, theoretical and substantive concerns that were urgent at the time of doing the research, and the dynamic of the research encounter.

To a large extent, qualitative research is co-constructed, its meanings jointly produced between the researcher and the research participant (Denzin and Lincoln, 2005). Rich specificity of material is a hallmark of qualitative enquiry, and data cannot be severed from context, as if it were a free-floating, objective aggregation of facts and findings. Indeed the choice of terms in these discussions is telling. The very descriptor 'data', slipping easily from the language of quantitative and positivist social science, is not particularly helpful, and is arguably counter-productive for understanding the epistemological and ethical processes that are involved when working with qualitative research. The term 'data' creates a sense of research as composed of a neat linear process of aims, methods and findings, with the latter understood as the objective 'facts and outcomes', the data that can be efficiently and tidily deposited in archives, extracted from context and the traces of their production (see too Bishop, 2007).

The terminology of 'primary' and 'secondary' sources risks creating false oppositions that minimize how the dilemmas linked to secondary analysis – context, attribution of significance, comparability, etc. - also bedevil so-called primary or original studies. With echoes of high school history, primary sources are implicitly invoked as more objective and reliable than secondary sources. The persistence of these distinctions among social scientists ignores, Moore argues, the diverse ways in which qualitative data are generated and reworked: temporal distinctions between primary – first, main – and secondary – later – readings are not necessarily clear-cut (Moore, 2007: para 2.2). Qualitative data are frequently revisited over the course of a project. They are reviewed, revised and discussed with research teams, at conference presentations, with colleagues working on related projects, in interaction with research literature, and even reviewed some years later by the same researcher/s, not as a new study but as part of an ongoing engagement with the project. Such evolving interpretive work troubles neat demarcations between primary and secondary analysis. This is made even more explicit in longitudinal studies, in which data is constantly reframed in different contexts, and even by different members of the research team (Henderson et al., 2006; McLeod, 2003).

Additionally, the language of 're-use' has instrumental connotations of mining inert data and downplays the creative role of the researcher in re-interpreting and re-engaging sources. It also sidelines major methodological currents regarding qualitative data as co-produced, not found – an insight that applies to both primary and secondary analysis. There are, of course, risks of glossing what was tenuous in the initial study, of being unable to capture tentative meanings or the vulnerabilities of the researcher. In re-analysis it is necessary to remain open to what the research is or could become, but also to be mindful of the kind of claims and analyses that the archives actually suggest or make possible (Bornat, 2005). In other words, one needs to negotiate, as with historical research, the relationship between 'evidence' – the archival materials available to build an argument and analysis – and the creative interpretive work of constructing meaning and significance.

Re-contextualizing research studies

Instead of debating the merits and difficulties of re-using data, others propose regarding it not as re-use per se, but as a process involving re-contextualization (Moore, 2007) or 'contextual reflexivity' (Temple et al., 2006: para 5). In this, the 'socially embedded nature of secondary data' requires 'not only analysis of the primary data, but also analysis of the context of their production (accessed through grant proposals, correspondence, interview schedules, field notes, reports and so on)'. The aim of re-contextualization is not so much to recreate the context of the 'primary' study but to reframe and contextualize the production of new data (Bishop, 2007: para 6.1).

Moore argues that the notion of data as pre-existing (or primary) obscures the way in which re-analysis represents a new research project, as well as 'the complexities of how data is co-constructed through a new research project':

> A new research project provides a new context for the creation and emergence of 'data', particularly through the contemporary production of the relationship between researcher and data. Thus secondary analysis is not so much the analysis of pre-existing data; rather secondary analysis involves the process of recontextualising, and reconstructing, data. Once that data is transformed through the process of recontextualisation, it is not so much that we now have a new entity to be termed 'secondary data' … rather that through recontextualisation, the order of the data has been transformed, thus secondary analysis is perhaps more usefully rendered a primary analysis of a different order of data. (Moore, 2007: para 2.3)

As we noted above, the imprint of the original researcher's identity permeates the archive – in notes, selection of materials and so forth. Archival collections are often organized around the papers of individuals, with access to research studies via their biography. Secondary analysis dramatically reverses this: the biography of the researcher is read from the archived project. Research identities blur, with the researcher becoming the researched, the object of enquiry. Some ambiguity can arise as to whether it is the project, the time period, or the researcher that is the focus of re-analysis. Moreover, the secondary analyst is not simply a miner of the archive, but brings to the analysis their research histories, emotional investments and vulnerabilities, co-producing meaning and re-contexualizing the research study. We are reminded here of our earlier discussion of Annette Kuhn's observation (Chapter 2) that memories involve 'secondary revision', whereby retrospective narratives are created to fit with present needs. We can readily apply this to what happens at the macro-level of crafting historical narratives, and to explanations of why some narratives have authority in particular periods. But secondary revision is also likely to shape how individual researchers revisit and re-use research studies. Methodological debate about re-analysis needs to engage with more than issues of consent, context and ethics; it needs to confront the intersubjective elements of research and their reverberation through the archive and its analysis.

Archiving and re-use opens up many possibilities for methodological innovation (Savage, 2005). Indeed, much commentary to date tends to be more concerned with methodological reflections than with illustrations of secondary analysis at work. (There are, of course, exceptions. See, for example, reports on studies from Bishop, 2007; Bornat, 2005 Goodwin and O'Connor, 2006.) One important consequence of revisiting research studies is that it allows us to see how research is actually done, compared to what is propounded in 'textbook' injunctions. Savage (2005) suggests that returning to the archives of 'classic studies' allows us to better 'understand how research actually advances. Given the normative character of much social science methodology texts, where the focus is on how researchers *should* conduct their research, rather than how they actually went about their research, this offers an important, much under-utilised, way of developing our methodological understanding' (Savage, 2005: 120). The creation of new methodological strategies is itself a valuable consequence of secondary analysis. It underlines the historicity of methodologies, showing that they are dynamic and evolving, rather than timeless formulas and techniques. Thompson speaks with great optimism about the potential of re-use to create links between different kinds of data (quantitative, qualitative, historical), declaring that this could 'release a powerful reinvigorating new force in social research' (Thompson, 2000: 13).

Historical methods and qualitative research

In regard to developing a productive dialogue between historical and qualitative enquiry, we highlight four issues. First, in many respects the very notion of 're-analysis' of sources is fundamental to historical method. Much historical enquiry involves acts of re-analysis and re-interpretation, of re-reading both primary and secondary sources, and interrogating the truth claims of each (Munslow, 1997). Historians need archives, and, to a large extent, archival collections drive what it is possible for historians to say (Fielding, 2004: 104). Archival records cannot capture the full texture of events or lives, which exceed what can be documented, and history is more than what is held in an archive (Ricoeur, 2004). Even so, given the prominence of archiving for historical research it may be more fruitful for secondary analysis and re-use of qualitative data to learn from historians' engagement with archives than to take the archiving of quantitative data as the guiding point of reference. Quantitative data allows for comparison at different points of time, which is useful for documenting and assessing social change. However, valuable lessons can be learnt from historical enquiry for establishing context and understanding the experience of change. Historians need to reconstruct and re-imagine, from multiple archived and other available sources, the context and time in which the material was produced – these are part of the creative and intellectual challenge, not regarded as obstacles or reasons to not undertake the work.

Second, the archiving of oral history records shares some of the characteristics of archiving qualitative data (Bornat, 2005; Thompson, 2000). Issues of consent, ownership, context, purposes and so forth are encountered in both. Both generate interview and ancillary material – images, sound, researcher notes – that can be revisited for different themes and purposes at different times. But there are also differences between the two, and delineating them clarifies the specific features of qualitative re-analysis. While oral historians may be the 'only qualitative researchers who archive their data as a matter of course', they have a somewhat different 'attitude towards data from that of a qualitative social scientist' and this leads to different 'disciplinary uses of data'. 'Whereas within oral history a main purpose of data collection is to secure an historical record for current and future access, social science data are seen mainly as a potential resource to generate new hypotheses, findings and theories' (Parry and Mauthner, 2004: 148–9). However valid such distinctions might be, we detect a new mood afoot among qualitative social science researchers – evident in our second case study below – away from immediate concerns towards conceiving their work as a potentially relevant source for future historical enquiry.

Third, these debates encourage a keen awareness of the history of methodological development within the social sciences, and offer further illustration of how methods to research social processes are themselves responsive to historical change. It may well remain an open question as to why or whether there is currently an intensified popular and scholarly interest in revisiting the past. But tracing the ebb and flow of different research methods provides an angle onto the shifting agendas of social researchers and the intellectual history of the social sciences. Further, the types of interpretations made from sources may also change over time. Even when sources remain the same, what is said about them in review and re-analysis is reflective of the times in which the researcher is working. For example, Joanna Bornat's (2005) re-analysis of interview transcripts with retired gerontologists, conducted in the early 1990s, draws out themes concerning cultural difference and racialization of the field of geriatrics (see also Bornat and Wilson, 2008), topics which have a particular salience in the current era but which were not an explicit focus of the original interviews.

Finally, approaching secondary analysis with a more historically-inflected gaze highlights how re-engaging with archived qualitative data offers a way of examining processes of social and historical change. As well, returning to and re-analysing a study can help 'ensure that the extent of social change is not overemphasised and provide a corrective to grand theoretical claims'; it thus also provides a basis for assessing commonly held views, such as the idea that 'family and community are no longer significant features of contemporary social life' (Charles et al., 2008: 131; see also Gillies, 2008). Further, Thompson (2000) observes that 'even when a historical perspective is explicit, earlier qualitative research data is not [traditionally] considered as a source' (2000: 1). Our second case study offers an example of such an approach, and continues the theme of changing class identities in historical and comparative perspective.

Revisiting understandings of social class in and over time

This case study draws on a relatively small piece of research, taken from a larger project of changing perceptions of social class in 20th-century Britain (Savage, 2007a, 2007b). Mike Savage, a British sociologist, reports on an analysis of two waves of interview data, 42 years apart, collected by other researchers as part of the British Mass Observation studies. While his observations on shifting views of class are of interest, the more novel and significant aspect of the study is his research strategy to revisit cohorts of data as a way of exploring shifts in collective and individual class identity, and accompanying trends in sociological research and theorizing. It shows the benefits that can flow from re-analysis and from bringing together sociological and historical frames of reference. Savage's analysis also highlights the richness of the Mass Observation archive, implicitly making a case for developing archives of the present to assist historical and social researchers in the future.

The Mass Observation studies

The Mass Observation archive is a collection of materials that record everyday life in Britain and associated documentation collected by the Mass Observation studies movement. Begun in 1937 by a group of three young men as a project to 'create an anthropology of ourselves', the initial Mass Observation studies continued until the early 1950s (www.massobs.org.uk/index.htm). During this period, material was gathered in a variety of ways – via letters in the *New Statesman,* and discussions in the press encouraging people to volunteer to keep daily diaries and write responses to questionnaires or directives. Paid and volunteer groups also observed and recorded people's everyday public activities (www.massobs.org.uk/original_massobservation_project.htm).

In 1970, the archives from the Mass Observation studies were transferred to the University of Sussex and in 1981 a new wave of Mass Observation studies was initiated, and these continue into the present. As with the initial study, people can donate their 'life stories' to the archive or volunteer to be an 'observer' and respond to 'directives' on specified topics. In rationales for the Mass Observation project there is a self-consciousness regarding both the need to preserve observations for posterity and the significance of any individual life. As the Mass Observation website explains:

> We send a panel of writers two themed directives each year on both opinion based and personal topics; from thoughts on the London bombings and education, to pets and close relationships. Correspondents may email, type or write by hand, draw, send photographs, diagrams, cuttings from the press, poems, stories, letters and so on. No stress is placed on 'good grammar', spelling or style. The emphasis is on self-expression, candour and a willingness to be a vivid social commentator, and tell a good story. (www.massobs.org.uk/becoming_an_ observer.htm)

These documents of everyday life hold much intrinsic interest, and the revival of the Mass Observation archive reveals something of a cultural mood for scrutinizing the everyday and grappling with the exigencies of ordinary life. It also represents an impulse to democratize research – it is not just the province of expert social scientists – and to secure a view of the ever-changing present for future generations. Since the 1970s, use of the Mass Observation materials has taken four main forms: 'as evidence in historical research; in the study of the Mass Observation movement itself; in methodological research; and to inform the development of related initiatives' (Heaton, 2004: 7).

Comparing class – 1948 and 1990

Mike Savage examined responses from mass observers to 'directives' regarding their views on social class and their class identities at two different points of time – 1948 and then again in 1990. Mass observers 'wrote about class changes in subtle and revealing ways between these periods', Savage claims (2007a: 1.3). Significantly, in contrast to quantitative survey evidence that tends to indicate 'relative stability in class identities', Savage found that the qualitative data 'suggests changes less in the class "labels" people use (middle and working class, most notably) but more in the forms through which class is articulated' (1.3). The case Savage makes for revisiting studies opens up several different types of comparative analysis – between views in two periods of time, between types of data, and between historical and contemporary social and identity processes.

One of the features of the Mass Observation material is that it has not been gathered from a 'representative sample' – participants volunteered and this meant that certain groups of people are more represented than others. Both the 1948 and 1990 groups of participants were predominantly well-educated, female, elderly and middle class (5.1). But the lack of 'representativeness' is not necessarily a limitation for this type of study – responses from similar groups of people living in different times could be compared. Further, even though similar types of people responded to the directives in 1948 and in 1990, there were significant differences in how they talked about class and described their class identity.

In 1948, class was understood as something one was born into, ascribed, and for middle-class people especially, both something taken for granted and something that one did not really talk about. In comparison, respondents in 1990 tended to write at more length about class, and to generate an extended autobiographical narrative to explain their views (5.4–5.6). There was also a more self-conscious use of 'class discourse', and this in itself became an indicator of sophistication and class identity. In 1948, respondents located their class identity in family lineage, and saw themselves as having little control over this. The 1990 respondents expressed the relationship between family and class in somewhat different terms, emphasizing perhaps an 'ambivalent' class position, or movement across classes, or family members being of a different class (5.7). Further, for these respondents, class is 'inscribed as part of an individual identity, albeit one which is fluid' (5.9). In other words, 'class is presented as part of agency rather than something handed down' (5.9):

> although there is considerable ambiguity about how people define themselves with respect to class, the sources of ambiguity [in 1990] are very different to those of 1948. In the earlier year, class is something which is un-stated, and correspondents do not like to talk about it. By 1990, they are happy to talk about it, in ways which emphasise their hybrid class identities, and which uses class as a set of external benchmarks around which they can announce their own individuality. (5.9)

Alongside these substantive arguments, Savage makes a case for the re-use of qualitative data to examine processes of historical and social change over time. Within re-use debates, there have been surprisingly 'few attempts to look at different qualitative studies at several time points to allow researchers to examine trends over time' (Savage, 2007a: 1.1). This is especially striking given that comparison at different time points drives much secondary analysis of quantitative data. Additionally, social and cultural historians 'of recent British history have also not shown much interest in how such data [from qualitative studies] can be used in their own studies' (1.1). This is particularly troubling, Savage observes, in light of the expansion of social science research in the postwar period and the subsequent proliferation of qualitative material on a multitude of aspects of social life. Moreover, historical accounts of social trends tend to rely heavily on quantitative data, which are seen as more reliable indicators of change than qualitative studies. It is thus widely held that 'social trends can be determined from abstract indicators' (such as numerical data) (2.2), and the 'absences which this data contain – about context, meaning, narrative – themselves become essential concomitant invisibilities around which abstract knowledge depends' (2.2). It is precisely in the messiness of qualitative data, its capacity to illuminate the texture and meaning of experience, that its strength as an historical source lies.

Savage calls for a more robust, historically-guided engagement with and re-use of *qualitative* social data, and this requires a different approach to reading data and attributing significance: 'Rather than providing abstract knowledge, they [qualitative data] can be read as relics revealing of the research process itself' (2.3). In reference to the vexed issue of context, Savage suggests that researchers take the lead from historians, attending less to the issue of re-use per se and more to *how* data are used, 'much in the same way that historians do when confronted with disparate sources' (2.3).

The above example of re-using archived qualitative data shows the potential of this strategy for examining historical change, and makes a compelling methodological case for using qualitative studies as sources for historical research. Qualitative sources allow for the excavation of ambiguities, and this is vital in identifying and understanding the nuances of change and for capturing it at the level of biographical and community experience. In this case, close attention to narratives from different generations showed that it is the 'form, rather than the content, of class talk which is important' (Savage, 2007a: 6.4).

Conclusion

Duration is a fundamental part of what makes revisiting studies so significant. As with ethnography and the benefits of extended time in the field, the lapse of time between the conduct of a study and returning to it gives clarity to its significance for re-analysis or follow-up. It sharpens what is distinctive, or common, or troubling and allows for sufficient distance for comparison, which in turn helps realize its benefits for historical research. Longitudinal research is also underpinned by temporal comparison – synchronic and diachronic – but the researcher often travels more closely alongside and in the time of the participant's journey. In follow-up studies there is typically a break in the research relationship, and more focus on the points of demarcation rather than on processes of change as they are happening, as is the case with longitudinal research. Comparison is also central to cross-generational research, but as with revisiting research, it is defined by temporal distance and contrasts.

In a period where there are greater calls and possibilities for archiving material, it is hard to know what kind of selective protocols should be in place or whether more democratic and inclusive strategies should prevail. Electronic communication threatened to destroy traditional paper-based archival collections. But the capacity to digitize vast amounts of records leads to other possibilities as well as to practical and philosophical challenges. Conventionally, the simple passage of time helped select what was archived: the importance of an event, a person, or its representativeness, or its ordinariness, became evident in the 'fullness of time'. Of course, there were and continue to be exclusions, and the politics of archiving and public memory have been discussed throughout this book. But the capacity and interest to archive ever more material poses new challenges. It calls for a speeding up of the time in which decisions about significance are made, and has consequences for how researchers gather, prepare and document their projects, with posterity and future audiences increasingly on their minds.

Revisiting research, in the form of either follow-up studies or re-analysis, dramatically captures the criss-crossing of past, present and future in research processes. Archiving takes from the present to preserve records for anticipated future audiences, and in doing so forecloses and allows some stories, some pasts, and not others. Re-analysis of previous studies underscores generational and historical change, and the temporality of conceptual and methodological moods and fashions. Follow-up studies similarly emphasize breaks and the power of duration to help re-frame research, to allow different themes to emerge in comparing the two periods of time, producing not only a follow-up study but also a different sense of the significance of the earlier study. Revisiting a study also represents a kind of intergenerational research in which contemporary researchers return to the studies of an earlier generation, or when follow-up studies chart generational shifts in their participants.

The strong interest in revisiting studies and the explosion of activity in archiving and re-analysis arises at a time when researchers are under pressure to maximize research benefits, and when there is the digital capacity and know-how to undertake some of these projects with greater ease than existed even 5 or 10 years ago. These orientations to research are also part of a cultural mood in which there is a heightened consciousness about generational change, a sense of an intensified break with a not-so-distant past, and risk and future uncertainty – ecological, geo-political, bio-medical – permeate everyday discussions. A 'collision of temporalities' (Harootunian, 2007: 474) is felt in mundane ways. Returning to, archiving and re-analysing qualitative projects amplifies the collision of temporalities in research methodologies, and underscores the role of the researcher as a kind of time traveller.

Summary points

- Revisiting studies include those where the researcher returns to an earlier study they conducted, or re-analyses a study originally conducted by someone else.

- In both cases, how the initial qualitative study is archived influences what is possible to say about it subsequently. Archiving preserves the present for the future (a future past) and constructs, forecloses and enables some stories rather than others.

- Digitization extends archiving possibilities, but the potential democratization of archives poses challenges for selection and significance and speeds up the time in which such judgements are to be made.

- Follow-up studies are valuable for showing contrasts and change at different points of time, rather than the change process.

- Re-use/re-analysis of qualitative projects and data can re-frame the initial study and represent a new or re-contextualized account of it.

- Context, ethics and consent are important aspects to re-analysis, but so too are intersubjective dimensions of the process, and the different experience of re-engaging with a project as either a secondary analyst or original researcher. This encompasses concerns of the original researcher about being exposed in unpredictable ways via secondary analysis, and of researchers adapting or censoring their projects in anticipation of an unknown future audience.

- The 'revisiting researcher' straddles different time zones and this affords distinctive opportunities for comparison and researching historical and generational change, including moves and fashions in social research methods.

- Re-analysis opens up a robust dialogue between sociological and historical methods, encourages the use of qualitative studies as sources for historical enquiry, takes lessons from historians' engagement with archives and re-creation of context, and promotes invigorated attention to the history of research methodologies in the social sciences.

Further resources

Ortner, S.B (2003) *New Jersey Dreaming: Capital, Culture and the Class of '58.* Durham, NC: Duke University Press.
A follow-up study in which the author, an anthropologist, tracks down her high school classmates and explores what they are doing as individuals and as a generation.

Heaton, J. (2004) *Reworking Qualitative Data.* London: Sage.
A useful guide and overview of terms, practices and debates involved in archiving, re-using and re-analysing qualitative research data.

Websites
Mass Observation Studies

www.massobs.org.uk/index.htm

Gives an overview and history of the studies, available collections, details on becoming an 'observer' and current directives and projects.

'Qualidata' Economic and Social Data Service (UK)

www.esds.ac.uk/qualidata/

Provides information and support for the archiving of qualitative data and access to a number of major social science archived data sets.

Films
Two film series that combine elements of both qualitative longitudinal and follow-up research.

7 Up, a series directed by Michael Apted, that began in the 1960s and follows a group of British children from diverse backgrounds, interviewing them every seven years: participants are now adults, aged 49 in the most recent film.

Smokes and Lollies (1975), *14's Good, 18's Better* (1980), *Bingo, Bridesmaids and Braces* (1988), *Not 14 Again* (1996). This is a series directed by Gillian Armstrong, beginning as a documentary of three 14-year-old South Australian girls. Follow-up films were made when the women were 18, 26 and 33.

8

Time, Emotions and Research Practice

In the previous chapters we have reviewed a series of methodologies that seek to make temporality explicit, not only the temporal flow of the lives and phenomena that are documented but also the temporal process of documentation itself. In this penultimate chapter we wanted to communicate some of the practical, embodied aspects of researching and generating 'data' as well as showing the ways in which interpreting that data and writing about it are practices that take place in specific places and times.

We faced the task of producing this chapter when working together on the final manuscript of the book in 2008. Rachel suggested that we consider a piece of unpublished writing on emotions in the research process that she had produced in 2004. In this example of 'secondary analysis' she returned to field notes and transcripts generated in a British secondary school in 1997 to revisit an incident 'remembered' as racist (Thomson, 2004). Working in Australian schools at the same time, Julie had also reflected on a troubling fieldwork encounter, and we also explore her account of this written in 2003. Together, these accounts capture the evolving, recursive, messy and even at times troubling dialogue between fieldwork, field notes and attempts to make sense of these 'in the moment' and 'on reflection' (Back, 2007; Law, 2004). That both Rachel and Julie identified a troubling research encounter – from among many experiences of fieldwork in their respective longitudinal studies – in which issues of racism were prominent is, we argue, more than a matter of idiosyncratic synchronicity.

The first account of fieldwork is explored in depth, involving a return to original data sources, and an explication of the different stages of responding to and making meaning from the research encounter. It includes samples of field notes written by Rachel immediately after the interview, her recollections of the episode, extended excerpts from the interview transcript, and several examples of 'secondary analysis', of revisiting the interview notes and transcripts, through the eyes of other colleagues, through conversations among Rachel and Julie and, for Rachel, with fresh eyes, afforded by distance and the lapse of time. The second example is briefer and offers a different style of response, one in which the various stages of struggling over meaning and of negotiating differences in interpretation over an extended period of time are synthesized, reflected upon to inform analysis, but not elaborated in detail. Consequently, some of the steps in the process may seem concealed, but they permeate the text, and the kind of interpretations that Julie and her co-researcher Lyn Yates eventually settled upon, writing in a particular time, place and genre. Together, these two examples from fieldwork provide an illustration of the coincidence of intellectual and methodological agendas that has been a recurrent motif in the book.

The chapter overall involves shifts in time, place and authorial voice: from the 'we' of 2008, to Rachel writing in 2004, and Julie writing in 2003, as well as voices captured in transcripts and field notes from the research that took place in parallel in Australia and England in 1997. Rather than transform the text through the passive voice into an abstract and extended present, or use a narrative gloss to erase the temporal gaps, we have preserved these 'jolts', making explicit the time travel that is part and parcel of the research and writing process. We ask our readers to bear with us as we take you through times and places to witness the research practice in process, giving glimpses of situated and embodied researchers at work.

London 2004 (reflecting on data collected in 1997)

When we are present in the data (as when we revisit an interview that we conducted ourselves), time is an unavoidable part of the interpretative process and with it memory. Where we have conducted fieldwork ourselves there is a living connection between the research encounter and the moment in which you revisit it – that connection is you. But as Natasha Mauthner and colleagues (1998) have discussed, the 'you' that conducts the analysis and the 'you' that was present in the interview may be very different – especially if a significant period of time has elapsed between. Within any research endeavour it is possible to trace different temporal narratives: *biographical time* (the speed at which life events unfold for researcher and researched), *research time* (the timetable of the research process) and *analytic time* (the longer and recursive project of thinking about and writing about data) (see Thomson and Holland, 2003).

Emotions may provide the link between these temporalities. A hermeneutic approach (that refuses the positivist separation of the subject from the object of knowledge) demands that we recognize that knowledge production *depends* on interpretation. Thus our route to knowledge of the social can be understood as mediated by our senses and our subjectivity. So we try to be aware that the 'perspective' that the analyst forges is informed, more or less consciously, by their own particular class and cultural location (Skeggs, 2004). As Walkerdine and colleagues observe, it is impossible to keep interpretations free from projections (Walkerdine et al., 2002: 190) and we can never fully disentangle the boundaries between. My concern with this kind of approach has always been that we give up on the possibility of knowing about the social and the world and settle instead for knowing about ourselves – a kind of solipsism (see too McLeod and Yates, 1997). But I am increasingly persuaded that these two projects are not mutually exclusive. In order to know about the world it is necessary and reasonable to use ourselves and our responses as a tool and a source of evidence.

Discomforts

Writing is an important part of the research process, and this is highly emotional, involving internal conversations about the relationship between the self and the Other. Writing collectively also involves complicated emotions between us as researchers. When I push myself to think about emotions in the research process I am drawn back to experiences of fieldwork, and research encounters that continue to discomfort me. This discussion is based on a journey that involved me going back to revisit fieldwork conducted in 1997, and a particular research encounter that troubled me, but which I have absorbed into my catalogue of 'things that I have learned about research': that things happen in groups and that control in research encounters is ethically, emotionally and morally fraught. Here I revisit the data from one of those groups, and introduce commentaries from the literature that I have found to be useful in making sense of what I found.

Going back

The instance that acted as a hook in my memory was a focus group conducted as part of a study of young people's moral landscapes, 'Youth values: identity, diversity and social change' (1996–9). The groups employed a game format, with participants reading out strong moral statements and discussing them (for more on the methodology see Thomson and Holland, 2004). The group discussed here was conducted in a white middle-class school. Three young people were present (less than had been expected), a boy and two girls, all in their 10th year of formal schooling. I was the group facilitator.

I remember the expression of racism that took place within the group, and feeling uncomfortable: concerned that I may have been complicit and wondering whether I had exploited the participants in some way. The unexplored memory had become a marker, of something – of some thinking that I needed to do. In their discussion of the theory and practice of memory-work, June Crawford and colleagues (whose work we discussed in Chapter 2) argue that we remember things for reasons: episodes that were problematic at the time and occasions when the responses of others were not congruent with our expectations (1992: 9). In retrieving the memories we are not working with the original events, but our own attempts to resolve these contradictions. Yet as researchers we have ways back into the encounter beyond (but including) the meaning making operations of memory. The simplest way is through the field notes that were used to capture the researcher's reflection on group dynamics. This field note would have been written immediately after the group and, as such, would capture contemporaneous feelings and interpretation provoked by the experience.

I have extracted only that part of the field note that relates to the discussion of the statement 'all white people are racist'. The three participants are identified as 1, 2 or 3 and the numbers along the continuum (a = agree, d = disagree) represent where these participants placed themselves in response to the statements.

Only white people can be racist:

agree 2——1—3———————————————————— disagree

1. Very blonde and blue eyed, long wavy hair in a tight bun, round featured, slight wc accent. Feminine looking. Very strong viewed and forward, leading on most questions, loud voice.
2. Tomboy looking. Mid length layered straight light brown hair. Slim, not traditionally 'pretty'. Strong viewed and 'macho' yet also lack of confidence. Rarely made eye contact, looked down a lot, mumbled and got giggly, especially around racism where she 'dared' to use the word 'Paki' then looked at friends each time and said 'don't make me laugh' at which point both would start laughing.
3. Dark haired blue eyed boy. Lots of spots, relatively tall. Quiet and dominated by the girls, but very different in his views. Where they were racist he was not, etc. When it came to discussion he would let them dominate but would contribute as invited. The girls did not give him any space, this had to come from the facilitator.

Other issues: Small group. The missing contingent were all yr 10 boys. Seating made things a little tricky. Sitting with back to clock and too close to 1 for comfort. Dynamics between 1 and 2 dominated the session. 3 was on side lines but seemed to enjoy himself. 1 and 2 were presenting themselves as 'bad girls' although 2 seemed to be taking most of the risks for 1. Small size was also good in allowing in-depth discussion. A range of non-pc views were expressed in this group in a way that they would not have been I felt in a larger group where 1 and 2 may not have been the most powerful people in the room. The discussion of racism was strange for me as torn between challenging their views and allowing discussion. Felt that they were waiting for me to challenge them/tell them off – especially in relation to the use of the word 'Paki'. My instinct was not to judge – sticking to the ethos of the game of listening to a range of different views. A bit worried that I might be 'setting them up' by not challenging them. 3 obviously did not share their views although agreed that the 'Paki jokes are funny' joining in the laughter. Interesting in exposing the racism that was silent in the questionnaire – the racist jokes did not appear nor the racist sentiment.

Only white people are racist:

Put stickers down at wrong end in terms of discussion. Consensus of 1 and 2 was that black people can be racist too and that this is the same as white racism, and really not that bad because racism makes sense! Towards the end of the discussion started to shift in discussion of their own families and how racist 1 and 2's families are. They described the kind of things they say, the same verbatim as the girls had said, and how they try to challenge their parents without success. Prompts on black popular culture came to nothing. Stuff on jokes. Centrality of family to values on racism.

All really enjoyed it. 3 said that glad that it was a small group as he would otherwise not have talked. 1 really enjoyed talking about her views and 2 agreed with 1.

Personally: I began really disliking these girls. Even though most of the racism came from 2, I disliked 1 the most as so pushy. Then felt a bit guilty that I was setting them up, then saw them shifting around a discussion of their families. It would be interesting to see how these girls develop in future.

One thing that I hope this field note might do is to reinforce the value of contemporaneous notes, particularly where a project is extended or archived. It is also an example of the kind of details that can be included in field notes. The notes are organized under set headings, but include more than observations about what was said by the participants; they incorporate my emotional reactions and 'hunches' as to what was going on. What I find most striking here is my description of the group, which suggests serious antagonism, particularly towards one of the girls.

Some tools for thinking about emotion

Before going on to look at the transcript, I want to talk a little about the work of Valerie Walkerdine, Helen Lucey and June Melody (2001) to which I turned to help me make sense of the emotional content of this fragment of data. Reflecting on their own research practice, which is influenced by psychoanalytic ideas and the practice of group analysis, they suggest that 'in order to examine other people's unconscious processes you must be willing and able to engage with your own' (Walkerdine et al., 2001: 85). The researcher herself is the primary instrument of this kind of enquiry, yet it is only through re-listening to interviews and sharing them with others that the 'layered nature of the encounter' becomes visible (p. 93). In their view researchers tend to 'hear what they expect to hear or feel comfortable with and screen out the rest'. They argue that a commitment to become aware of the emotional dynamics of research encounters requires a 'willingness to engage (way beyond the point of "comfort")' in what are sometimes very difficult emotions' (p. 107).

The following extract outlines the process that Walkerdine and colleagues employed in their longitudinal study 'Growing Up Girl' in order to disentangle researcher subjectivity from their interpretations of the motives and meanings of the young women whose lives they were documenting:

At the first level, common to much qualitative analysis we looked at the face value of the subjects' 'story'; one containing events, characters and subplots. The second level of analysis moved towards an initial exploration of the unconscious processes at play by paying attention to words, images and metaphors. ... Here we looked at the interview alongside the researcher's recorded emotional responses to the interview. ... [In] the third level of analysis ... we reflected as a team on our individual responses to and interpretations of cases in an effort to shed light on unconscious to unconscious communication. Integral to this level of our analysis was the working premise that our experience of the intra-psychic dynamic could tell us something important about this person's relationship to the social world. Crucially we went beyond what the researcher herself recorded. This was neither a simple or technical matter, or confession or self revelation, but required a willingness to consider sometimes extremely difficult feelings and experiences that were heavily defended against at the level of the unconscious – feelings that were unwanted, denied and/or felt to belong to others. (Lucey et al., 2003: 282)

I find this work challenging but also inviting and useful. I am not entirely comfortable with the psychoanalytic paradigm that it brings with it, yet many of the comments resonate for me. I agree that researchers are instruments of enquiry. I agree that we connect with participants through common elements of experience – the more varied these are, the richer the connection. I also agree that some of the connections and traffic are unconscious and that our feelings for our interviewees may be the manifestation of this process. What we like/dislike about them is linked to our own biography. And finally, I agree that data needs to be interrogated again and again at different levels and over time. The work of Walkerdine, Lucey and Melody is uncompromising on the limits of the individual analyst. They argue that the group has a unique role in naming interpretations that would be too uncomfortable for the individual to perceive. This is the very stuff of collective scholarship and helps me understand why such collectives are themselves such emotionally dynamic experiences that play a unique role in forging insights and interpretations that go beyond what is possible in individual scholarship.

When I returned to look at this field note I was embarrassed by the obviousness of what Lucey and colleagues call 'the unconscious processes at play'. My negative feelings about the young women are clear, as are my protective feelings towards the young man. There are hints of jealousy in my description of their relationship and concern to distance myself from the one in particular. When I take the risk of thinking about our points of contact I become aware that of all the schools in which we conducted the research, this school is closest to my own experience. It is a predominantly white school, in a semi-rural middle-class area. These are working-class girls who know that they don't quite fit in, and I know this too. Their racism can be understood as an expression of their exclusion from the middle-class liberal consensus that characterized all other focus group discussions at that school, yet which was starkly contradicted by the many racist jokes we collected via the questionnaires that also formed part of our methodology. My interpretation of these young women as performing racism as a way of 'showing off' and being 'bad girls' may be a defence against a better understanding, rooted in common experience. My ethical deliberations about whether I had exploited them may have protected me from less comfortable identifications and feelings.

In their discussion of emotions as analysed through memory-work, June Crawford and colleagues (1992) observe that emotional memories tend to be associated with moral judgements, as we seek to make sense of experiences in relation to the wider moral order and social relations that define acceptable and predictable behaviour. The fact that we remember at all suggests that the moral order may have been transgressed, and the work that we do on these memories seeks to bring our own constructions of self within an intelligible moral order. What is then at stake when we worry over the ethics of such an encounter?

In order to look a little more closely at this remembered research encounter I want to share a lengthy extract from the transcript. The extract includes the discussion prompted by the statement that 'all white people are racist'.

*3: Only white people can be racist.
OOOOO – LAUGHTER AND INDISTINCT COMMENTS
*2: No, black people are racist as well, they go 'f'kin whites' [in accent]
*1: Yea, but I'm not racist but, well, you do find Paki jokes funny and I'm sure Pakis tell jokes about you and I'm sure black people tell jokes about us, and they go like 'you .... bitch' [in accent/voice].
LAUGHTER AND INDISTINCT COMMENTS
2*: Oh, my God!
LAUGHTER AND INDISTINCT COMMENTS
*INT: Explain, come on explain more.
*1: Because when there is white people on a show – just white people – like, say, it was a soap opera and it was just white people – black people always phone up and say, it's not fair, they're racist, they don't have any black people (Yea) – white people never do that.
*2: Mmm yea they don't.
*3: They might not even notice that there's only white people on there – they – well, they always notice but they would deliberately do it.
*INT: Say that again.
*3: They might not deliberately not put black people on it – they might sort of accidentally –
*INT: Just not notice?
*3: Yea.
*1: I mean black people seem to take it in more than white people do. ...
*INT: What, they notice racism or they notice.
*1: They notice – they take it more offensive than white people do because – but the reason – I think the reason black people are against white people is because they used to be slaves, their ancestors were slaves – and I think that's what started it all off – the racism and things – and if that didn't happen I think we'd all get along with each other. And I think that black people and white people – I think they're equal but I think the black people are just as racist because, like when somebody's racist to them they can be even worse back (Yes 3) sometimes they'll do something really stupid to a white person because – sorry, a white person's

been racist to them then they'll get them back somehow.
*INT: Why do you think that black people are so sensitive then?
*3: 'Cos they've had it for so long.
*1: Yes, because white people and black people have been enemies for so long that they just think it's the right thing to do to be enemies with us but like some black people they want to be friends with everybody – they want to be equal, they want to be known as equal person but some people white people ...
*3: They won't allow it.
*1: They don't want to know black people but sometimes white people actually hang around with black people and sometimes they try and actually be like them, try and get in with their culture and stuff because they just want to know what a black person's like.
*INT: What do you think of that?
*1: Well, sometimes I think that black people should stick with black people and white people should stick with white people, but that's just my opinion – and – but my step-dad, he's really racist and he doesn't like black people at all but umm, I shouldn't be saying this.
*INT: No, no, no, it's interesting. When you say that they should stick with each other – why – why is that? – because it's easier or –
*1: I don't know because it's easier then there won't be so much racism. If black people stuck to their country and stuck to their culture and stuff and white people stuck to their country and their culture there might not be as much racism because they'd be in a country of their own, the white people would be in a country of their own –
*INT: So there's no use trying to mix people together – that leads to trouble?
*3: Yea, but then they would lose all their houses and homes and things.
*2: The thing is the whites started it really – they brought them over.
*1: Yea.
*2: I don't know how the Pakis came over but ...
LAUGHTER
*2: But they are funny the Paki jokes though.
*INT: So when you are talking about black people you are mostly talking about people from the Caribbean – something like that – from Jamaica and from Africa, yea – but when you're talking about Pakis you're talking about people from Pakistan, India, whatever – so people who are Asian. Do you think there's a big difference between the different groups? I mean would you class all black people as black?
*1: I think that white people have got more against Pakis than they have against –
*3: Black people.
*INT: Why?
*3: There's more jokes about them.
*INT: So why are there more jokes? What's ...
*3: I don't know ...
*INT: I am asking about jokes because we asked in the questionnaire for jokes – you can't remember 'cos you didn't do it – was about jokes and we got lots, like you say, 'Paki jokes'. We got loads and loads and loads from all over the country and ... interesting – you know, why are there these jokes and why are they about a certain group of people? What do you think?
INDISTINCT COMMENTS

*2: They probably do say things about white people as well but the white people think Paki jokes and the Paki people think white jokes – it's just the way it is really and 'cos how many white people are there in Pakistan and India, I reckon there aren't really all that many. But here, they're in all the corner shops and the petrol stations – [3 laughs]. Well, people don't like that – some people don't like that so the Paki jokes start and some people find them funny – like I've got to admit I do (laughs) sometimes find them funny. I didn't used to though, now there's more and more of them about you do find them funny.

*3: You get used to it.

*2: You don't mean to hurt the Pakis or anything –

*1: But –

*INT: What about Asian people who are liked, there are Asian people at this school aren't there?

*3: Yea.

*INT: What do they think of them?

*1: Can I just say something. If we went over to Africa or something they'd be annoyed – they'd think, what are they doing in our country? – they just don't fit into our country – that's exactly what we do to them but they don't like it and – because we say to them, what are you doing over here? – you have to go back to Africa – and stuff like that – that's not actually what I say but some people who are so racist say, oh, go back to your own country, you don't deserve to be here – that's definitely what black people would do to us. If we went to Africa and we was a white person they'd think, they don't fit in. But like there is quite a lot of people who are white and live in Africa but some of the black people there don't like it at all and some of the white people over here don't like Pakis owning petrol stations and corner shops and things.

*INT: You said something about religion, when we were asking about why is it do you think people from Pakistan get the – really they're the group that get most attacked ...

*3: It's 'cos they have different ways to the Christian people and they believe in totally different things and ...

*INT: So it's their differentness?

*3: Yea.

*INT: Whereas what, people from the Caribbean, there's more shared culture.

*3: Yea.

*2: There's all sorts of different Christians though – there's like orthodox Christians, then there is Catholic people.

*INT: Yea. But I mean, for instance, like would you perhaps think the same things about the Caribbean culture? I mean 'cos it seems in some ways that the Caribbean culture's got quite a lot of people look up to it in terms of music, it is seen to be quite cool.

*3: Yea.

*1: Yea, I think that the reason that we're all against black people is because of the way they talk and what sort of music they have – it's completely different to us and it's just that the way they are – in Pakistan they're Muslims and things and they've got a different religion and I think that's what people see – it's like ... their religion or their kind of music or the way they talk and like some people find it funny when a black person will talk to you how[?] they talk – it's much different – and they'll laugh at them and they'll say, why do you talk like that? Because they'll be different to you because they – say, they've just come down here for a holiday or something and they start talking in English but they are actually South African – people do like say to them, why do you talk like that? But the way we talk is probably weird to them too and –

*INT: Is it? I mean do you think it's good, take the example of a school like this – is it difficult to be different? If you're different than the majority is that something that's actually –

*3: Yea.

*2: There are very few like black people or Paki, oh, sorry – Indian people here.

*INT: Say, use your own words.

*2: Pakis we call them [laughs] but it doesn't sound very nice though does it.

*INT: No, it doesn't.

*1: It just sounds awful.

*2: But that's what we're used to saying.

*INT: That's fine, it's, well we are talking about values.

*2: They might say white people or something, or coconuts ...

*1: Or slave drivers or something – some black people will call us slave drivers or something or they'll call us polo mints.

*INT: But I mean it's interesting how you use the word Paki, so you'd only use that obviously amongst white friends so is there no sort of official way that people talk about differences so that you don't – do you know what I mean? – there's no way that you would talk to somebody who was Indian or Asian (No. 3) about their Indianness or their Asianness – is that just not spoken about?

INDISTINCT COMMENTS

*1: I wouldn't talk to them like that.

*2: I'll talk to them about their culture.

*1: Yea, you wouldn't say that to their face – I mean you think it's funny to your friends but you think – when you see them you think, well, maybe it's not that nice and you try and be friends with them but sometimes they – and they say, no, we don't like white people, we don't hang around with white – we don't like, we don't want you to be near us.

[...]

*INT: No, so some differences you can see visually and some you can't but, you know, for instance, there may be lots of differences actually between people in terms of their religious background or the cultures they come from or, you know –

*2: Some black people are English and have English cultures and things and some Pakis are English and have English cultures and things.

*INT: and some white people are not English (Yea) and will have a very different cultural background.

*1: It's just that I think that the racism between black people, Paki people and white people is exactly the same –

[End of Audio Tape Side A/Start Side B]

[...]

*INT: But I mean is that about how we react to differences, isn't it? – 'cos I mean in one way you could react to difference is to say, 'that's really

cool' and everyone wants to be that person's friend 'cos they're different and (Yea) whatever – that's one way – and the other way is not liking, being scared of, or, you know, thinking they're funny 'cos they're
different. I'm just wondering why is it that it always goes that way rather
than the other way that, you know, somebody is seen to be interesting
'cos they're different? That doesn't happen, does it?
*1: No, I don't know why.
*2: It's really what kind of person they are.
*INT: Right, so if they've got a strong personality or something ...
INDISTINCT COMMENT
*3: Yea, if they're quiet then you tend to take the mick out of them and
stuff but –
*2: If they are like a Paki down the corner shop in your road and they're
like saying, well, you, get out of here, I don't like the look of you, or, don't
touch that – 'cos you're white – not because you're white, just because
you're ...
*INT: Going to nick something?
LAUGHTER AND INDISTINCT COMMENTS
*2: Yea, or not 'cos you are going to nick something, but because you've
been standing in the shop for a while choosing something, or you're acting suspiciously they just go, hey, you, get out – and then you're like, oh,
Pakis are all like that then, aren't they? Oh – let's go get more Paki jokes.
LAUGHTER AND INDISTINCT COMMENTS
*1: Sometimes you stand in the corner shop and they'll tell you to get out
and you'll say to them, shut up, you Paki. Look at you, you're the colour
of – poo
*INT: And what will they say?
*1: And they'll turn round and say to you, and they'll find it so offensive
that they'll ban you from the shop for the rest of your life. And you say, oh,
you're a Paki, shut up, you Paki, or something like that 'cos they find it
really offensive.
*3: Shut up and eat crisps or something.
*1: Or they say, shut up you pigeons – 'cos that's what they call us some-
times – you'd just laugh at them, wouldn't you? You'd just say, fine ...

[...]

*INT: This is very interesting, you've got your lunch now, haven't you?
*2: Break.
*INT: Oh, sorry – break ... feels like it. Can I just ask you one quick question
before. ... One of the things that's interesting in what you're saying is I
think probably a lot of the people, if they were being honest, would, you
know, say what you're saying but would you also say that – if someone
asked you were you racist what would you say?
*3: I'd say no.
*1: I'd probably say half and half.
*INT: You'd say?
*3: No, probably – but I do find the jokes funny though but I don't think
I'm racist.
*1: What would you say?
*2: I'd say no. I'm not actually racist – I wouldn't go up to a black person
and say, Oh, get away from me you nigger.
*1: Yea, no I wouldn't say, oh, go away, you nigger. I'd say to them,
oh – I'd say to them, if they were like really friendly I'd be friends with

them, there's nothing wrong with being friends with a black person, but there's always a problem with boyfriends and girlfriends being – one being black and one being white – there's always problems between family because the white family might have something against black people and the black people will think well why's he going out with a white person – 'cos normally black people would want a black person to go out with a black person, not a white families – they wouldn't expect you to go for someone who's a different colour to you.

INDISTINCT COMMENTS

*2: My family wouldn't really mind that much 'cos they are not really English.

*1: My family would because my family –

*INT: Say if there were two different cultures together they wouldn't mind. But would they mind if it was someone[?] from Pakistan?

INDISTINCT COMMENTS AND LAUGHTER

*2: Hmm, I don't know really!

*1: Her face!

*2: ... Pakis as well.

*1: My family, the whole of my family has something against black people, and Pakis because they just don't like them.

*INT: ... your family?

*3: My family – my parents wouldn't really mind, I don't think, but my grandparents would feel ashamed maybe.

*INT: Right, so like it's the generation.

*3: Yea.

*INT: Do you think it's changing? Do you think young people are less racist than old people?

*3: Yea, I think so actually 'cos they're getting more used to it.

*INT: What – more used to it being a mixed culture?

*3: Yea.

*2: My grandad is like old, and he calls them like chocolate drops and that and I tell him 'don't call them that' – like that. I don't, I just call them black – I wouldn't call them Paki or anything.

*1: Yea, I'd say to my step-dad, well, you shouldn't really say things like that – and he'll go, why? – they're niggers – what are they doing in this country? And I'll say, yea, well, you don't like it when they say it to us – and like he'll start on me and he'll say, yea, well, you're not supposed to stick up for them, you're supposed to – and he'll say to me like, they're black, you're not supposed to like hang round them and stuff – like with my dad, my dad's not like that but this is my step-dad – my mum, she's not too keen on black people ...

*INT: So it's quite difficult, isn't it? You're all in different worlds basically (Yea) – you've got your parents, you've got your school, you've got your friends. We're going to have to stop now but thank you loads. [...]

This is a long extract, much longer than we use when we are writing up research. For the purposes of this book and space constraints, we have deleted some small sections from the transcript – indicated by [...] – but even that proved difficult as it involved isolating sections which could be regarded as 'less important' than others, and even that relatively simple task is already an act of interpretation. Further, we wanted to show

how meanings from transcripts are not easily located in single phrases or responses, and that the flow, sequence and even awkwardness of an interview need to be considered. The entire extract is itself a fragment of the overall focus group discussion (which in reality should be understood as a single document) but also in terms of the research encounter and what it means for us to enter and intervene in these young people's worlds in this way.

When I look at this material now I am aware of the strangeness of the intervention. If we focus our analytic attention on the researcher we can see my role in attempting to forge the language and structure of the discourse, and the part that the group participants play in negotiating this. The group begins with their pleasure at the transgression effected by using racist language, 'Oh my God', and my clear response that this language is OK, 'explain more' I say. But of course it is not an acceptable way for students and an adult to talk in school, and I intervene to introduce new language:

*INT: So when you are talking about black people you are mostly talking about people from the Caribbean – something like that – from Jamaica and from Africa, yea – but when you're talking about Pakis you're talking about people from Pakistan, India, whatever – so people who are Asian. Do you think there's a big difference between the different groups? I mean would you class all black people as black?

In a pedagogic mode I go further to interrogate the logic of their argument, challenging the idea that there is 'equivalence' between the racism of the oppressed and the oppressor. Having put up a serious fight, the girls submit:

*2: There are very few like black people or Paki, oh, sorry – Indian people here:
*INT: Say, use your own words.
*2: Pakis we call them [laughs] but it doesn't sound very nice though does it?
*INT: No, it doesn't.
*1: It just sounds awful.

Negotiations continue, the young people's own ethnicity is brought explicitly into the discussions (one is Greek, the other two Anglo-British), positions are reasserted. On looking at the material again I was drawn to a particular moment in the proceedings when one of the young women asks, via the assumed voice of an imagined black person:

With black people, the black person that you're bullying, they'd say to you, why are you bullying me? I'm black – look, I'm the same colour as you.

And I wonder if I was bullying them, and if so, why? Could it be my discomfort about bullying rather than ethical doubts over inciting a racist discourse that makes me remember this group, that means it continues to have a hold on me? The final positioning is a clear victory. The young women disown their racism, blame it instead on their families from whom they then dissociate themselves.

My memory of this group is that something *happened* during the group process. I remembered it in terms of the girls' bravado and my own feelings of both not being and being too much in control. I also remembered it as a group in which there was some movement and that by the end of the session the young women had found a resolution. When I went back to the data these memories were reinforced by what I found. It was not until I opened the process up to others that the more difficult picture emerged.

I am lucky to work with Helen Lucey and talked the case over with her on a car journey to Milton Keynes (where we both worked at the Open University). Helen asked me what was so frightening about the girls expressing racism. Why couldn't I let them? She also asked me to think about who the resolution was for. On one hand, it is possible to see my intervention as promoting a lesson in cultural capital. I explain:

*INT: So it's quite difficult, isn't it? You're all in different worlds basically (Yea) – you've got your parents, you've got your school, you've got your friends.

The message being that although I have invited them to bring the discourse of home and peer culture into the research encounter, in doing so they have made a mistake. Why I felt compelled to intervene so actively is something that will take more interpretative labour to understand.

These themes are taken up by the British scholar Les Back in an article entitled 'Politics, Research and Understanding' (2002, 2004). In this article Back explores his own motives for and feelings produced by undertaking research with racists. Unlike the work of Lucey and colleagues, which maintains a focus on emotion and on the defended researcher self, Back's commentary gravitates towards the ethical and political. He observes that the journey from his south London past to his metropolitan present has involved the shedding of cultural layers that would enable a point of contact between him and his research subjects. He also worries that he is not entirely in control of the experience of researching these people whose views he finds repugnant yet which he must comprehend. Back's resolution is erudite and elegant. Drawing on George Marcus' work on ethnography, he exposes our assumptions about the nature of the relationship between researcher and researched by questioning whether we really want a dialogic relationship with racists. He draws on the philosophy of Levinas and Taylor, the anthropology of Clifford Geertz and the essays of Primo Levi to suggest that moral *complicity* need not be a feature of understanding.

Back (2004) describes his project as a search for an 'ethics of interpretation'. For him, the only way in which an ethnographer can generate the 'reflexive interpretative reading that arises within the space between what is familiar and what is alien' (p. 266) is to learn through the instrument that is ourself. His argument is constructed in response to a politics of research ethics that is dominated by the duty to empower the research subject and a desire to eradicate difference by 'matching' researcher and researched on criteria of ethnicity, gender and so forth. Instead, what (following Ruth Frankenberg) Back calls 'inevitable betrayal' must be accepted as part of the research relationship and the human condition. For Back:

the task of reflexive interpretative analysis is to establish the plausibility of each account, while remaining attentive to the discursive and rhetorical moves utilized to both enunciate and legitimate a particular view of the world. Critical insight was produced where common ground was established, or equally in moments when our respective worldviews came into direct confrontation. (2004: 269)

I have found Les Back's writing useful in that he not only acknowledges the shameful feelings and punitive political discourse that are associated with expressions of racism, but he also points towards ways in which an excavation of and engagement with personal feelings may contribute to understanding. Looking at the researcher self is not simply a form of reflexive lip service, nor is it autobiographical indulgence; it is evidence – the manifestation of the space between what is familiar and what we are seeking to know. His approach encourages me to return to data such as those that I have shared here and to find connections and ruptures in the pursuit of understanding. If we add to this the contribution of Lucey and colleagues that the boundaries between the self and the Other are not as clear as we might want them to be, it may be possible to take a further step towards understanding without being paralysed by the powerful feelings that police such borders.

The writing present: 2008

Returning to the 'writing present', to the time of writing this chapter, a range of different themes struck us as prominent in the transcript, giving rise to new interpretations. The reader will no doubt have been drawn in by the data extract and as a result have your own ideas about what was going on then and ways of making sense of it in the here and now. Rachel worked with this example from her fieldwork as a jumping-off point to consider the work of emotions in research. However, there are many ways of thinking about the data given that it is revealed in a relatively unmediated way. In the process of preparing this manuscript we shared it with several people, one of whom, Mary Jane Kehily, provided us with a number of insights into this data fragment in the context of the wider themes of the book. She alerted us to the coincidence of temporal frames captured in the transcript: the political climate that makes a study of youth values meaningful and fundable; the 'special' time constituted by the focus group that is both within but partially exempt from the institutionalized timetable and codes of conduct of the formal school; and the biographical episode that is 'youth' in which 'acting out' becomes a medium for improvising and testing the limits and contradictions of identifications with family, peers and forms of authority. Mary Jane also observed the extent to which the focus group method produced an abstract and binary discourse of race, which the participants occasionally broke through with expressions of their own experience – moments often marked by laughter. A good example of this can be found in the mention of the corner shop, a space in which they feel that they are viewed as potential thieves. Here, for a brief moment, we can glimpse the context for their investment and pleasure in forms of resistance that are also racist.

Mary Jane also commented on the unease of the interviewer, who moves between pedagogic, liberal listener and ethical researcher roles: seeking both to 'know' whilst not liking what is said.

We have resisted the urge to rework the presentation of this data extract in line with Mary Jane's insights. Instead, we offer her interpretations as an example of the way in which secondary analysis can work, with new perspectives allowed by distance, which reveal some things while occluding others. The time and place of doing the interview, of returning to analysis and iterative and cumulative attempts to construct meaning all matter. So too does the way in which fieldwork leaves a mark, and stays with you, emotionally and intellectually, even long after the research project is officially finished and its outcomes and findings documented. In this respect, fieldwork is dynamic and biographical and its visceral effects exceed the research time of the project. Similarly, the ethics of research practice, the ongoing engagement with 'data' and the fits and starts of building interpretations, are all central considerations for the reflexive methodologies we have been discussing. This attempt to reveal something of the research and writing process makes concrete the arguments we have been making about the spatial and temporal dimensions of research and interpretation.

Coincidence and cultural climate

But beyond these characterizations of the temporal and emotional aspects of the research process, we were struck by what at first appeared a rather uncanny coincidence, but which we now see as an example of how the political and cultural climate not only frames the kind of research we undertake but also the interpretations we make and the matters we find troubling. At much the same time that Rachel and her colleagues were conducting their research in schools in the UK, Julie and her colleague Lyn Yates were interviewing students in Australian schools for their longitudinal study (discussed in Chapter 4). They too had been deeply troubled by a series of interviews in which the topic was racism. Lyn and Julie subsequently wrote about the dilemmas and difficulties one incident in particular provoked and their attempt to draw methodological and substantive insight from that (McLeod and Yates, 2003, 2006).

These interviews were conducted in schools in 1997, and the choice of topic was partly prompted by the intense media and public discussions about race and national identity in Australia at that time. This was linked to the rise of a prominent leader of a small political party, Pauline Hanson, who vocally opposed immigration and special treatment of Aboriginal people. In terms of the longitudinal study, the questions about racism were tied into a set of related questions on political values, with the aim of gaining insight into both the cultural logic of racism in one national setting and the formation and make-up of young people's political values and social orientations. We turn to an excerpt from this discussion in order to show an example of another way in which an unsettling episode was defined and negotiated, and how the slow working through of this research encounter was felt through various attempts to write about it. The extract also shows the lingering impact of fieldwork and the repeated returning to episodes and conversation to understand their meaning. The extract below begins with a reflection from Lyn and Julie on their difficulties in researching racism and then shifts to an account of a particular interview exchange.

Melbourne 2003 (reflecting on data collected in 1997)

What is meant by being 'racist' is not necessarily clear or agreed upon, even though much discussion proceeds as if there were taken-for-granted criteria for determining racism. This was also the case in our interviews in that neither we, nor the students, really explained what we, or they, meant by the term 'racism'. On the one hand, a shared commonsense understanding was presumed, but, on the other, students were explicitly concerned with trying to work out the protocols and form of race discourses and when they were or were not being racist. These were ongoing tensions for us as well, in terms of how we formulated and posed questions about racism, analysed responses and wrote about young people's discourses of race and racism.

Like the students we talk about, we struggle with protocols and problems of how to talk about and write about this: what is proper, what is at issue, what is not appropriate to say? In this project, we two researchers have done all the interviews together, and have spent a lot of time together discussing what we are doing and trying to 'make sense' of it. Our process in writing is normally to begin with a discussion, then one of us will do an initial draft, followed by exchange to the other who will comment and do a second draft, and this continues, sometimes including further meetings and discussions. But no aspect of writing about the project has proved more difficult for us than attempting to write about race, racism and the issues we discuss in this chapter. An attempt to write an article on this continued for over three years before it was produced, and included long periods when we avoided even trying to talk about it. The topic seemed to produce for us much deeper tension than intellectual disagreements about which theorists and recent writings could help make sense of. To take one example … one of us used the phrase 'the etiquette of racial discourse'. To the other, this phrase was viscerally shocking in what seemed to be its depoliticization of the topic. Yet it also captured something of what seemed relevant about the particular perspective available on this topic from the type of interview-based study we had conducted. The phrase had been intended to convey the intense anxiety and uncertainty the participants expressed in trying to work out what was the right way to speak about racism; what language was available, what was it possible to say in this historical period and political climate? This was also a concern being played out in media commentary, amidst the explosion of debate about race, identity and nation. Our guilt and our own desire to say the right thing, our ability to avoid the issue if we wanted to, or to make the easy cosmopolitan judgements about racism in others, at the same time as knowing how much we too could be judged wanting, is similar to the tensions we analyse in those others. …

Researching racism and constructing the other

… A different kind of response to racial discourses in Australia was offered by a student from Suburban High, Talik, who was born in Australia, has Arabic parents and is identified as 'ethnic' by physical appearance and accent. He attends weekend school to study his family culture and language, he mixes socially and at school with kids from the same background. In interviews, he is often reticent, and sometimes awkward with our style of questioning, but he keeps coming voluntarily to all the interviews, even those conducted after he finishes school. Throughout the interview he positions himself as someone who comments on racism, rather than someone who has experienced racism.

> Int: What are your views about her [Pauline Hanson] and the debate that she's generating?
> Talik: I don't like it.
> Int: Have you talked about it much with your friends? Does it come up at home and
>   do you talk about it at home?
> Talik: At home? It has come up a couple of times at home. Um, not with friends.
> Int: Do you think there is much racism in Australia?
> Talik: Um, besides Pauline Hanson, no.
> Int: You think not?
> Talik: No. (Talik, Suburban High, Year 10)

One possible explanation for Talik's reluctance to say more and his description of there not being much racism in Australia is that it locates him less as an outsider. Or it might be that Talik is simply conforming to rules of polite behaviour both in his own family and in mainstream schools: he is avoiding making us feel uncomfortable by not insisting on racism being associated with those of Anglo background.

But Talik's responses also raise methodological issues about the effect of asking questions in particular ways, and of unintentionally inciting and producing certain responses. In retrospect, and in listening to and reading the interview transcripts, it was clear that our mode of questioning made it difficult for Talik to respond in other ways. (Here too we need to acknowledge the accumulated history and effects of our interviews over the preceding four years, where two white women came twice a year to conduct social science research interviews with him at school. In these interviews Talik is polite and cooperative but also a little uncertain as to what we actually want and what kind of responses he should be giving.) His responses to our questions in this interview are noticeably briefer than usual, often a couple of words, and he appears uncomfortable, pausing in responses, laughing nervously, looking away from us, and he is obviously relieved when the questioning stops. During the interview we too felt awkward, and unsure of how to manage the silences and uneasiness. We could see that he was uncomfortable but ending the interview early did not seem the right thing to do either, as that too could be another form of silencing.

In retrospect it is evident that we asked questions about Pauline Hanson and migration as if he were an expert on the experience of racism (an Other) and he responded in a way that showed his mastery of polite and proper discourse about racism when speaking with white women in a relatively formal setting. It is possible as well that his responses reflected a sense of (or desire for) national belonging as an Australian. He does not take up the position of 'discriminated-against Other' who might tell us as researchers some truth about racism. This was the position our line of questioning, unconsciously perhaps, wanted him to speak from. We did not regularly ask other students if they spoke about Pauline Hanson and One Nation at home, but by posing this question to Talik ('the ethnic family must have encountered racism, tell us all about it') we betrayed our own desire for him to speak as, and be positioned as, the Other. In his answers too there was another kind of second-guessing of our desire to hear certain answers (that multi-culturalism works? that Australia is a tolerant society?) and to not offend us as white Australians. So the dynamics of the research interview simultaneously produced a form of official multi-cultural discourse and an Othering of the research participant; and also revealed some of Talik's reasoning about the context-specific and appropriate way to respond to questions to racism and some of our own complicity in discursive constructions of the Other … (McLeod and Yates, 2006: 154–6).

Writing present: 2008

We want to conclude this chapter with some final reflections on temporality and emotions in the research process, drawing on the insights generated for us in returning to these examples from our respective fieldwork. The methodologies we have discussed throughout this book can be distinguished from most other social science methods by the way in which they are explicitly temporalized. Many qualitative research techniques take snatches of data and abstract them – from the times which the researcher and researched inhabit, from the time of the research, of analysis, of returning to and building interpretations. It thus becomes possible to study an interview in terms of discourse, subject position, rhetorical moves and so forth. It also becomes possible to establish a relationship between the particular (be it a phrase, an object, an image) and the structural and abstract. One of the things that makes this kind of abstraction possible is the distancing of a relationship between the researcher and the researched. We can contain what we know, which in turn facilitates focus and a form of objectification. This move, as we have suggested throughout, is much more difficult in the kind of methodologies we have been reviewing in this book.

In qualitative longitudinal and ethnographic research, for example, there is an unbroken temporal relationship between the present tense of fieldwork and the kinds of dynamics and transactions that are captured in a transcript, and then the more recursive temporality that is a feature of attempts at interpretation and analysis. Thus the field note is the first stage of such recursivity as the researcher self who has returned to the office is able to attempt to make sense of the experience in the school that afternoon. Over time, we return again and again to the same data, each time with the benefit of more hindsight and the new resources of a changing present. It is important to keep going back to data, in its rawest forms, as the past can easily become a fantasy supporting a particular present. In many cases we forge a working narrative and move on. In methodologies that involve repeated field work over a period of time, such as longitudinal, follow-up or intergenerational studies, we more often find ourselves revisiting data with new eyes. And in some cases memory pulls us back, those troublesome examples that we just cannot shake, which keep popping up to remind us that we need to look again. As researchers we are lucky that we can do this – that is, of course if we keep good records. We can take our lead here from memory-work. The episodes are remembered since they remain significant and the engagement with the past in the present represents a continuing search for intelligibility:

> one's self engages with one's memories, has a conversation with them, responds to them, as another responds to oneself. The 'I' reflects back on the 'me' and together they constitute the self. Memories contain the traces of the continuing process of appropriation of the social and the becoming, the constructing, of self. (Crawford et al., 1992: 39)

Emotional resonances

Addressing emotions in the research process does not signal a retreat from the materiality of historical and social contexts. On the contrary, historical and emotional dimensions of research are intermeshed, in the sense of the biographical history of the researcher and the cultural setting in which some topics, rather than others, are likely to have emotional resonance. This encompasses what is noticed, or not, in fieldwork, and what strikes a chord or unsettles a researcher, as we found in the two examples discussed above. In another historical period, perhaps even only two decades ago, as researchers we might have been particularly aware of or more sensitized to gender dynamics and gender marginalization, and consequently we might have more vividly remembered fieldwork incidents that pertained to gender, or perhaps to sexuality, and in the 1950s and 1960s we might have been more attuned to class inequality. But, in the late 1990s, the touchstone of a methodologically troubling incident for both of us, researching in different parts of the world – although with some shared history (!) – was racism. This was a time when not only national and global politics but also academic theory and social and educational policy were rhetorically attuned to racism and race/ethnic-based differences. Of course, this is not to say that these matters were being or have been addressed adequately, but there was nevertheless a discursive intensity and political immediacy to discussions about race and racism at that time. The point here is that our emotional response to the difficulties of researching racism arises at a political and historical time when 'race' is on the political agenda and when feminist social scientists, such as ourselves, are also attuned to the exclusions, omissions and devastating silences of our disciplines and politics in this regard, and the lived advantages and normalization of our own white privilege. That racism was the touchstone issue for both of us is a coincidence, but one that registers the cultural mood in which we write and research.

Emotions contribute to the historical record and the ways in which we narrate processes of continuity and change. Feelings are not timeless responses, but are generated in particular times and places. It is in this sense also that we have been arguing for a thoroughly temporalized, situated approach to methodologies for researching social change.

Conclusion

> *Time expresses the nature of what subjects are ... being is made visible in its temporal character. (John Urry, 1996: 372)*

> *Making the social world hold still for its portrait can seem like gross violence, reducing its mutable flow to frozen moments preserved in the hoarfrost of realist description. (Les Back, 2007: 17)*

We write this book at a moment in which *change* has become a highly charged social and political category, emphasized in social theory (Heaphy, 2007), policy (Corden and Millar, 2007) and, increasingly, methodology (Edwards, 2008). It has been argued that contemporary times are characterized by acceleration, projection into the future (Adam, 2003) and a radical re-imagining of the temporal order that disrupts the presumed linearity of past–present–future (Harootunian, 2007). The same technologies that have enabled the emergence of risk management, futurology and anticipatory marketing (if-you-liked-that-you-might-like-this) have also provided us with ways of documenting the present, creating prospective archives that presume the value of 'data' to future generations. Yet this moment is also characterized by a nostalgia, a looking back at the studies, theories and intellectual communities of the past.

In this book we have indulged our desire to remember, to revisit earlier moments in the history of the social sciences in order to inform our present predicaments. Our selection reflects much about the contemporary moment and our personal communities of interpretation. Our journey has involved us passing through something akin to the three orders of nostalgia characterized by Fred Davis (1979) as firstly *simple* (producing a warm glow), secondly *reflexive* (provoking questions as to whether it really was that way) and thirdly *interpreted* – demanding an analysis of experience and an interrogation of why we feel this way. And although we do not feel that we have 'arrived', we certainly have a better idea of why we felt compelled to write this book, and an even stronger sense of the value of exploring temporality in social research methodologies.

Our approach has been to locate our chosen methods within wider intellectual histories, imagining the audiences to which they were oriented and the problems that they hoped to solve. This stands in some tension with traditional academic approaches in which research methods are seen to exist in isolation from people, times and places – posed within an abstract landscape, and judged in relation to philosophical criteria and contemporary values. Placing memory-work, oral history, qualitative longitudinal research, ethnography, generational research and revisiting studies within a 'timescape' involves attending to associated timeframes, tempos, synchronizations, sequences, extensions and the operations of past, present and future (Adam, 2004: 144). In this respect we have produced something that is rather different from the usual methods textbook, while at the same time attempting to provide an accessible understanding of the components and contributions of particular approaches to researching change.

Looking in two directions

In the Introduction (Chapter 1) we outlined four methodological motifs implicated in our theoretical orientation: historicizing methods, historicizing subjects, dynamic temporal relations, and an articulation of contingency and relatedness. Each of these motifs in some way seeks to escape the powerful binaries that structure a positivist model of social enquiry – between knowledge and the world; between subject and object; and between agency and structure. Yet, in reviewing our final manuscript, we became aware of another set of binaries that had grown up in their wake: distinctions between space and time; between diachronic and synchronic analysis; between *temps* and *durée* (or objective and subjective time); and between juxtaposition and linearity.

In these concluding words we do not attempt to resolve our particular iteration of this most basic and comforting analytic practice. Instead, we remind ourselves that while it may be hard to escape binaries, we can refuse to split them, recognizing that they are mutually constituting, with the expression of one aspect revealed in the concealment of the other. The binaries that we are left with at the end of this book are products of our desire to privilege the temporal, yet paradoxically they speak to the impossibility of isolating this project – demanding that we attend to both the spatiality of the temporal and the temporality of the spatial (Massey, 1994). Our approach has been to look both ways: employing linear accounts as well as juxtaposing approaches; capturing the sensuality of *durée*, yet locating it with an objective clock time; pointing to questions of synchronization as well as sequence; and understanding continuity and change as integral to each other.

Making temporality visible

Making temporality visible demands that we go against many elements of the genre of sociological writing. In selecting examples for this book we have struggled to find accounts of research design that make the temporal aspects of the process explicit. Questions of timing and synchronization tend to be glossed over when researchers report their methodologies, other than the reflexive accounts that gesture towards the juggling of academic and family timetables, or of the place of research within their wider biographies. Temporality is less visible in accounts of analysis, with styles of academic writing tending to occupy an extended present within which claims to generalization and validity appear to make sense. The messiness of real-life research continues to be marginalized within mainstream academic writing genres, so that we rarely see collisions between data collection and analysis, the provisional character of interpretation or the ways in which acts of reporting impose analytic closure. As we show in the previous chapter ('Time, Emotions and Research Practice'), in making temporality visible we expose other conventions of academic writing, including the personal voice and location of the author.

Making temporality visible also brings certain ethical dilemmas to the fore. In the case of projects conducted over time, such as qualitative longitudinal or follow-up fieldwork, ethical complexity is amplified due to the long-term engagement of the researcher, and the changing demands of consent, perspective and representation. Re-analysing data and working with archived projects poses distinctive ethical challenges for the secondary analyst regarding context and what it means to enter into someone else's intellectual project. This is in addition to questions of whether consent endures, or what it means for participants to give consent and whether that holds for archived projects and re-use of their 'data' some time later. Yet, in all the methodologies we have discussed, the close relation between researcher and researched, developed in and over time, carries with it particular ethical challenges for how we interpret, represent and write about 'informants'. Daily immersion in the ethnographic field site, evoking and listening to a life story told in the intensity of a single interview, or entering into the life and history of family dynamics through intergenerational interviews, creates intimacy and underscores the situated and embodied nature of research. The idea of a located researcher (whether or not one constituted in a continuous relationship with data) allows us to develop historically situated *and* mobile perspectives that change over time, between research projects and research teams.

Conversation and collaboration

Writing this book has been a collaborative exercise, and a challenging one given our locations on opposite sides of the planet. It has been made possible by email, study leave, cheap and dirty air travel, by a common mother tongue and shared cultural references. There have been key moments within the writing of the book when the authorial 'we' that we mostly use in our text has been a reality – when we have been able to sit, talk and walk together, checking out our understandings and interpretations. At other times we have worked more independently. Thinking about the disjunctions between these grammatical – and embodied – positions, and sharing them with others, has been a productive part of the final stages of writing and editing the manuscript.

Many of the studies that we have featured as exemplars in this book are also collaborations. In some cases these have brought people together across disciplines; in others it is the methods that are mobile, moving between traditions and academic communities. History, sociology, psychology, cultural and gender studies all feature as backdrops, yet are complicated by nation, giving us French family sociology, British cultural studies, American ethnography, Australian social psychology and Nordic gender studies. Location, moment and audience are important, and shape the relationship between academia and wider political processes.

Part of the nostalgia involved in writing this book has been to revisit times and places when researchers could take their time, do their own fieldwork, and when the lines between academic, intellectual, artist and activist were less clearly drawn than they seem today. The identity of the poet sociologist (ascribed to members of the group who established the Mass Observation archive) feels distant yet inspiring in an era when performance review and just-in-time delivery dominate academic cultures. We hope that we have enabled readers to see the part played by academic knowledge claims within socialist, feminist, queer and postcolonial political projects, helping us to recognize the ongoing potential of social research for making change as well as simply recording it.

The contemporary moment may be marked by a certain distance between academic knowledge-production and formal politics, yet it is also marked by a proximity with popular culture and commercial knowledge practices. This has been a cause for anxiety as reality television enacts populist psychological experiments in the name of entertainment (Woods and Skeggs, 2004), and as property searching websites outperform national statistics in linking a diverse range of data sets (Savage and Burrows, 2007). Savage and Burrows have characterized this joining-up of information sources as heralding a descriptive turn in social research. Yet the kind of descriptions that we produce is open to negotiation. As Les Back has argued, research can be imagined as a craft as well as a science, with 'sociological listening tied to the art of description' (Back, 2007: 21). This suggests a different kind of descriptive turn, one that privileges the evocation of understanding over explanation (or prediction), that is emotionally engaged and employs elegance as a criterion of validity.

Research as time travel ...

Thinking and writing about time is a humbling experience. It is easy to get out of your depth, and to find yourself lurching between profundity and banality. In order to grasp temporality we have tried to be specific, descriptive and reflexive, 'nurturing awareness of the possibilities and vulnerabilities implied in these simple words, am, are, is' (Farrell Krell, 1993: 35). A powerful metaphor for this kind of approach can be found in Heidegger's idea of the 'woodpath' (*holzwege*): ways that lead somewhere that cannot be predicted or controlled. At times we have experienced ourselves as wandering through a forest, attempting to follow 'the path, never the product', ensuring that 'the enquiry, just like its subject matter, is fundamentally and irreducibly temporal' (Adam, 2004: 58). Our interest in historicizing social research methods has included situating ourselves, both as qualitative researchers and as writers of this book. Our tendency to *describe ourselves describing methodologies* is, in part, an attempt to trace this route, making our path through the 'methodological woods' visible to others.

As researchers we engage in time travel, whether this be through our explorations of memory, contracting the 'fever' of the archive, or becoming entangled in the complexities of revisiting our own or other's data. The nature of social science practice demands that we think about the relationship between researchers, their methods and the resulting 'data', as well as the substance of what is recorded. We believe that the subjectivity of the researcher provides an important mechanism through which the temporal can be encountered and mediated. This need not mean indulging ourselves, or reducing the sociological record to intellectual biography. By accounting for the presence of the researcher we can begin to locate the data-generation process and restore contemporary relevance to material that might otherwise be seen as 'out of date'.

Throughout this book we have been arguing for greater attention to the timing and location of research methodologies. We have attempted to show the significance of studying temporal processes – in both the practice and the topics of research. Historical, biographical and generational time – the context and time in which we write, read, research and analyse – are inextricably and productively linked to the research methodologies we adopt and the kind of knowledge and understanding they make possible. In different ways, and in different chapters, we have shown some of the non-linear ways in which time collides and is experienced, apprehended and imagined in research practices. Methodologies oriented to the future may in practice produce hindsight as their analytic dividend. Methodologies which seem oriented to the past are as much about the present, and the past–present relation, and even infer the future in the sense of an anticipated time and audience for the research.

References

Adam, B. (2003) 'Reflexive modernization temporalized', *Theory, Culture and Society*, 20 (2): 59–78.

Adam, B. (2004) *Time*. Cambridge: Polity Press.

Adkins, L. (2002a) *Revisions: Gender and Sexuality in Late Modernity*. Buckingham: Open University Press.

Adkins, L. (2002b) 'Reflexivity and the politics of qualitative research', in T. May (ed.), *Qualitative Research in Action*. London: Sage. pp. 332–48.

Alastalo, M. (2008) 'The history of social research methods', in P. Alasuutari, L. Bickman and J. Brannen (eds), *The Sage Handbook of Social Research Methods*. London: Sage. pp. 36–41.

Alexander, B.K. (2005) 'Performance ethnography: the re-enacting and inciting of culture', in N.K. Denzin and Y.S. Lincoln (eds), *The Sage Handbook of Qualitative Research* (3rd edn). Thousand Oaks: Sage. pp. 411–41.

Andrews, M. (2007) *Shaping History: Narratives of Political Change*. Cambridge: Cambridge University Press.

Ansell Pearson, K. and Mullarkey, J. (eds) (2002) *Bergson: Key Writings*. London: Continuum.

Appadurai, A. (ed.) (2001) *Globalization*. Durham, NC: Duke University Press.

Atkinson, P., Coffey, A., Delamont, S., Lofland, J. and Lofland, L. (eds) (2002) *Handbook of Ethnography*. London: Sage.

Attwood, B. (2001). ' "Learning about the truth": the stolen generations narrative', in B. Attwood and F. Magowan (eds), *Telling Stories: Indigenous History and Memory in Australia and New Zealand*. Crows Nest, Sydney: Allen and Unwin. pp. 183–212.

Back, L. (2002) 'Guess who's coming to dinner? The political morality of investigating whiteness in the gray zone', in V. Ware and L. Back (eds), *Out of Whiteness: Color, Politics and Culture*. Chicago: University of Chicago Press. pp. 33–59.

Back, L. (2004) 'Politics, research and understanding', in C. Seale, G. Gobo, J.F. Gubrium and D. Silverman (eds), *Qualitative Research Practice*. London: Sage. pp. 249–64.

Back, L. (2007) *The Art of Listening*. Oxford: Berg.

Baker, B. and Heyning, K. (2004) 'Dangerous Coagulations? Research, education and a travelling Foucault', in B. Baker and K. Heyning (eds), *Dangerous Coagulations? The Uses of Foucault in the Study of Education*. New York: Peter Lang. pp. 1–79.

Beck, U. (1992) *Risk Society: Towards a New Modernity*. London: Sage.

Behar, R. (1996) *The Vulnerable Observer: Anthropology that Breaks Your Heart*. Boston, MA: Beacon Press.

Bertaux, D. (1981a) 'Introduction', in D. Bertaux (ed.), *Biography and Society: The Life Historical Approach in the Social Sciences*. London: Sage. pp. 5–15.

Bertaux, D. (1981b) 'From the life historical approach to the transformation of sociological practice', in D. Bertaux (ed.), *Biography and Society: The Life Historical Approach in the Social Sciences*. London: Sage. pp. 29–45.

Bertaux-Wiame, I. (1993/2005) 'The pull of family ties: intergenerational relationships and life paths' in D. Bertaux and P. Thompson (eds), *Between Generations: Family Models, Myths and Memories*. Oxford: Oxford University Press/Transaction Books. pp. 39–50.

Bertaux, D. and Bertaux-Wiame, I. (1997/2003) 'Heritage and its lineage: a case history of transmission and social mobility over five generations', in D. Bertaux and P. Thompson (eds), *Pathways to Social Class: A Qualitative Approach to Social Mobility*. Oxford: Calrendon Press. pp. 62–97.

Bertaux, D. and Thompson, P. (1993/2005) 'Introduction', in D. Bertaux and P. Thompson (eds), *Between Generations: Family Models, Myths and Memories*. London: Transaction Books. pp. 1–12.

Bertaux, D. and Thompson, P. (1997/2003) 'Introduction', in D. Bertaux and P. Thompson (eds), *Pathways to Social Class: A Qualitative Approach to Social Mobility*. Oxford: Clarendon Press. pp. 1–31.

Biersack, A. (1989) 'Local knowledge, local history: Geertz and beyond', in L. Hunt (ed.), *The New Cultural History: Essays*. Berkeley: University of California Press. pp. 72–96.

Bishop, L. (2005) 'Protecting respondents and enabling data sharing: reply to Parry and Mauthner', *Sociology*, 39 (2): 333–6.

Bishop, L. (2007) 'A reflexive account of reusing qualitative data: beyond primary/secondary dualism', *Sociological Research Online*, 12 (3).

Bjerrum Nielsen, H. (1996) 'The magic writing pad – on gender and identity', *Young: Journal of Nordic Youth Studies*, 4 (3): 2–18.

Bjerrum Nielsen, H. (2003) 'Historical, cultural, and emotional meanings: interviews with young girls in three generations', *NORA: Nordic Journal of Women's Studies*, 11 (1): 14–26.

Bjerrum Nielsen, H. and Rudberg, M. (1994) *Psychological Gender and Modernity*. Oslo: Scandinavian University Press.

Bjerrum Nielsen, H. and Rudberg, M. (2000) 'Gender, love and education in three generations', *European Journal of Women's Studies*, 7 (4): 423–53.

Blaxter, M. (2007) 'Commentary on a "reflexive account of reusing qualitative data: beyond primary/secondary dualism" (Libby Bishop)', *Sociological Research Online*, 12 (3).

Bornat, J. (2003) 'A second take: revisiting interviews with a different purpose', *Oral History* (Spring): 47–53.

Bornat, J. (2005) 'Recycling the evidence: different approaches to the reanalysis of geron-tological data', *Forum: Qualitative Sozialforschung/Forum: Qualitative Social Research*, 6 (1).

Bornat, J. and Diamond, H. (2007) 'Women's history and oral history: developments and debates', *Women's History Review*, 16 (1): 19–39.

Bornat, J. and Wilson, G. (2008) 'Recycling the evidence: different approaches to the re-analysis of elite life histories', in R. Edwards (ed.), *Researching Families and Communities: Social and Generational Change*. London: Routledge. pp. 95–113.

Bourdieu, P. (1993) 'Youth is just a word', *Sociology in Question*. London: Sage. pp. 94–102.

Bourdieu, P. (2001) *Masculine Domination* (trans. R. Nice). Stanford, CA: Stanford University Press.

Bourdieu, P. and Wacquant, L.J.D. (1992) *An Invitation to Reflexive Sociology*. Chicago: University of Chicago Press.

Brannen, J. (2005) 'Time and the negotiation of work-family boundaries: autonomy or illusion?', *Time and Society*, 14 (1): 113–31.

Brannen, J. and Nilsen, A. (2006) 'From fatherhood to fathering: transmission and change among British fathers in four-generation families', *Sociology*, 40 (2): 335–52.

Brannen, J., Moss, P. and Mooney, A. (2004) *Working and Caring over the Twentieth Century: Change and Continuity in Four-Generation Families*. Basingstoke: Palgrave Macmillan.

Bringing Them Home: Report of the National Inquiry into the Separation of Aboriginal and Torres Strait Islander Children from their Families (1997) Commissioned by the Commonwealth government, and conducted by the Australian Human Rights and Equal Opportunity Commission. Retrieved from: www.humanrights.gov.au/social_justice/bth_report/index.html.

Britzman, D. (2000) ' "The question of belief ": writing poststructural ethnography', in E. St Pierre and W. Pillow (eds), *Working the Ruins: Feminist Poststructural Theory and Methods in Education*. London: Routledge. pp. 27–40.

Brown, S. (2003) 'Desire in ethnography: discovering meaning in the social sciences', in M. Tamboukou and S. Ball (eds), *Dangerous Encounters: Genealogy and Ethnography*. New York: Peter Lang. pp. 69–90.

Brown, W. (1995) *States of Injury: Power and Freedom in Late Modernity*. Princeton, NJ: Princeton University Press.

Brown, W. (2001) *Politics Out of History*. Princeton, NJ: Princeton University Press.

Burawoy, M. (2000) *Global Ethnography: Forces, Connections, and Imaginations in a Postmodern World*. Berkeley: University of California Press.

Burchall, G. (1993) 'Liberal government and techniques of the self ', *Economy and Society*, 22 (3): 267–82.

Burke, P. (1992) *History and Social Theory*. Ithaca, NY: Cornell University Press.

Byng-Hall, J. (1995) *Rewriting Family Scripts: Improvizations and Systems Change*. New York: Guilford Press.

Chamberlayne, P., Bornat, J. and Wengraf, T. (eds) (2000) *The Turn to Biographical Methods: Comparative Issues and Examples*. London: Routledge.

Charles, N., Aull Davies, C. and Harris, C. (2008) 'The family and social change revisited', in R. Edwards (ed.), *Researching Families and Communities: Social and Generational Change*. London: Routledge. pp. 114–32.

Clendinnen, I. (2006) 'The history question: who owns the past?', *Quarterly Essay*, 23: 1–72.

Clifford, J. (1986) 'Introduction: partial truths', in J. Clifford and G.E. Marcus (eds), *Writing Culture: The Poetics and Politics of Ethnography*. Berkeley: University of California Press. pp. 1–26.

Clifford, J. (2003) *On the Edges of Anthropology (Interviews)*. Chicago: Prickly Paradigm Press.

Clifford, J. and Marcus, G. (eds) (1986) *Writing Culture: The Poetics and Politics of Ethnography*. Berkeley: University of California Press.

Coffey, A. (1999) *The Ethnographic Self: Fieldwork and the Representation of Identity*. London: Sage.

Comaroff, J. and Comaroff, J. (1992) *Ethnography and the Historical Imagination*. Boulder, CO: Westview Press.

Connerton, P. (1989) *How Societies Remember*. Cambridge: Cambridge University Press.

Corden, A. and Millar, J. (2007) 'Time and change: a review of the qualitative longitudinal research literature for social policy', *Social Policy and Society*, 6 (4): 583–92.

Corsaro, W.A. and Molinari, L. (2000) 'Entering and observing children's worlds: a reflection on longitudinal ethnography of early education in Italy', in P. Christensen and A. James (eds), *Research with Children: Perspectives and Practices*. London: Sage. pp. 179–200.

Corti, L. (2000) 'Progress and problems of preserving and providing access to qualitative data for social research: the international picture of an emerging culture', *Forum: Qualitative Sozialforschung/Forum: Qualitative Social Research*, 1 (3).

Corti, L. and Thompson, P. (2003) 'Secondary analysis of archive data', in C. Seale, G. Gobo, J.F. Gubrium and D. Silverman (eds), *Qualitative Research Practice*. London: Sage. pp. 279–313.

Coslett, T., Lury, C. and Summerfield, P. (eds) (2000) *Feminism and Autobiography: Texts, Theories, Methods*. London: Routledge.

Cousins, M. (2006) 'The aesthetics of documentary', *Tate Etc*, 6 (Spring): 41–7.

Crang, M. and Cook, I. (2007) *Doing Ethnographies*. London: Sage.

Crawford, J., Kippax, S., Onyx, J., Gault, U. and Benton, P. (1992) *Emotion and Gender: Constructing Meaning from Memory*. London: Sage.

Crotty, M. (1998) *The Foundations of Social Research: Meaning and Perspective in the Research Process*. St Leonards: Allen and Unwin.

Crow, G. (2008) 'Thinking about families and communities over time', in R. Edwards (ed.), *Researching Families and Communities: Social and Generational Change*. London: Routledge. pp. 11–24.

Dale, R. (2006) 'From comparison to translation: extending the research imagination', *Globalisation, Societies and Education*, 4 (2): 179–92.

Darian-Smith, K., and Hamilton, P. (eds) (1994) *Memory and History in Twentieth Century Australia*. Melbourne: Oxford University Press.

Davies, C.A. (2008) *Reflexive Ethnography: A Guide to Researching Selves and Others* (2nd edn). London: Routledge.

Davis, F. (1979) *Yearning for Yesterday: A Sociology of Nostalgia*. New York: The Free Press.

De Beauvoir, S. (1949/1997) *The Second Sex*. London: Vintage.

Denzin, N.K. and Lincoln, Y.S. (eds) (2005) *The Sage Handbook of Qualitative Research* (3rd edn). Thousand Oaks, CA: Sage.

Desai, K. (2006) *The Inheritance of Loss*. London: Penguin.

Dwyer, P. and Wyn, J. (2001) *Youth Education and Risk: Facing the Future*. London: RoutledgeFalmer.

Edmunds, J. and Turner, B. (2002) *Generations, Culture and Society*. Buckingham: Open University Press.

Edwards, R. (ed.) (2008) *Researching Families and Communities: Social and Generational Change*. London: Routledge.

Eisenhart, M. (2001) 'Changing conceptions of culture and ethnographic methodology: recent thematic shifts and their implications for research on teaching', in V. Richardson (ed.), *Handbook of Research on Teaching* (4th edn). Washington, DC: AERA. pp. 209–23.

Elias, N. (1992) 'Time: an essay', in N. Elias, S. Mennell and J. Goudsblom (eds), *On Civilization, Power, and Knowledge: Selected Writings*. Chicago, IL: University of Chicago Press. pp. 253–68.

Elliott, J., Holland, J. and Thomson, R. (2007) 'Qualitative and quantitative longitudinal research', in L. Bickman, J. Brannen and P. Alasuutari (eds), *Handbook of Social Research Methods*. London: Sage. pp. 228–48.

Ellis, C. (2004) *The Ethnographic I: A Novel about Autoethnography*. Walnut Creek, CA: AltaMira Press.

Erben, M. (1998) *Biography and Education: A Reader*. London: Falmer.

Farrell Krell, D. (1993) 'General introduction: the question of being', in M. Heidegger (ed.), *Basic Writings*. London: Routledge. pp. 3–35.

Ferri, E., Bynner, J. and Wadsworth, M. (eds) (2003) *Changing Britain, Changing Lives: Three Generations at the Turn of the Century*. London: Institute of Education, University of London.

Fielding, N. (2004) 'Getting the most from archived qualitative data', *International Journal of Social Research Methodology*, 7 (1): 97–104.

Finch, J. and Mason, J. (1993) *Negotiating Family Responsibilities*. London: Routledge.

Fine, M. and Weis, L. (1998) *The Unknown City: The Lives of Poor and Working-Class Young Adults*. Boston, MA: Beacon Press.

Foster, G.M., Scudder, T., Colson, E. and Kemper, R. (1979) *Long Term Field Research in Social Anthropology*. New York: Academic Press.

Foucault, M. (1982) 'Afterward: the subject and power', in H.L. Dreyfus and P. Rabinow (eds), *Michel Foucault: Beyond Structuralism and Hermeneutics*. Chicago: University of Chicago Press. pp. 208–26.

Foucault, M. (1984) 'Nietzsche, genealogy, history', in P. Rabinow (ed.), *The Foucault Reader*. New York: Pantheon Books. pp. 76–100.

Fraser, R. (1984) *In Search of a Past: The Manor House, Amnersfield, 1933–1945*. London: Verso.

Frisch, M. (1990) *A Shared Authority: Essays on the Craft and Meaning of Oral and Public History*. Albany, NY: State University of New York Press.

Frosh, S., Phoenix, A. and Pattman, R. (2002) *Young Masculinities*. Basingstoke: Palgrave Macmillan.

Geertz, C. (1973) *The Interpretation of Cultures: Selected Essays*. New York: Basic Books.

Geisen, B. (2004) 'Noncontemporaneity, asynchronicity and divided memories', *Time and Society*, 13 (1): 27–40.

Gelder, K. (2007) *Subcultures: Cultural Histories and Social Practice*. London: Routledge.

Gergen, K.J. (1984) 'An introduction to historical social psychology', in K.J. Gergen and M.M. Gergen (eds), *Historical Social Psychology*. Mahwah, NJ: Lawrence Erlbaum Associates. pp. 3–36.

Giddens, A. (1991) *Modernity and Self Identity: Self and Society in the Late Modern Age*. Cambridge: Polity Press.

Gillies, V. (2008) 'Secondary analysis in investigating family change: exploring substantive and conceptual questions', in R. Edwards (ed.), *Researching Families and Communities: Social and Generational Change*. London: Routledge. pp. 77–94.

Gillies, V. and Edwards, R. (2005) 'Secondary analysis in exploring family and social change: addressing the issue of context', *Forum: Qualitative Sozialforschung/Forum: Qualitative Social Research*, 6 (1).

Gillies, V., Harden, A., Johnson, K., Reavey, P., Strange, V. and Willig, C. (2004) 'Women's collective constructions of embodied practices through memory work: Cartesian dualism in memories of sweating and pain', *British Journal of Social Psychology*, 43 (1): 99–112.

Gillies, V., Harden, A., Johnson, K., Reavey, P., Strange, V. and Willig, C. (2005) 'Painting pictures of embodied experience: the use of non-linguistic data in the study of embodiment', *Qualitative Research in Psychology*, 2 (3): 199–212.

Gluck, S.B. and Patai, D. (eds) (1991) *Women's Words: The Feminist Practice of Oral History*. New York: Routledge.

Goldbart, J. and Hustler, D. (2005) 'Ethnography', in B. Somekh and C. Lewin (eds), *Research Methods in the Social Sciences*. London: Sage. pp. 16–23.

Goodwin, J. and O'Connor, H. (2006) 'Contextualising the research process: using interviewer notes in the secondary analysis of qualitative data', *The Qualitative Report*, 11 (2): 374–92.

Greenwood, D. and Levin, M. (2006) *Introduction to Action Research: Social Research for Social Change*. London: Sage.

Grosz, E. (2004) *The Nick of Time: Politics, Evolution and the Untimely*. Durham, NC: Duke University Press.

Grosz, E. (2005) *Time Travels: Feminism, Nature, Power*. Durham, NC: Duke University Press.

Hacking, I. (1995) *Rewriting the Soul: Multiple Personality and the Sciences of Memory*. Princeton, NJ: Princeton University Press.

Haebich, A. (2002) 'Between knowing and not knowing: public knowledge of the stolen generations', *Aboriginal History*, 25: 70–90.

Hagestad, G.O. (1985) 'Continuity and connectedness', in V.L. Bengtson and J.F. Robertson (eds), *Grandparenthood*. London: Sage. pp. 31–48.

Halbwachs, M. (1950/1992) *On Collective Memory* (trans. L.A. Coser). Chicago: University of Chicago Press.

Hall, S. and Jefferson, T. (eds) (1976) *Resistance through Rituals*. London: Hutchinson.

Halpern, D., Bates, C., Beales, G. and Heathfield, A. (2004) *Personal Responsibility and Changing Behaviour: The State of Knowledge and its Implications for Public Policy*. London: Cabinet Office, Prime Minister's Strategy Unit.

Hamilton, P. (1994) 'The knife edge: debates about memory and history', in K. Darian-Smith and P. Hamilton (eds), *Memory and History in Twentieth-Century Australia*. Melbourne: Oxford University Press. pp. 9–32.

Hamilton, P. and Shopes, L. (2008) 'Introduction: building partnerships between oral history and memory studies', in P. Hamilton and L. Shopes (eds), *Oral Histories and Public Memories*. Philadelphia, PA: Temple University Press. pp. vii–xvii.

Hammersley, M. (1997) 'Qualitative data archiving: some reflections on its prospects and principles', *Sociology*, 31 (1): 131–41.

Hammersley, M. (1998) *Reading Ethnographic Research: A Critical Guide* (2nd edn). London: Longman.

Hammersley, M. and Atkinson, P. (2007) *Ethnography: Principles in Practice* (3rd edn). London: RoutledgeFalmer.

Harootunian, H. (2007) 'Remembering the historical present', *Critical Inquiry*, 33 (Spring): 471–94.

Harper, D. (1992) 'Small n's and community studies', in S. Ragan and H.S. Becker (eds), *What is a Case? Exploring the Foundations of Social Inquiry*. Cambridge: Cambridge University Press. pp. 139–58.

Haug, F. (2001) 'Sexual deregulation or, the child abuser as hero in neoliberalism', *Feminist Theory*, 2 (1): 55–78.

Haug, F., Andresen, S., Bunz-Elfferding, A., Hauser, K., Lang, U., Laudan, M. et al. (1999). *Female Sexualization: A Collective Work of Memory* (trans. E. Carter) (1987, 2nd edn). London: Verso.

Heaphy, B. (2007) *Late Modernity and Social Change: Reconstructing Social and Personal Life*. London: Routledge.

Heath, R. (2006) *Please Just F* Off, It's Our Turn Now: Holding Baby Boomers to Account*. Melbourne: Pluto Press.

Heaton, J. (2004) *Reworking Qualitative Data*. London: Sage.

Henderson, S., Holland, J. and Thomson, R. (2006) 'Making the long view: perspectives on context from a qualitative longitudinal (QL) study', *Methodolgical Innovations On Line*, 1 (2).

Henderson, S., Holland, J., McGrellis, S., Sharpe, S. and Thomson, R. (2007) *Inventing Adulthoods: A Biographical Approach to Youth Transitions*. London: Sage.

Henderson, S., McGrellis, S. and Sharpe, S. (2004) 'Capitalising on both sides: experiences in a longitudinal research project', in R. Edwards (ed.), *Social Capital in the Field: Researchers' Tales* (Working Paper 10). London: Families and Social Capital ESRC Research Group, London South Bank University.

Heron, L. (1993) *Truth, Dare or Promise: Girls Growing Up in the Fifties*. London: Virago.

Hey, V. (1997) *The Company She Keeps: An Ethnography of Girls' Friendships*. Buckingham: Open University Press.

Hirsch, J. (2003) *Portrait of America: A Cultural History of the Federal Writers' Project*. Chapel Hill: University of North Carolina Press.

Hobsbawm, E. (1994) *Age of Extremes: The Short Twentieth Century*. London: Michael Joseph.

Hockey, J. (2008) 'Lifecourse and intergenerational research'. Paper presented at the Launch of Timescapes Study, University of Leeds, 31 January.

Hodgson, S.M. and Clark, T. (2007) 'Sociological engagements with computing: the advent of e-science and some implications for the qualitative research community', *Sociological Research Online*, 12 (3).

Holland, J., Thomson, R. and Henderson, S. (2006) 'Qualitative longitudinal research: a discussion paper', Working Paper 21, Families and Social Capital ESRC Research Group, London South Bank University.

Hollway, W. (1994) 'Beyond sex differences: a project for feminist psychology', *Feminism and Psychology*, 4 (4): 538–46.

Hollway, W. and Jefferson, T. (2000) *Doing Qualitative Research Differently: Free Association, Narrative and Interview Methods*. London: Sage.

Huggins, J. (2005) 'So what is memory and the task of recording memory?' Paper presented at the Deadly Directions Conference, AITSIIS Library Conference, Adelaide.

Human Rights and Equal Opportunity Commission Australia (2008) Bringing them home. The 'Stolen Children' report (1997) www.humanrights. gov. au/social_justice/bth_report/about/personal_stories.html [accessed 22 August 2008].

Hunt, L. (ed.) (1989) *The New Cultural History: Essays*, Berkeley: University of California Press.

James, H. (1981) *The Notebooks of Henry James,* ed. P.O. Matthiessen, and B. Murdock Chicago: University of Chicago Press.

James, J. and Sorensen, A. (2000) 'Archiving longitudinal data for future research: why qualitative data add to a study's usefulness', *Forum: Qualitative Sozialforschung/Forum: Qualitative Social Research*, 1 (3).

Jedlowski, P. (2001) 'Memory and sociology: themes and issues', *Time and Society* 10 (1): 29–44.

Jones, G. (2005) *The Thinking and Behaviour of Young Adults (Aged 16–25)*. Literature review for the Social Exclusion Unit.

Kehily, M.J. (2002) *Sexuality, Gender and Schooling: Shifting Agendas in Social Learning*. London: Routledge.

Kemper, R. and Peterson Royce, A. (eds) (2002) *Chronicling Cultures: Long-Term Field Research in Anthropology*. Walnut Creek, CA: AltaMira Press.

Kennedy, R. (2001) 'Stolen Generations testimony: trauma, historiography, and the question of "truth" ', *Aboriginal History*, 25: 116–31.

Kenway, J. and McLeod, J. (2004) 'Bourdieu's reflexive sociology and "spaces of points of view": whose reflexivity, which perspective?', *British Journal of Sociology of Education*, 25 (4): 525–44.

Kenway, J., Kraack, A. and Hickey-Moody, A. (2006) *Masculinity Beyond the Metropolis*. London: Palgrave Macmillan.

Kilby, J. (2002) 'Redeeming memories: the politics of trauma and history', *Feminist Theory*, 3 (2): 201–10.

Kluge, S. and Opitz, D. (2000) 'Computer-aided archiving of qualitative data with the database system "QBiQ" ', *Forum: Qualitative Sozialforschung/Forum: Qualitative Social Research*, 1 (3).

Kohli, M. (1996) 'The problem of generation: family, economy, politics', Public Lectures No. 14 Collegium Budapest: Institute for Advanced Studies. Available at www.colbud.hu/main_old/PubArchive/PL/PL14-Kohli.pdf [accessed 4 February 2008].

Koselleck, R. (1985) *Futures Past: On the Semantics of Historical Time*. Cambridge, MA: MIT Press.

Kuhn, A. (1995) *Family Secrets: Acts of Memory and Imagination*. London: Verso.

Lamb, S. and McKenzie, P. (2000) *Patterns of Success and Failure in the Transition from School to Work in Australia, Longitudinal Survey of Australian Youth*, Research Report 18. Australian Council for Educational Research, Camberwell, Victoria.

Laslett, P. (1965) *The World We Have Lost*. London: Methuen.

Latour, B. (2005) *Reassembling the Social: An Introduction to Actor-Network-Theory*. Oxford: Oxford University Press.

Law, J. (2004) *After Method: Mess in Social Science Research*. London: Routledge.

Lawler, S. (2000) *Mothering the Self: Mothers, Daughters, Subjects*. London: Routledge.

Leiserling, L. and Walker, R. (eds) (1998) *The Dynamics of Modern Society: Poverty, Policy and Welfare*. Bristol: Policy Press.

Leonard, D. (1980) *Sex and Generation: A Study of Courtship and Weddings*. London: Tavistock.

Lewis, J. (2007) 'Analysing qualitative longitudinal research in evaluations', *Social Policy and Society*, 6 (4): 545–56.

Lucey, H., Melody, J. and Walkerdine, V. (2003) 'Project 4:21: transitions to womanhood: developing a psychosocial perspective in one longitudinal study', *International Journal of Social Research Methodology*, 6 (3): 279–84.

Macintyre, S. and Clark, A. (2003) *The History Wars*. Melbourne: Melbourne University Press.

MacLure, M. (2003) *Discourse in Educational and Social Research*. Buckingham: Open University Press.

Mannheim, K. (1952) 'The problem of generations', in P. Kecskemeti (ed.), *Essays on the Sociology of Knowledge*. London: Routledge & Kegan Paul. pp. 276–323.

Marcus, G.E. (1992) 'Past, present and emergent identities: requirements for ethnographies of late twentieth century modernity worldwide', in S. Lasch and J. Friedman (eds), *Modernity and Identity*. Oxford: Blackwell. pp. 309–30.

Marker, C. (1998) *Immemory*, CD ROM. Berkeley, CA: Exact Change.

Massey, D. (1993) 'Power geometry and a progressive sense of space', in J. Bird, B. Curtis, G. Putnam, G. Robertson and L. Tickner (eds), *Mapping the Futures: Local Cultures, Global Change*. London: Routledge. pp. 59–69.

Massey, D. (1994) 'Politics and space/time', in D. Massey (ed.), *Space, Place and Gender*. Cambridge: Polity Press. pp. 249–72.

Mauthner, N., Parry, O. and Backett-Milburn, K. (1998) 'The data are out there, or are they? Implications for archiving and revisiting qualitative data', *Sociology*, 32 (4): 733–45.

McLeod, J. (2000) 'Metaphors of the self: searching for young people's identity through interview', in J. McLeod and K. Malone (eds), *Researching Youth*. Hobart: Australian Clearing House for Youth Studies. pp. 45–58.

McLeod, J. (2003) 'Why we interview now – reflexivity and perspective in a longitudinal study', *International Journal of Social Research Methodology*, 6 (3): 201–12.

McLeod, J. and Yates, L. (1997) 'Can we find out about girls and boys today – or must we settle for talking about ourselves? Dilemmas of a feminist, qualitative, longitudinal research project', *Australian Educational Researcher*, 24 (December): 23–42.

McLeod, J. and Yates, L. (2003) 'Who is "us"? Students negotiating discourses of racism and national identification in Australia', *Race, Ethnicity and Education*, 6 (1): 29–49.

McLeod, J. and Yates, L. (2006) *Making Modern Lives: Subjectivity, Schooling and Social Change*. Albany, NY: State University of New York Press.

McRobbie, A. and McCabe, T. (1981) *Feminism for Girls: An Adventure Story*. London: Routledge & Kegan Paul.

Middleton, S. (1998) *Disciplining Sexuality: Foucault, Life Histories and Education*. New York: Teachers College Press.

Molloy, D., Woodfield, K. and Bacon, J. (2002) 'Longitudinal qualitative research approaches in evaluation studies', Working Paper 7. London: HMSO.

Moore, N. (2005) (Re)using qualitative data?', CRESC Working Paper. Presented at the CRESC Methods Workshop, University of Manchester, 23 September.

Moore, N. (2007) '(Re)using qualitative data?', *Sociological Research Online*, 12 (2).

Munslow, A. (1997) *Deconstructing History*. New York: Routledge.

Nayak, A. and Kehily, M.J. (2008) *Gender, Youth and Culture: Young Masculinities and Feminities*. Basingstoke: Palgrave Macmillan.

Neale, B. and Flowerdew, J. (2003) 'Time, texture and childhood: the contours of longitudinal qualitative research', *International Journal of Social Research Methodology*, 6 (3): 189–99.

Neale, B., Flowerdew, J., Smart, C. and Wade, A. (2003) *Enduring Families? Children's Long Term Reflections on Post Divorce Family Life*. Research report for ESRC (No. R000239248).

Nora, P. (1996) 'General introduction: Between memory and history', in P. Nora (ed.), *Realms of Memory: Rethinking the French Past. Vol. 1: Conflicts and Divisions*, English version edited by L. D. Kritzman, trans. A.B. Goldhammer. New York: Columbia University Press. pp. 1–20.

O'Brien, E. (2006) *The Light of Evening*. Boston, MA: Houghton Mifflin.

O'Farrell, C. (2005) *Michel Foucault*. London: Sage.

Okley, J. and Callaway, H. (eds) (1992) *Anthropology and Autobiography*. New York: Routledge.

Ortner, S.B. (2003) *New Jersey Dreaming: Capital, Culture and the Class of '58*. Durham, NC: Duke University Press.

Ortner, S. (2006) *Anthropology and Social Theory: Culture, Power and the Acting Subject*. Durham, NC: Duke University Press.

Parry, O. and Mauthner, N.S. (2004) 'Whose data are they anyway? Practical, legal and ethical issues in archiving qualitative research data', *Sociology*, 38 (1): 139–52.

Parry, O. and Mauthner, N.S. (2005) 'Back to basics: who re-uses qualitative data and why?', *Sociology*, 39 (2): 337–42.

Passerini, L. (1987) *Fascism in Popular Memory: The Cultural Experience of the Italian Working Class*. Cambridge: Cambridge University Press.

Passerini, L. (1990) 'Mythobiography in oral history', in R. Samuel and P. Thompson (eds), *The Myths We Live By*. London: Routledge. pp. 49–60.

Passerini, L. (2002) 'Shareable narratives? Intersubjectivity, life stories and reinterpreting the past'. Paper presented at the Advanced Oral History Summer Institute, Berkeley, CA, 11–16 August.

Perks, R. and Thomson, A. (eds) (2006) *The Oral History Reader* (2nd edn). Abingdon: Routledge.

Peterson Royce, A. and Kemper, R. (2002) 'Long term field research: metaphors, paradigms and themes' (eds), in R. Kemper and A. Peterson Royce (eds), *Chronicling Cultures: Long Term Field Research in Anthropology*. Walnut Creek, CA: AltaMira Press. pp. xiii–xxxviii.

Pilcher, J. (1995) *Age and Generation in Modern Britain*. Oxford: Oxford University Press.

Plummer, K. (1995) *Telling Sexual Stories: Power Change and Social Worlds*. London: Routledge.

Plummer, K. (2001) *Documents of Life 2: An Invitation to Critical Humanism*. London: Sage.

Pollard, A. and Filer, A. (1996) *The Social World of Children's Learning: Case-Studies of Pupils from Four to Seven*. London: Cassell.

Pollard, A. and Filer, A. (1999) *The Social World of Pupil Career: Strategic Biographies through Primary School*. London: Continuum.

Popkewitz, T. (1998) *Struggling for the Soul: The Politics of Schooling and the Construction of the Teacher*. New York: Teachers College Press.

Popular Memory Group (1982) 'Popular memory: theory, politics, method', in R. Johnson, G. McLennan, B. Schwarz and D. Sutton (eds), *Making History: Studies in History-Writing and Politics*. London: Hutchison in association with the Centre for Contemporary Cultural Studies University of Birmingham. pp. 205–52.

Portelli, A. (1990) 'Uchronic dreams: working-class memory and possible worlds', in R. Samuel and P. Thompson (eds), *The Myths We Live By*. London: Routledge. pp. 143–60.

Powell, A. (1997) *A Dance to the Music of Time: Winter*. London: Mandarin.

Powell, A. (2000) *A Dance to the Music of Time: Spring*. London: Mandarin.

Rabinow, P. (2003) *Anthropos Today: Reflections on Modern Equipment*. Princeton, NJ: Princeton University Press.

Radstone, S. (ed.) (2000) *Memory and Methodology*. Oxford: Berg.

Ramazanoglu, C. and Holland, J. (1999) 'Tripping over experience: some problems in feminist epistemology', *Discourse: Studies in the Cultural Politics of Education*, 20 (3): 381–92.

Read, P. (1982) 'The stolen generations: the removal of Aboriginal children in New South Wales 1883 to 1969', Occasional Paper, New South Wales, Ministry of Aboriginal Affairs; No. 1, Government Printer, Sydney.

Reavey, P. and Brown, S.D. (2006) 'Transforming agency and action in the past, into the present time: adult memories and child sexual abuse', *Theory and Psychology*, 16: 170–202.

Reavey, P. and Warner, S. (eds) (2003) *New Feminist Stories of Child Sexual Abuse: Sexual Scripts and Dangerous Dialogues*. London: Routledge.

Reay, D. (2005) 'Doing the dirty work of social class? Mothers' work in support of their children's schooling', in M. Glucksmann, L. Pettinger, J. Parry and R. Taylor (eds), *A New Sociology of Work*. Oxford: Blackwell. pp. 104–15.

Ricoeur, P. (2004) *Memory, History, Forgetting* (trans. K. Blamey and D. Pellauer). Chicago: University of Chicago Press.

Rose, N. (1999) *Powers of Freedom: Reframing Political Thought*. Oxford: Oxford University Press.

Rosenthal, G. (1998) *The Holocaust in Three Generations: Families of Victims and Perpetrators of the Nazi Regime*. London: Cassells.

Rubin, G. (1975) 'The traffic in women: notes on the political economy of sex', in R. Reiter (ed.), *Toward an Anthropology of Women*. New York: Monthly Review Press. pp. 157–210.

Saldana, J. (2003) *Longitudinal Qualitative Research: Analyzing Change through Time*. Walnut Creek, CA: AltaMira Press.

Samuel, R. (1994) *Theatres of Memory. Vol. 1: Past and Present in Contemporary Culture*. London: Verso.

Samuel, R. and Thompson, P. (eds) (1990) 'Introduction', in R. Samuel and P. Thompson (eds), *The Myths We Live By*. London: Routledge. pp. 1–22.

Savage, J. (2008) *Teenage: The Creation of Youth Culture*. London: Pimlico.

Savage, M. (2005) 'Revisiting classic qualitative studies', *Historical Social Research*, 3 (1): 118–39.

Savage, M. (2007a) 'Changing social class identities in post-war Britain: perspectives from Mass Observation', *Sociological Research Online*, 12 (3).

Savage, M. (2007b) 'Revisiting class qualitative studies', *Forum: Qualitative Sozialforschung/Forum: Qualitative Social Research*, 6 (1).

Savage, M. and Burrows, R. (2007) 'The coming crisis of empirical sociology', *Sociology*, 41 (5): 885–9.

Schostak, J.F. (2006) *Interviewing and Representation in Qualitative Research*. Buckingham: Open University Press.

Scott, J.W. (1992) 'Experience', in J. Butler and J.W. Scott (eds), *Feminists Theorize the Political*. London: Routledge. pp. 22–40.

Simon, R.I. (2005) *The Touch of the Past: Remembrance, Learning and Ethics*. London: Palgrave Macmillan.

Skeggs, B. (1997) *Formations of Class and Gender: Becoming Respectable*. London: Sage.

Skeggs, B. (2004) *Class, Self, Culture*. London: Routledge.

Smart, C. (2007) *Personal Life: New Directions in Sociological Thinking*. Cambridge: Polity Press.

Smith, D. (2005) *Insitutional Ethnography: A Sociology for People*. Lanham, MD: AltaMira Press.

Spence, J. (1986) *Putting Myself in the Picture: A Political, Personal and Photographic Autobiography*. London: Camden Press.

Spry, T. (2001) 'Performing autoethnography', *Qualitative Inquiry*, 7 (6): 706–32.

St Pierre, E.A. and Pillow, W. (2000) *Working the Ruins: Feminist Poststructural Theory and Methods in Education*. New York: Routledge.

Stanley, L. (1992) *The Auto/biographical I: Theory and Practice of Feminist Auto/biography*. Manchester: Manchester University Press.

Stanley, L. (2007) 'Epistolarity, seriality and the social: letters – between "biography" and "history"'. Paper presented at Constructing Lives: Biographical Methodologies in Social and Historical Research, The Open University, 4 December.

Steedman, C.K. (1986) *Landscape for a Good Woman*. London: Virago.

Stephenson, N. and Papadopoulos, D. (2006) *Analysing Everyday Experience: Social Research and Political Change*. Basingstoke: Palgrave Macmillan.

Stephenson, N., Kippax, S. and Crawford, J. (1996) 'You and I and she: memory work, moral conflict and the construction of self', in S. Wilkinson (ed.), *Feminist Social Psychologies*. Buckingham: Open University Press. pp. 182–200.

Summerfield, P. (2000) 'Dis/composing the subject: intersubjectivities in oral history', in T. Cosslett, C. Lury and P. Summerfield (eds), *Feminism and Autobiography: Texts, Theories, Methods*. London: Routledge. pp. 91–106.

Tamboukou, M. and Ball, S. (eds) (2003) *Dangerous Encounters: Genealogy and Ethnography*. New York: Peter Lang.

Temple, B., Edwards, R. and Alexander, C. (2006) 'Grasping at context: cross language qualitative research as secondary qualitative data analysis', *Forum: Qualitative Sozialforschung/Forum: Qualitative Social Research*, 7 (4).

Thompson, P. (1978) *The Voice of the Past: Oral History*. Oxford: Oxford University Press.

Thompson, P. (1988) *The Voice of the Past: Oral History* (2nd edn). Oxford: Oxford University Press.

Thompson, P. (1981) 'Life histories and the analysis of social change', in D. Bertaux (ed.), *Biography and Society: The Life Historical Approach in the Social Sciences*. London: Sage. pp. 289–306.

Thompson, P. (1993/2005) 'Family myth, models and denials in the shaping of individual life plans', in D. Bertaux (ed.), *Between Generations: Family Models, Myths and Memories*, Second edition. Oxford: Oxford University Press. pp. 13–38.

Thompson, P. (2000) 'Re-using qualitative research data: a personal account', *Forum: Qualitative Sozialforschung/Forum: Qualitative Social Research*, 1 (3).

Thomson, A. (2007) 'Four paradigm transformations in oral history', *Oral History Review*, 34 (1): 49–71.

Thomson, R. (2000) 'Dream on: the logic of sexual practice', *Journal of Youth Studies*, 4 (4): 407–27.

Thomson, R. (2004) 'Finding and keeping emotions in the research process'. Paper presented at 'Reflexive Methodologies Seminar', 21–22 October, Helsinki Collegium for Advanced Studies, Finland.

Thomson, R. (2007) 'The qualitative longitudinal case history: practical, methodological and ethical reflections', *Social Policy and Society*, 6 (4): 571–82.

Thomson, R. (forthcoming 2009) *Unfolding Lives: Youth, Gender and Change*. Bristol: Policy Press.

Thomson, R. and Holland, J. (2003) 'Hindsight, foresight and insight: the challenges of longitudinal qualitative research', *International Journal of Social Research Methodology*, 6 (3): 233–44.

Thomson, R. and Holland, J. (2004) 'Youth values and transitions to adulthood: an empirical investigation', Working Paper 4, Families and Social Capital ESRC Research Group, London South Bank University.

Thomson, R. and Holland, J. (2005) 'Thanks for the memory: memory books as a methodological resource in biographical research', *Qualitative Research*, 5 (2): 201–91.

Thomson, R., Henderson, S. and Holland, J. (2002) 'Imagining adulthood: resources, plans and contradictions', *Gender and Education*, 14 (4): 337–50.

Thomson, R., Plumridge, L., and Holland, J. (2003) 'Longitudinal qualitative research: a developing methodology', *International Journal of Social Research Methods: Theory and Practice*, 6 (3): 185–7.

Timescapes (2007) Retrieved 5 February 2008, from www.timescapes.leeds.ac.uk.

Urry, J. (1996) 'Sociology of time and space', in B. Turner (ed.), *Blackwell Companion to Social Theory*. Oxford: Blackwell. pp. 416–43.

Walkerdine, V., Lucey, H. and Melody, J. (2001) *Growing Up Girl: Psychosocial Explorations of Gender and Class*. London: Palgrave Macmillan.

Walkerdine, V., Lucey, H. and Melody, J. (2002) 'Subjectivity and qualitative method', in T. May (ed.), *Qualitative Research in Action*. London: Sage. pp. 179–96.

Weeks, J. (2007) *The World We Have Won: The Remaking of Erotic and Intimate Lives*. London: Routledge.

Weis, L. (2004) *Class Reunion: The Remaking of the American White Working Class*. New York: Routledge.

Wengraf, T. (2001) *Qualitative Research Interviewing: Biographic, Narrative and Semi-Structured Method*. London: Sage.

Wengraf, T. (2006) 'The biographical interpretive method: principles and procedures', in SOSTRIS Working Papers, No. 2. London: Centre for Biography in Social Policy. Available at: www.uel.ac.uk/cnr/Wengrafo6.rtf-.

Williamson, H. (2004) *The Milltown Boys Revisited*. Oxford: Berg.

Willis, P. (1981) *Learning to Labor: How Working Class Kids Get Working Class Jobs*. New York: Columbia University Press.

Willis, P. (2000) *The Ethnographic Imagination*. Cambridge: Polity Press.

Woods, H. and Skeggs, B. (2004) 'Notes on ethical scenarios of self on British reality TV', *Feminist Media Studies*, 4 (1): 205–8.

Woolcott, H.F. (2002) *Sneaky Kid and Its Aftermath: Ethics and Intimacy in Fieldwork*. Walnut Creek, CA: AltaMira Press.

Yates, L. (2003) 'Interpretive claims and methodological warrant in small-number qualitative longitudinal research', *International Journal of Social Research Methodology*, 6 (3): 223–32.

Yetman, N.R. (n.d.) 'An introduction to the WPA slave narratives', www.memory.loc.gov/ammem/snhtml/snintro00.html.

Yow, V. (1997) ' "Do I like them too much?" Effects of the oral history interview on the interviewer and vice-versa', *Oral History Review*, 24 (1): 55–79.

Index

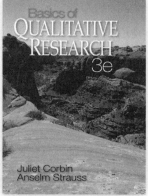

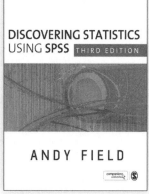
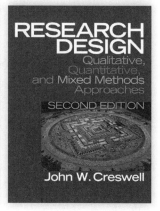

The Qualitative Research Kit

Edited by Uwe Flick

Read sample chapters online now!

Supporting researchers for more than forty years

Research methods have always been at the core of SAGE's publishing. Sara Miller McCune founded SAGE in 1965 and soon after, she published SAGE's first methods book, Public Policy Evaluation. A few years later, she launched the Quantitative Applications in the Social Sciences series – affectionately known as the "little green books".

Always at the forefront of developing and supporting new approaches in methods, SAGE published early groundbreaking texts and journals in the fields of qualitative methods and evaluation.

Today, more than forty years and two million little green books later, SAGE continues to push the boundaries with a growing list of more than 1,200 research methods books, journals, and reference works across the social, behavioral, and health sciences.

From qualitative, quantitative, mixed methods to evaluation, SAGE is the essential resource for academics and practitioners looking for the latest methods by leading scholars.

www.sagepublications.com